Two-Story Homes
For Active, Growing Families

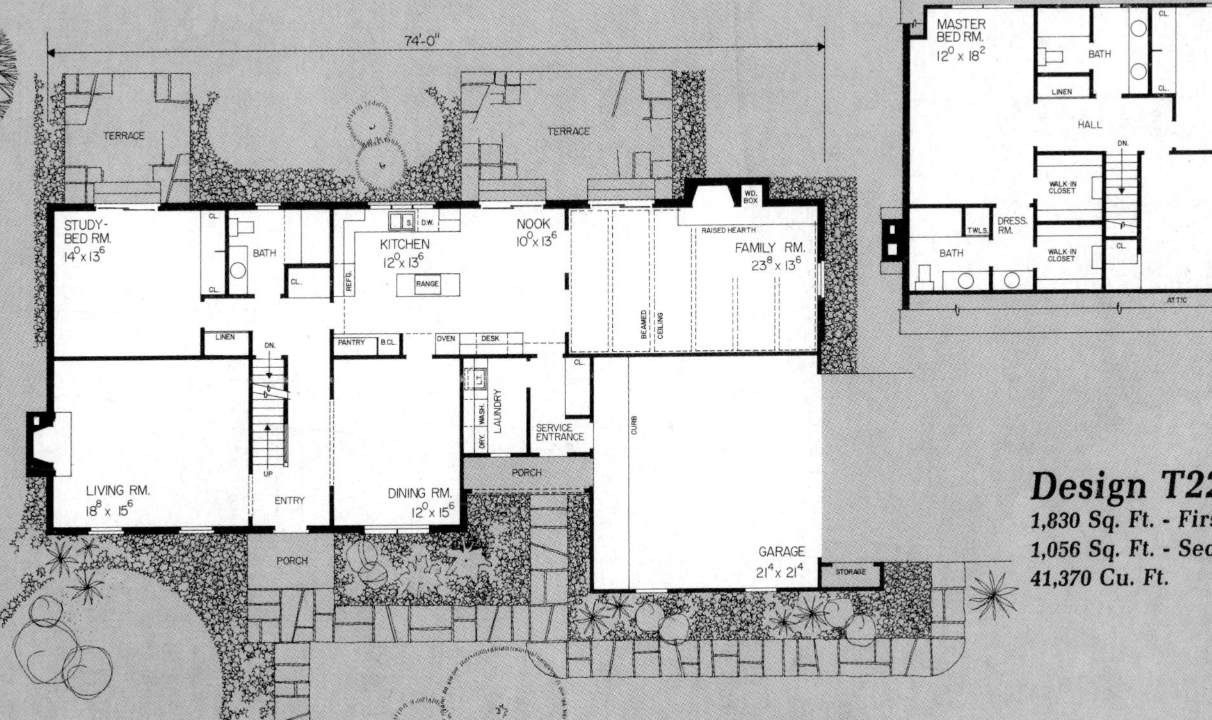

Design T22713

1,830 Sq. Ft. - First Floor
1,056 Sq. Ft. - Second Floor
41,370 Cu. Ft.

● This home with its Gambrel roof and paned windows is sure to be a pleasure for the entire family. Along with the outside, the inside is a delight. The spacious family room creates an inviting atmosphere with sliding glass doors to the terrace, beamed ceilings and a raised-hearth fireplace that includes a built-in wood box. A spectacular kitchen, too. Presenting an island counter/range as well as a built-in oven, desk and storage pantry. A sunny breakfast nook, too, also with sliding glass doors leading to the terrace. Note the size of the formal dining room and the fireplace in the living room. A first floor study/bedroom with a private terrace. Upstairs, there is the master suite and two more bedrooms and a bath.

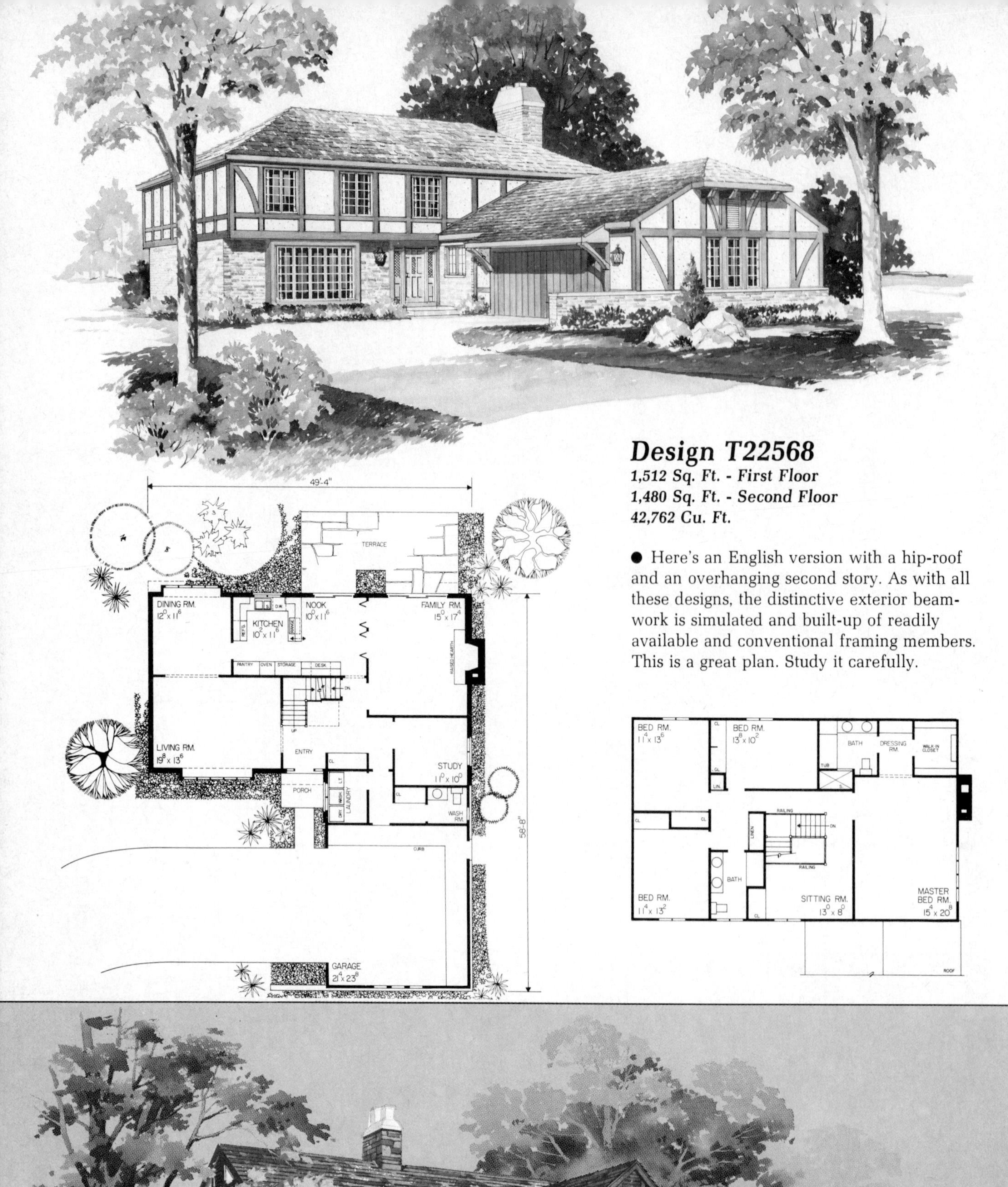

Design T22568

1,512 Sq. Ft. - First Floor
1,480 Sq. Ft. - Second Floor
42,762 Cu. Ft.

● Here's an English version with a hip-roof and an overhanging second story. As with all these designs, the distinctive exterior beamwork is simulated and built-up of readily available and conventional framing members. This is a great plan. Study it carefully.

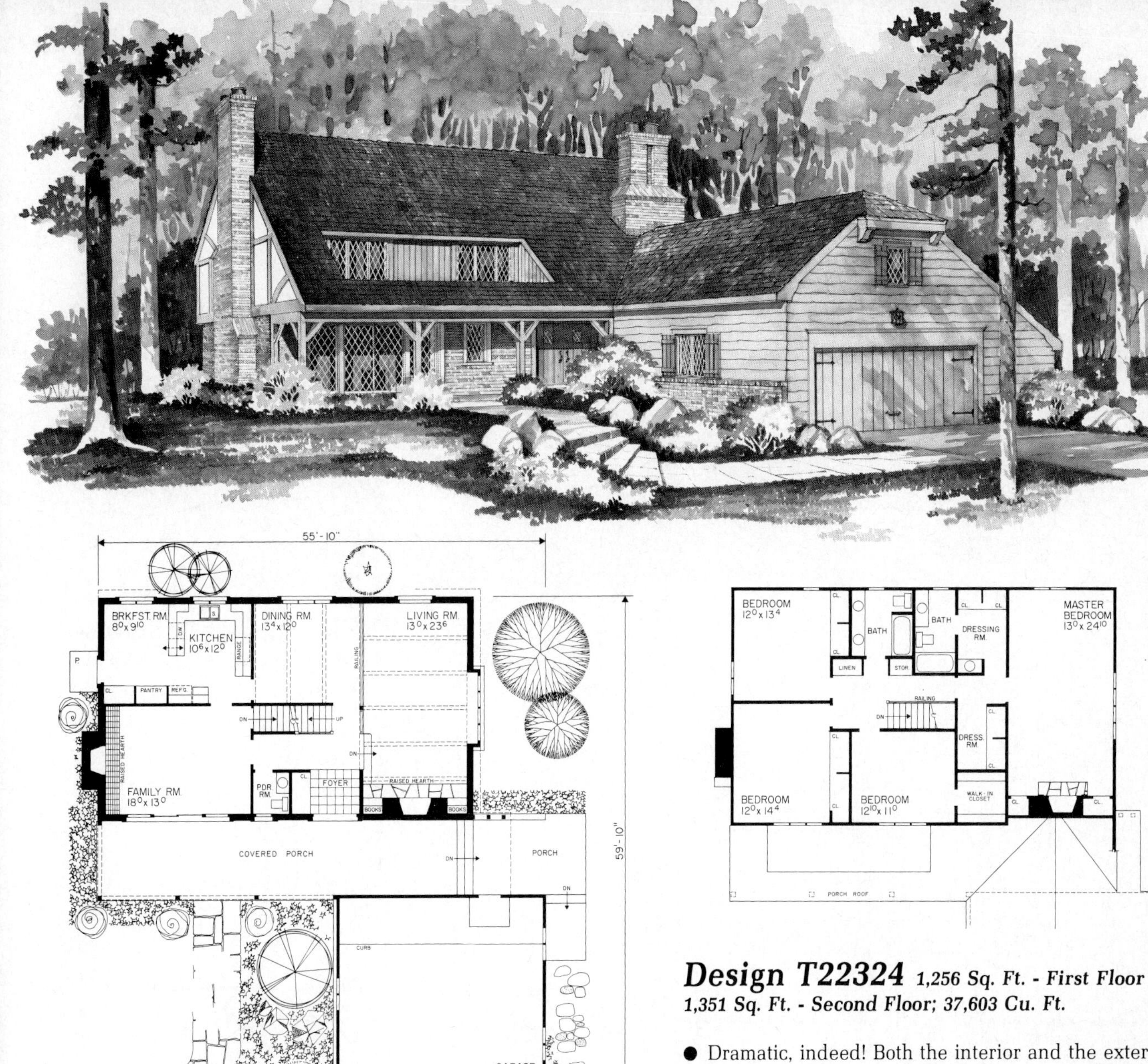

Design T22324 *1,256 Sq. Ft. - First Floor*

1,351 Sq. Ft. - Second Floor; 37,603 Cu. Ft.

● Dramatic, indeed! Both the interior and the exterior of these three Tudor designs deserve mention. Study each of them closely. The design featured here has a simple rectangular plan which will be relatively economical to build. This design is ideal for a corner lot.

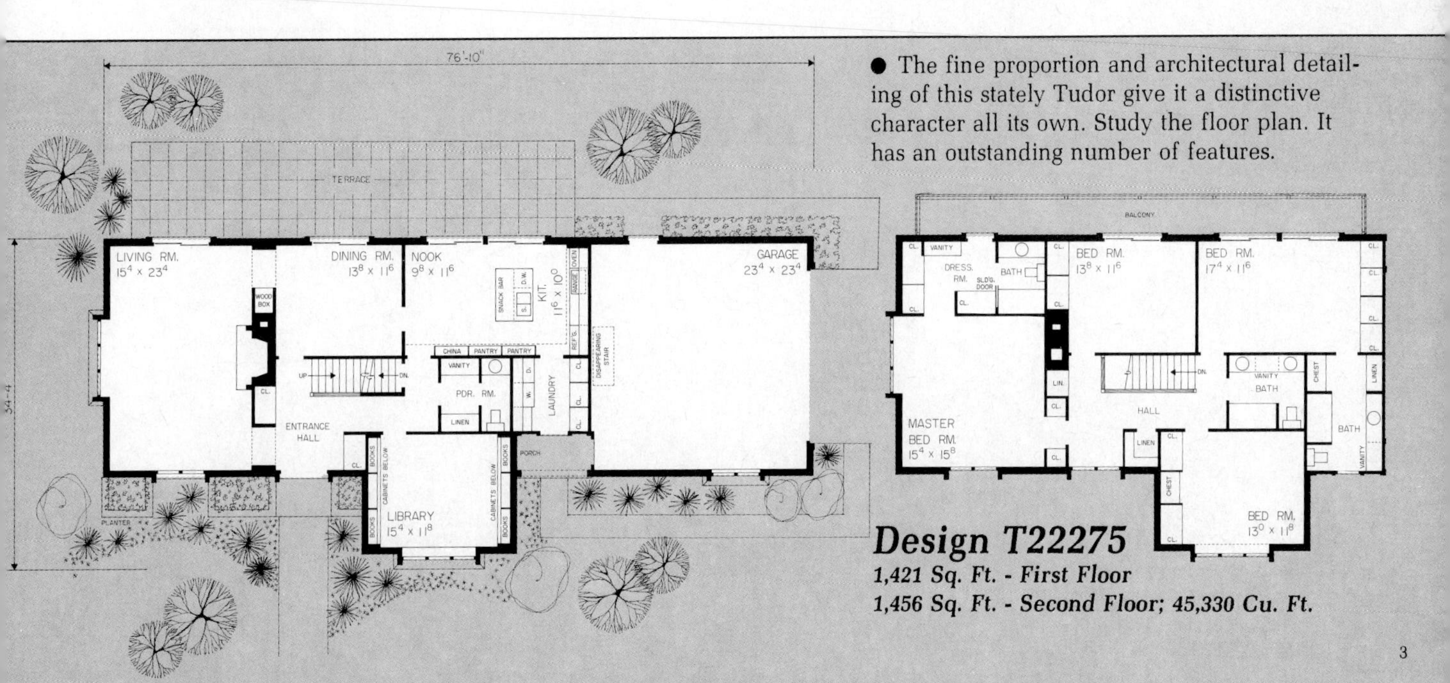

● The fine proportion and architectural detailing of this stately Tudor give it a distinctive character all its own. Study the floor plan. It has an outstanding number of features.

Design T22275

1,421 Sq. Ft. - First Floor

1,456 Sq. Ft. - Second Floor; 45,330 Cu. Ft.

Design T22530 *1,616 Sq. Ft. - First Floor 997 Sq. Ft. - Second Floor; 41,925 Cu. Ft.*

● This exciting contemporary has dramatic roof lines and appealing glass areas. The interior planning is, indeed, unique. Study this plan carefully and consider how your family would function in it. The sunken gathering room is a delightful area with its dramatic raised hearth fireplace and planter, and access to two terraces. The spaciousness of the dining/family room will make entertaining a memorable occasion.

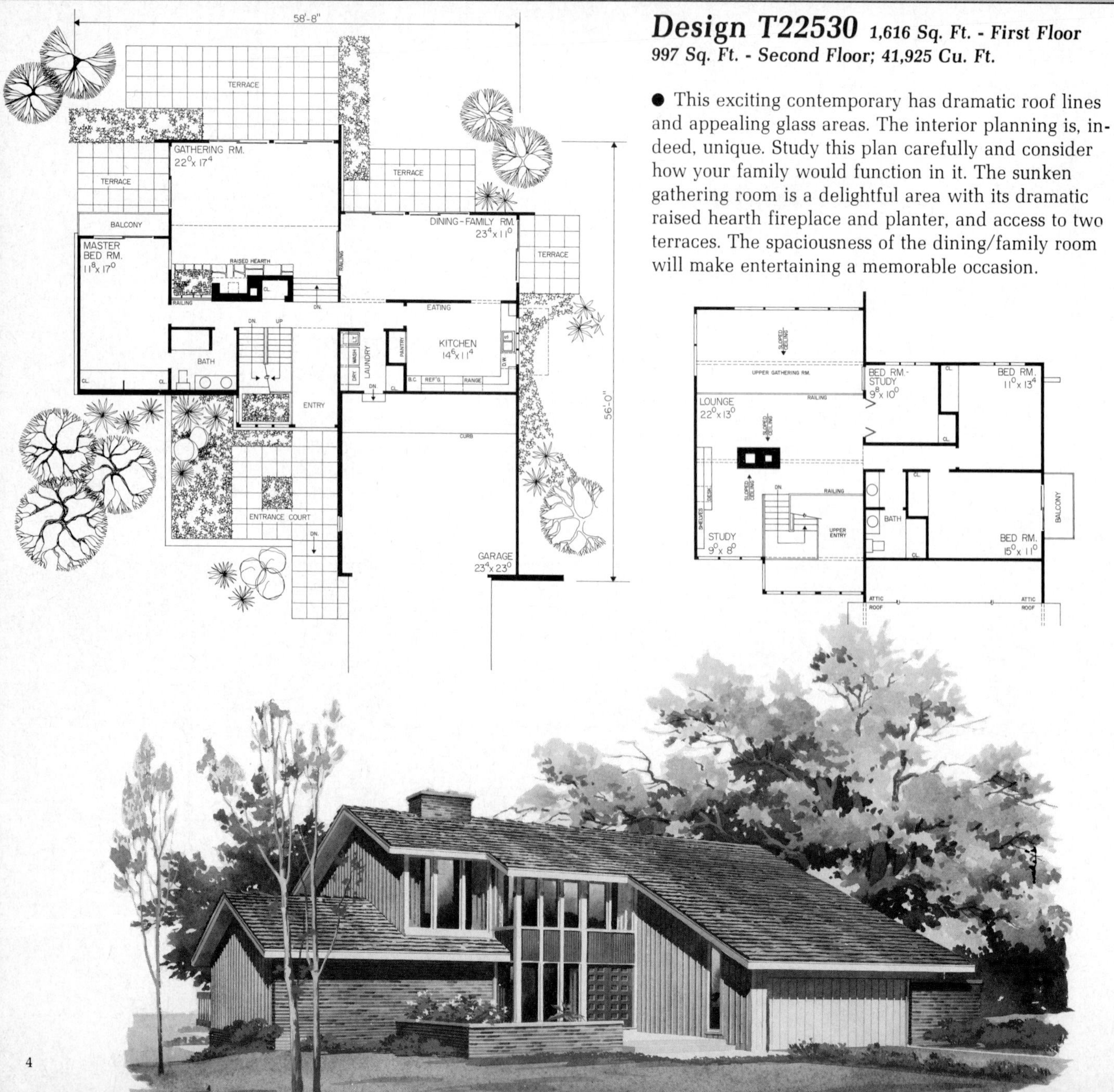

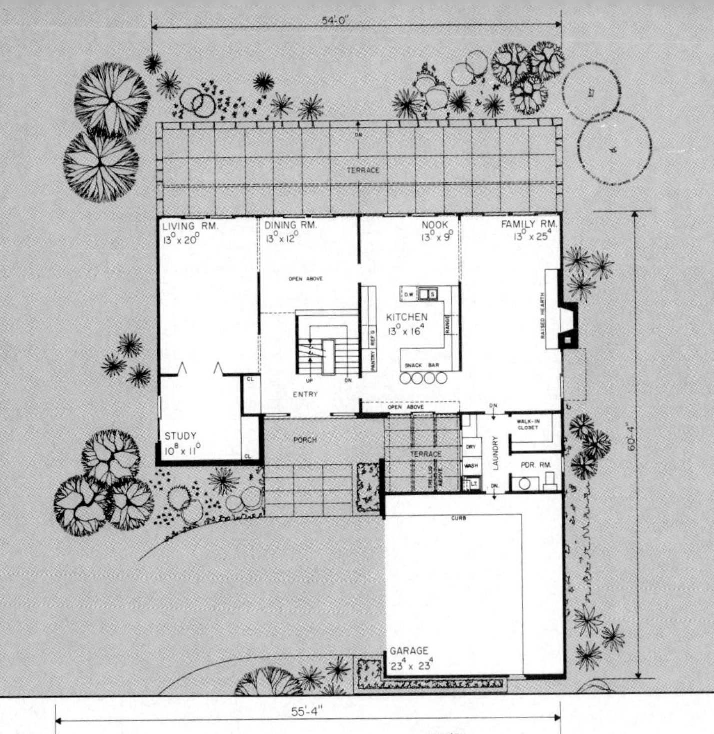

Design T22509 1,634 Sq. Ft. - First Floor
1,304 Sq. Ft. - Second Floor; 44,732 Cu. Ft.

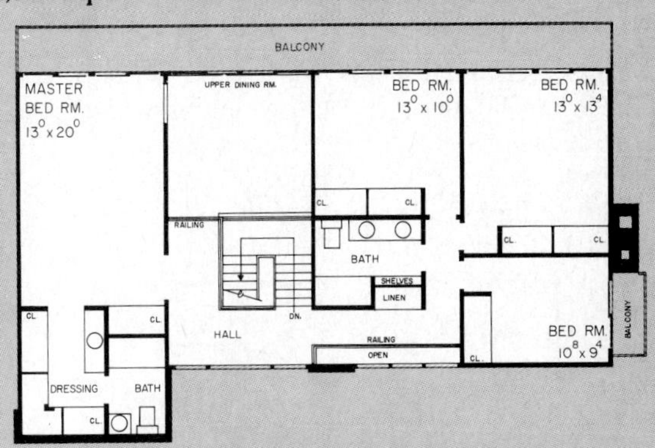

● A two-story with more livability will be hard to find. Notice how the various rooms are oriented with the terrace and balcony. Count all of the sliding glass doors. The family room is large and has a raised hearth fireplace as its focal point.

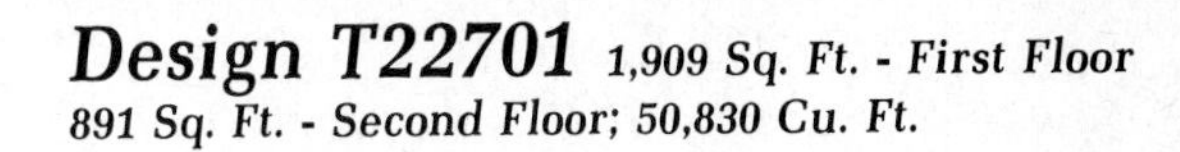

Design T22701 1,909 Sq. Ft. - First Floor
891 Sq. Ft. - Second Floor; 50,830 Cu. Ft.

● A snack bar in the kitchen! Plus a breakfast nook and formal dining room. Whether it's an elegant dinner party or a quick lunch, this home provides the right spot. There's a wet bar in the gathering room. Built-in bookcases in the study. And between these two rooms, a gracious fireplace. Three large bedrooms. Including a luxury master suite. Plus a balcony lounge overlooking gathering room below.

Design T22538

1,503 Sq. Ft. - First Floor
1,095 Sq. Ft. - Second Floor; 44,321 Cu. Ft.

● This Salt Box is charming, indeed. The livability it has to offer to the large and growing family is great. The entry is spacious and is open to the second floor balcony. For living areas, there is the study in addition to the living and family rooms.

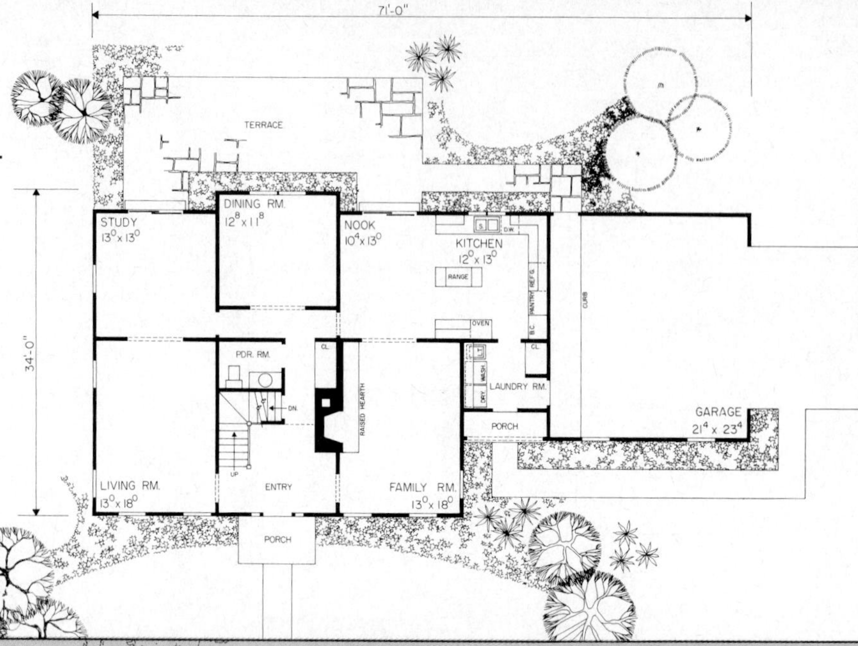

Design T22188

1,440 Sq. Ft. - First Floor
1,280 Sq. Ft. - Second Floor; 40,924 Cu. Ft.

● This design is characteristic of early America and its presence will create an atmosphere of that time in our heritage. However, it will be right at home wherever located. Along with exterior charm, this design has outstanding livability to offer its occupants.

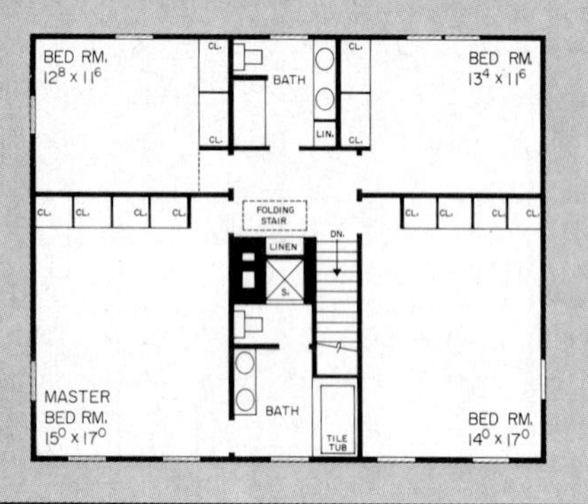

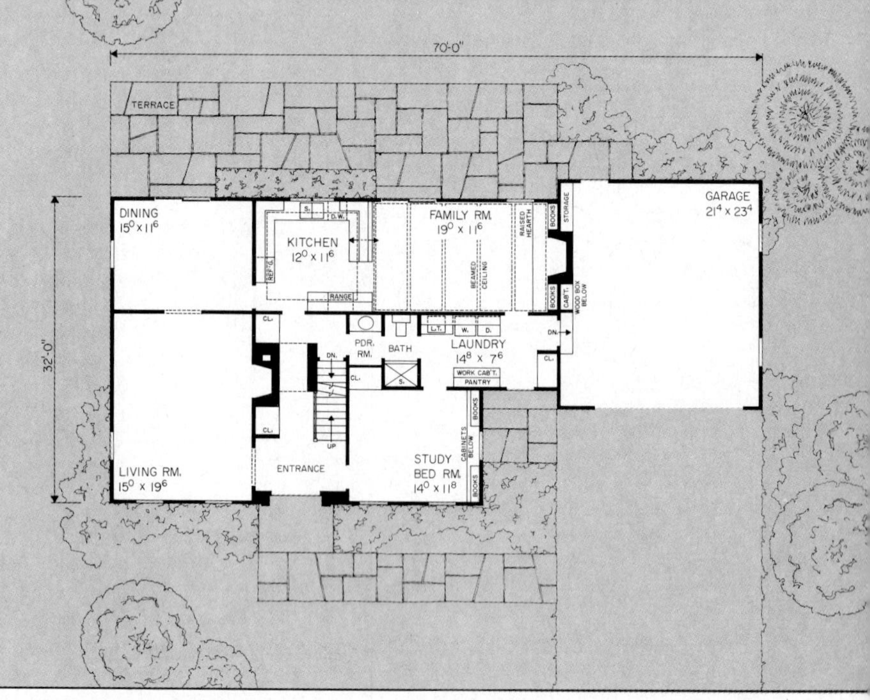

Design T22253

1,503 Sq. Ft. - First Floor
1,291 Sq. Ft. - Second Floor; 44,260 Cu. Ft.

● The overhanging second floor sets the character of this Early American design. Study the features, both inside and out.

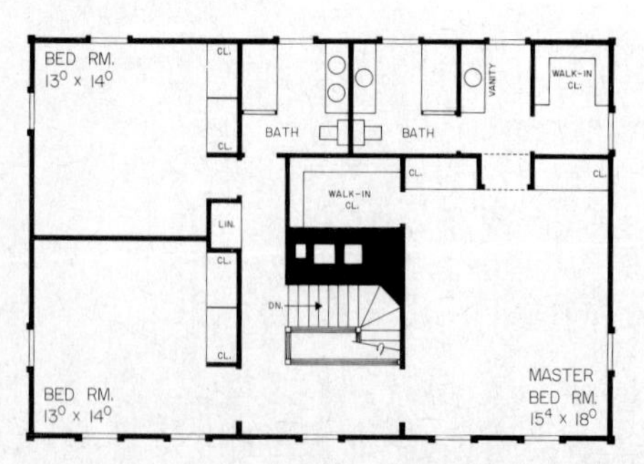

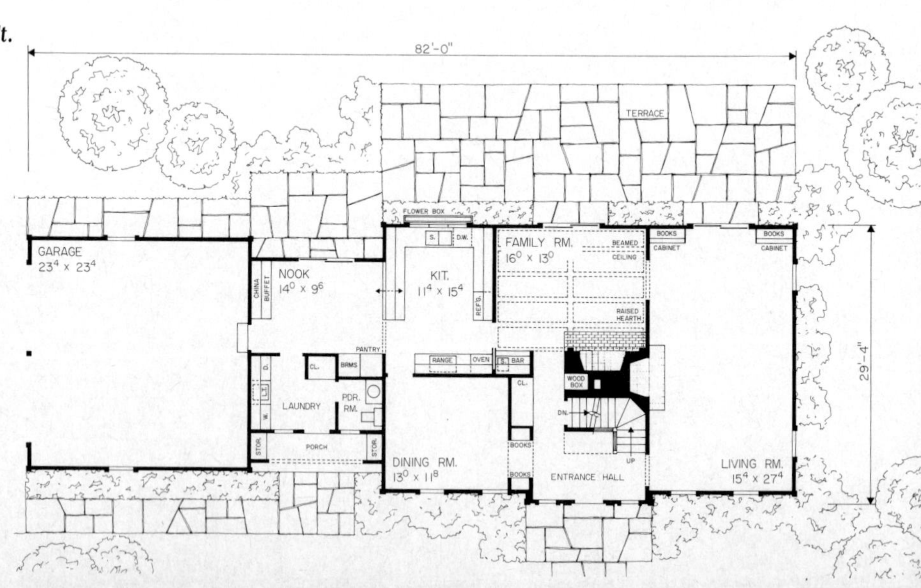

Design T22123

1,624 Sq. Ft. - First Floor; 1335 Sq. Ft - Second Floor
42,728 Cu. Ft.

● Inside there is close to 3,000 square feet of uniquely planned floor area. The spacious, well-lighted entry has, of course, a high sloping ceiling. A second floor balcony looks down from above. This area features two walk-in closets. Between the dining and living rooms is a thru fireplace which may be enjoyed from either room. Between the garage and the family room is the laundry and the compartmented powder room. The second floor ceilings slope and, consequently add to the feeling of spaciousness.

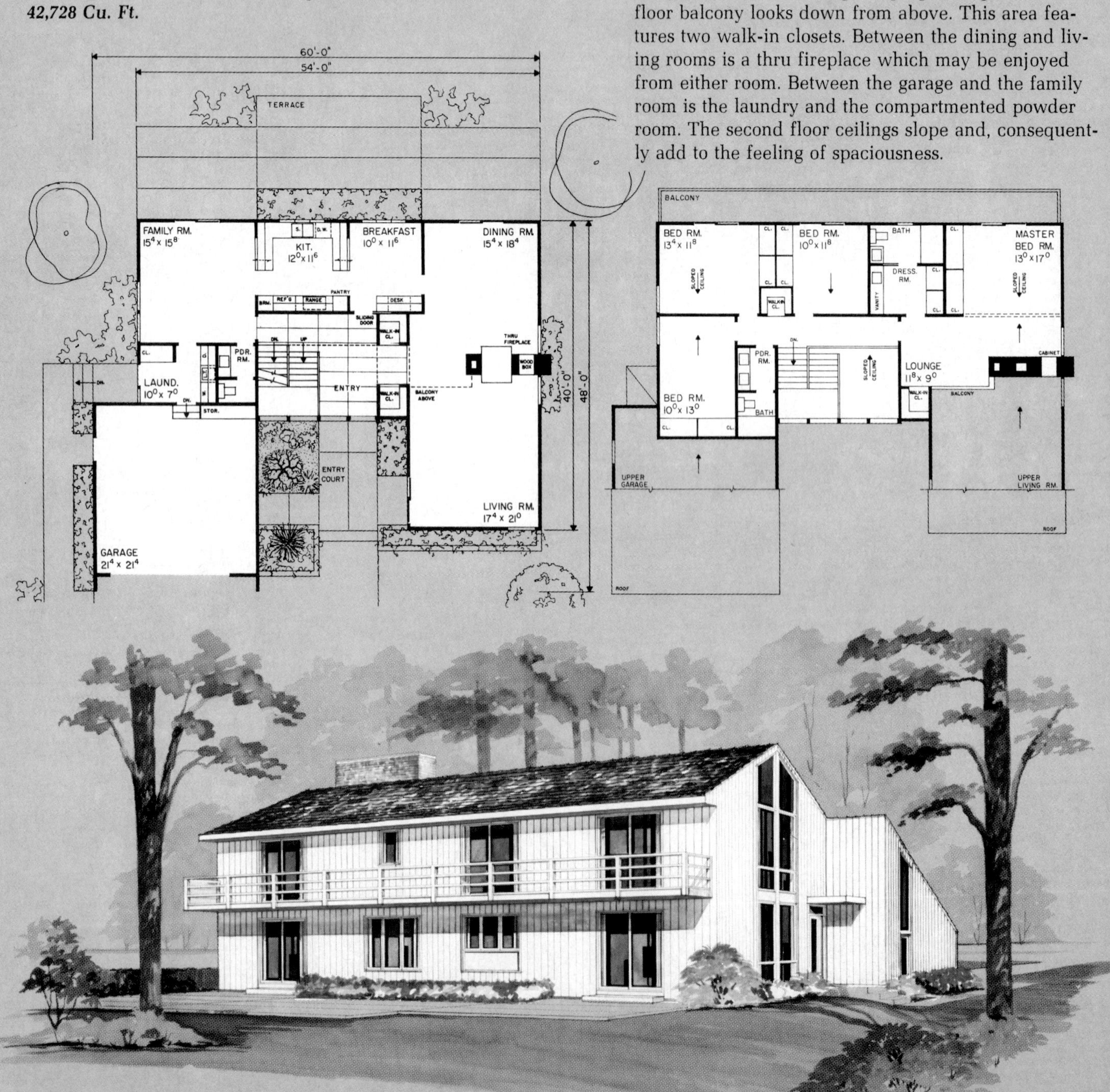

Design T22828 *First Floor: 817 Sq. Ft. - Living Area; 261 Sq. Ft. - Foyer & Laundry Second Floor: 852 Sq. Ft. - Living Area; 214 Sq. Ft. - Foyer & Storage; 34,690 Cu. Ft.*

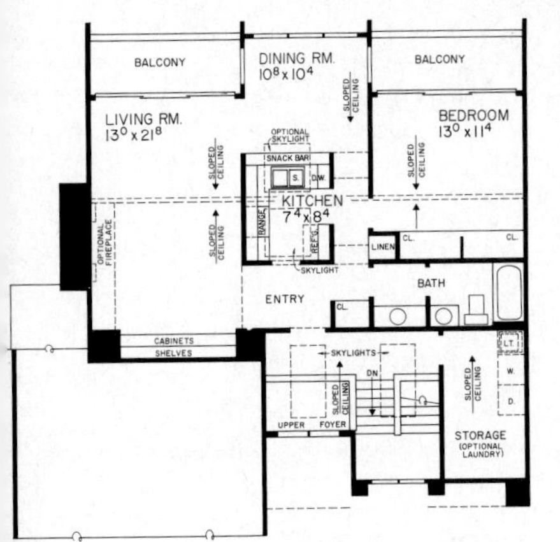

TWO COUPLES/SINGLES RESIDENCE

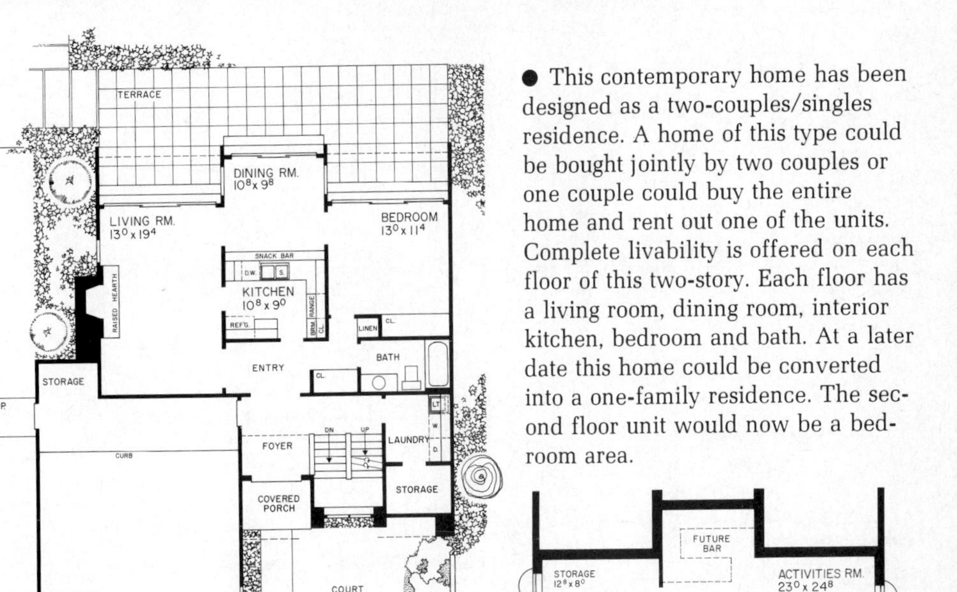

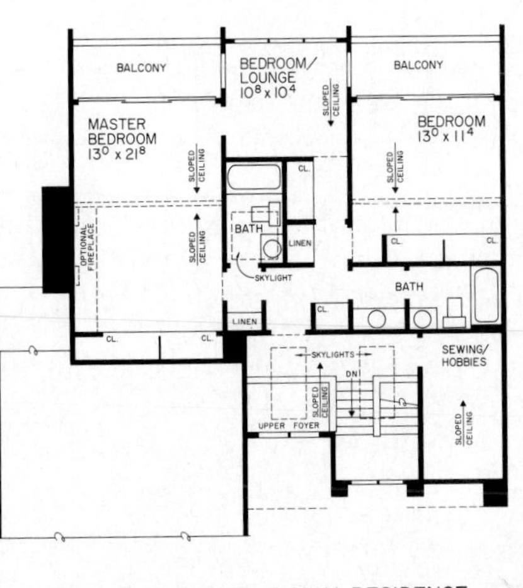

CONVERTIBLE ONE- FAMILY RESIDENCE

● This contemporary home has been designed as a two-couples/singles residence. A home of this type could be bought jointly by two couples or one couple could buy the entire home and rent out one of the units. Complete livability is offered on each floor of this two-story. Each floor has a living room, dining room, interior kitchen, bedroom and bath. At a later date this home could be converted into a one-family residence. The second floor unit would now be a bedroom area.

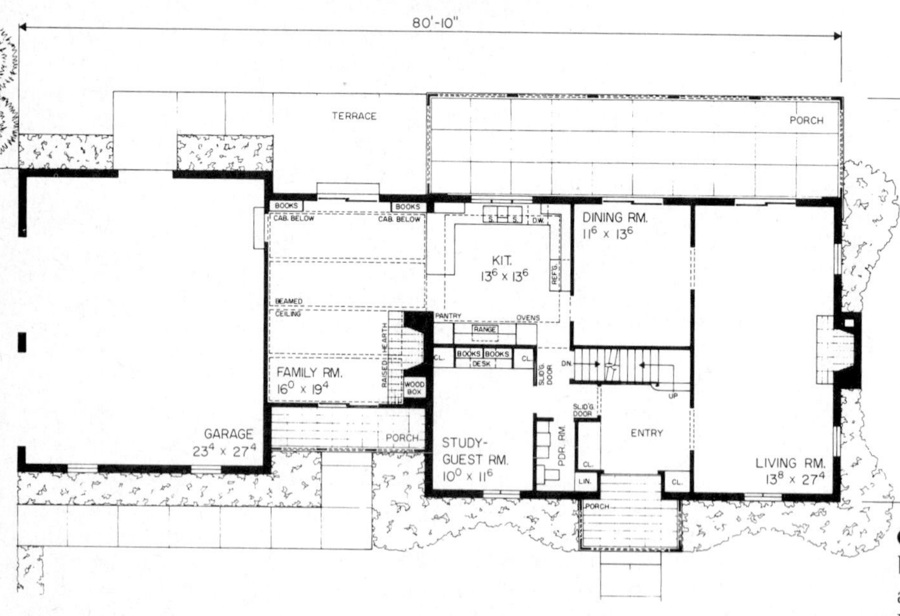

Design T22222

1,485 Sq. Ft. - First Floor
1,175 Sq. Ft. - Second Floor
45,500 Cu. Ft.

● Gracious, formal living could hardly find a better backdrop than this two-story French adaptation. The exterior is truly exquisite. Inside, living patterns will be most enjoyable.

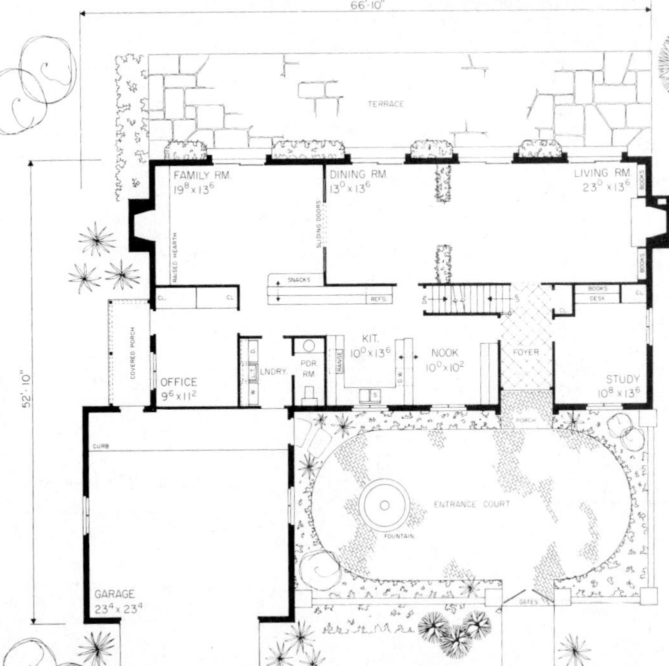

Design T22326

1,674 Sq. Ft. - First Floor
1,107 Sq. Ft. - Second Floor
53,250 Cu. Ft.

● If your family enjoys the view of the backyard, then this is the design for you. The main rooms, family, dining and living, are all in the back of the plan, each having sliding glass doors to the terrace. They are away from the confusion of the work center, yet easily accessible. A study and separate office are also available. Four bedrooms are on the second floor. Be sure to note all of the features in the master bedroom suite.

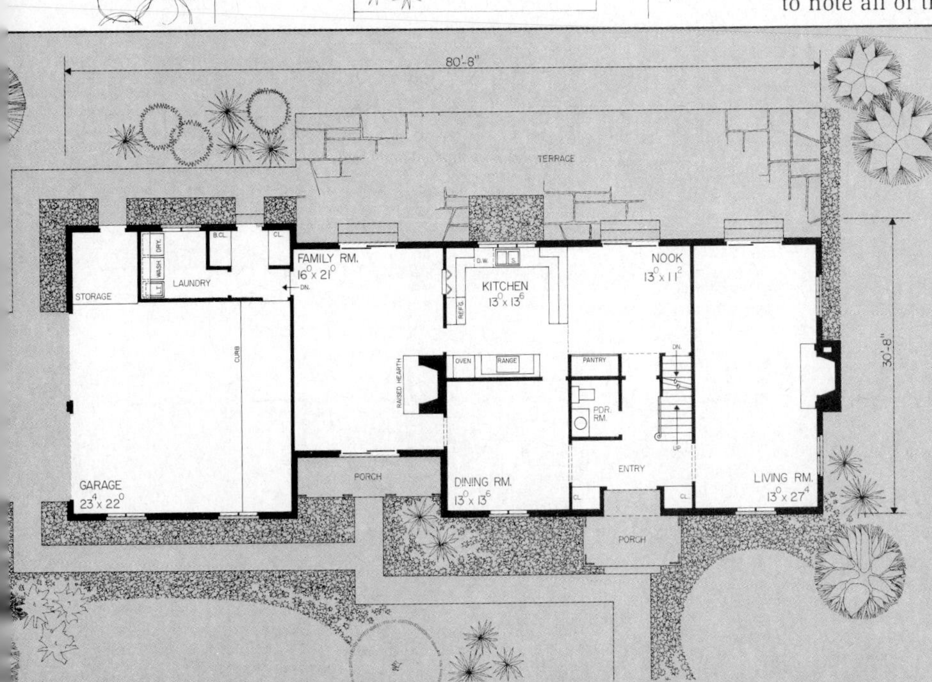

Design T22564

1,706 Sq. Ft. - First Floor
1,166 Sq. Ft. - Second Floor
48,640 Cu. Ft.

● French tone! Here's a home with Old World charm! But liveable in the American style. Formal and informal areas each have a fireplace. Three (optional four) bedrooms upstairs.

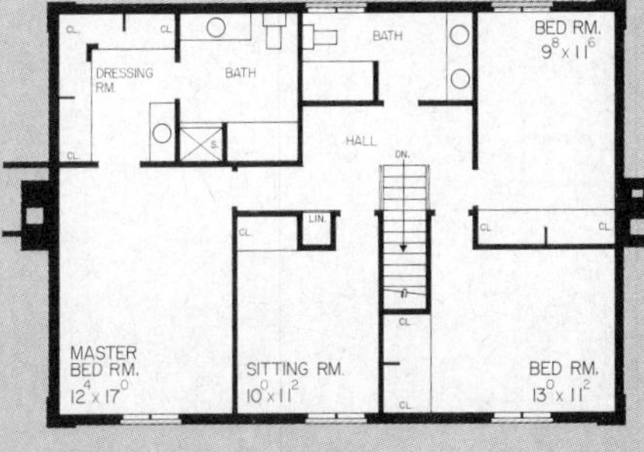

Design T22539

1,450 Sq. Ft. - First Floor
1,167 Sq. Ft. - Second Floor; 46,738 Cu. Ft.

● This appealingly proportioned Gambrel exudes an aura of coziness. The beauty of the main part of the house is delightfully symmetrical and is enhanced by the attached garage and laundry room. The center entrance routes traffic directly to all major zones of the house.

70'-0"
TERRACE
PORCH
NOOK 13^0x11^0
FAMILY RM. 25^8x13^0
KITCHEN 13^0x10^0
LAUNDRY RM.
GARAGE 21^4x23^4
PDR. RM.
DINING RM. 13^0x12^8
ENTRY
LIVING RM. 13^0x18^0
PORCH
34'-4"

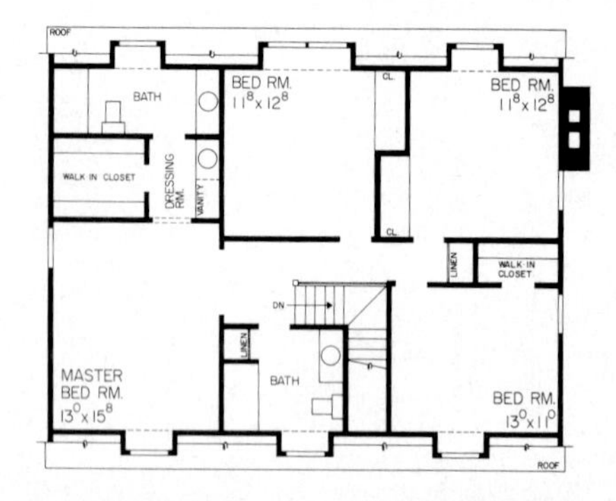

● This Gambrel roofed design has its roots in the early history of New England. While its exterior is decidedly and purposely dated, the interior of this design reflects an impressive 20th Century floor plan. All of the elements are present to guarantee outstanding living patterns for the large, active family of today.

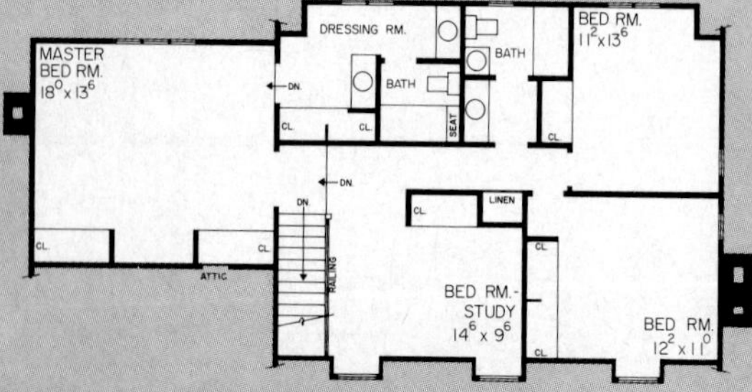

Design T22531 ***1,353 Sq. Ft. - First Floor***

1,208 Sq. Ft. - Second Floor; 33,225 Cu. Ft.

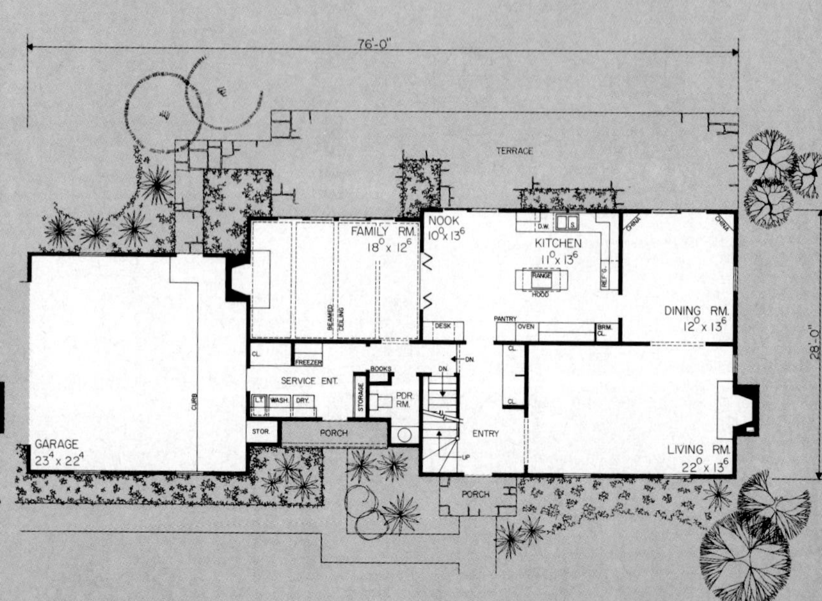

Design T21142 *1,525 Sq. Ft. - First Floor*

952 Sq. Ft. - Second Floor (1,053 Sq. Ft. - Four Bedroom Option); 32,980 Cu. Ft.

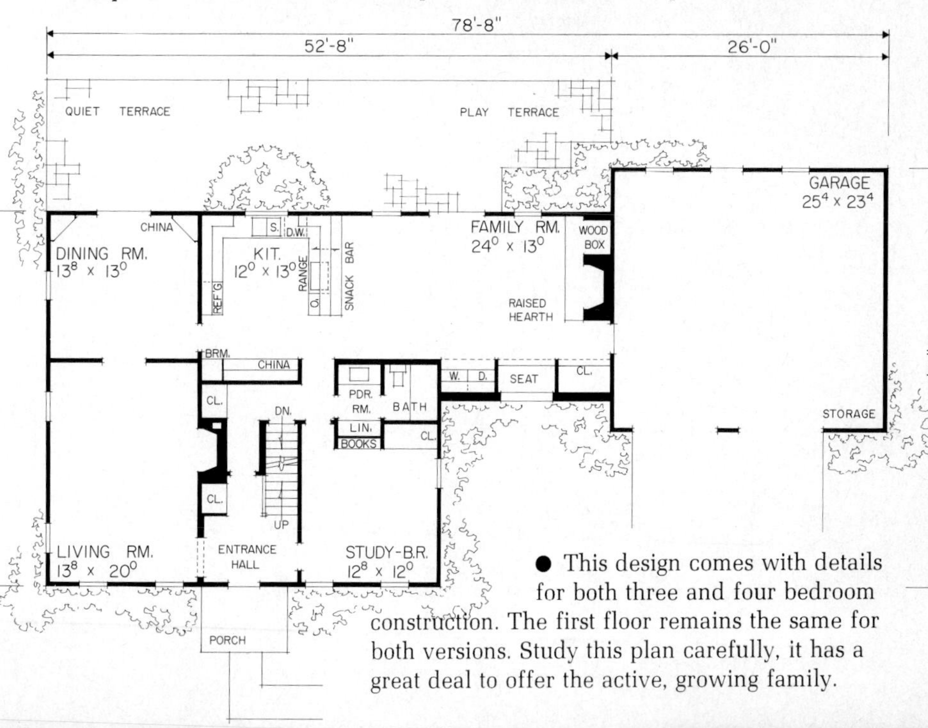

● This design comes with details for both three and four bedroom construction. The first floor remains the same for both versions. Study this plan carefully, it has a great deal to offer the active, growing family.

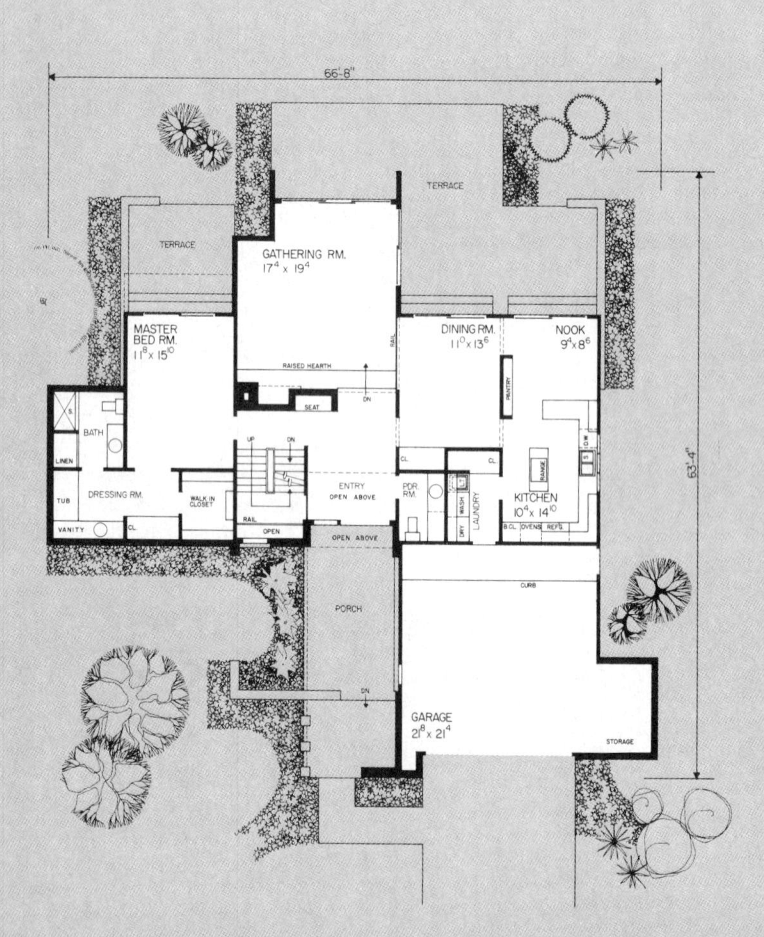

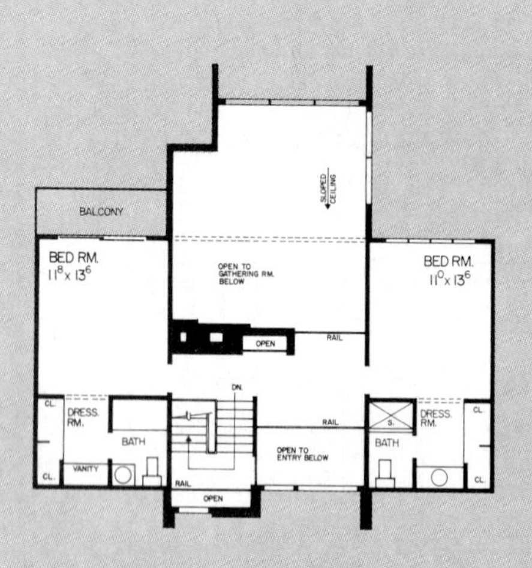

Design T22729

1,590 Sq. Ft. - First Floor
756 Sq. Ft. - Second Floor
39,310 Cu. Ft.

● Entering this home will surely be a pleasure through the sheltered walk-way to the double front doors. And the pleasure and beauty does not stop there. The entry hall and sunken gathering room are open to the upstairs for added dimension. There's even a built-in seat in the entry area. The kitchen-nook area is very efficient with its many built-ins and the adjacent laundry room. There is fine indoor-outdoor living relationship in this design. Note the private terrace off the luxurious master bedroom suite, a living terrace accessible from the gathering room, dining room and nook plus the balcony off the upstairs bedroom. Upstairs there is a total of two bedrooms, each having its own private bath and plenty of closets.

Design T22379 *1,525 Sq. Ft. - First Floor; 748 Sq. Ft. - Second Floor; 26,000 Cu. Ft.*

● A house that has "everything" may very well look just like this design. Its exterior is well-proportioned and impressive. Inside the inviting double front doors there are features galore. The living room and family room level are sunken. Separating these two rooms is a dramatic thru fireplace. A built-in bar, planter and beamed ceiling highlight the family room. Nearby is a full bath and a study which could be utilized as a fourth bedroom. The fine functioning kitchen has a pass-thru to the snack bar in the breakfast nook. The adjacent dining room overlooks the living room and has sliding doors to the covered porch. Upstairs three bedrooms, two baths and an outdoor balcony. Blueprints for this design include optional basement details.

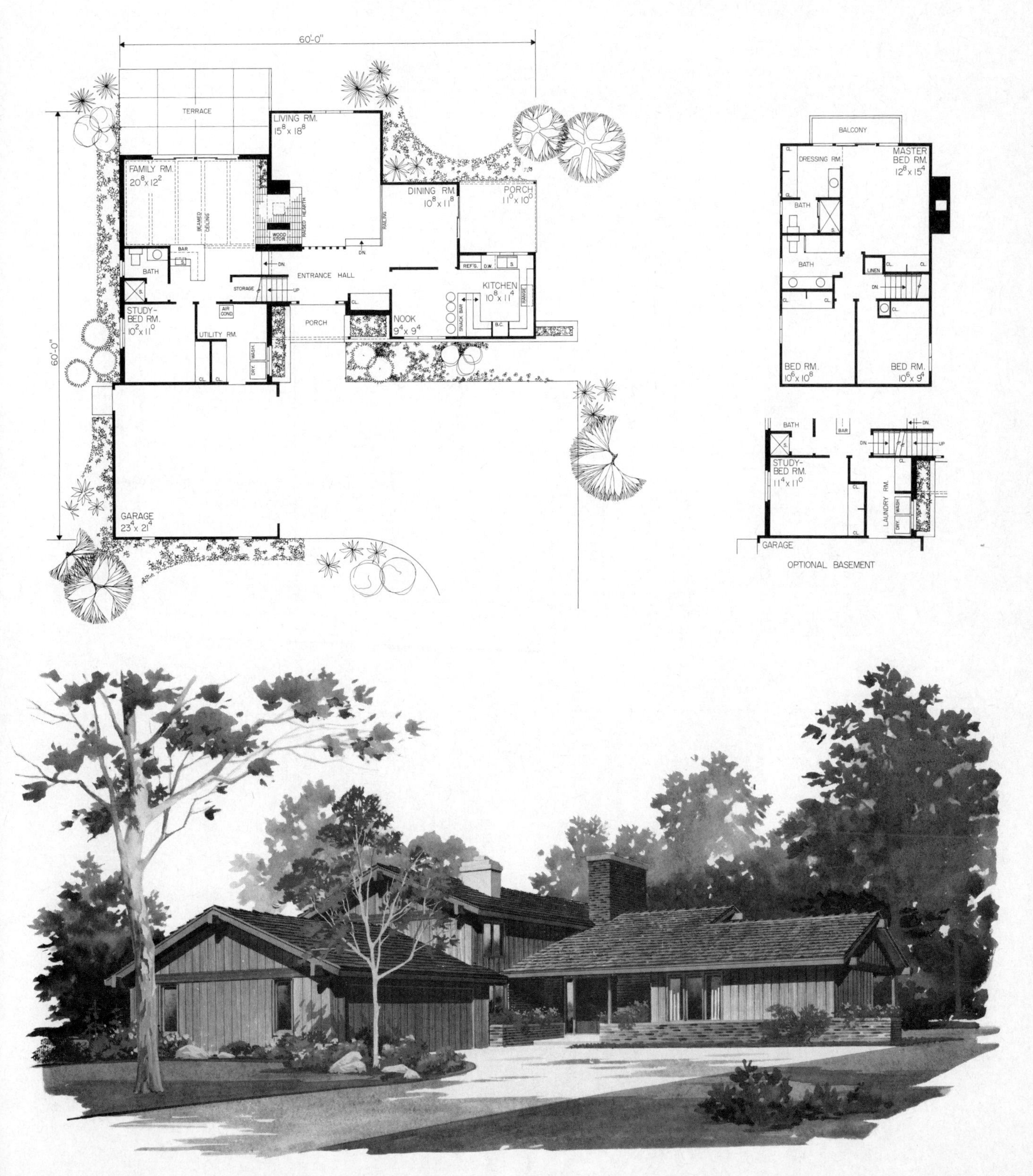

Design T22518

1,630 Sq. Ft. - First Floor
1,260 Sq. Ft. - Second Floor
43,968 Cu. Ft.

● For those who have a predilection for the Spanish influence in their architecture. Outdoor oriented, each of the major living areas on the first floor have direct access to the terraces. Traffic patterns are excellent.

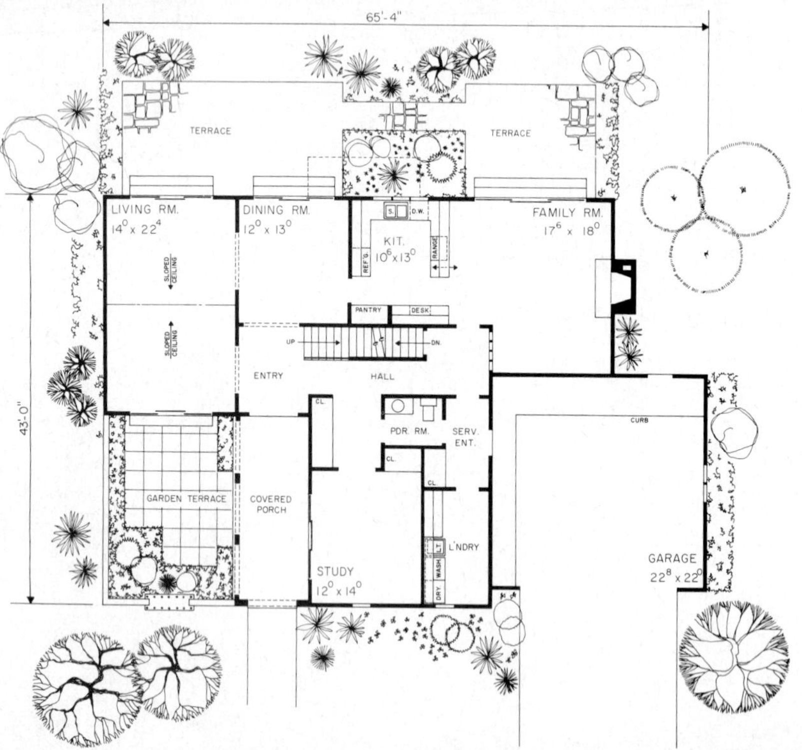

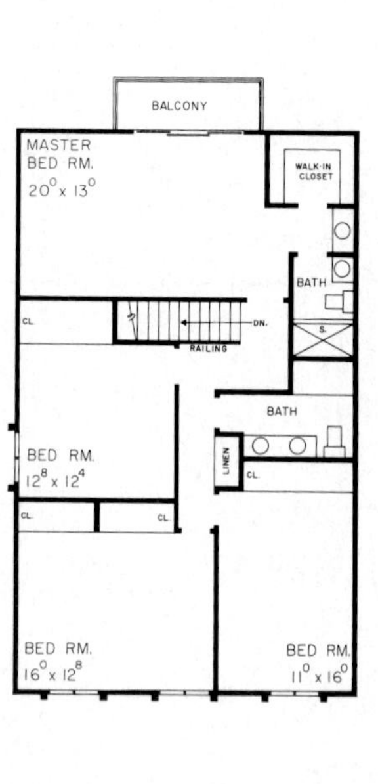

Design T22390 ***1,368 Sq. Ft. - First Floor***

1,428 Sq. Ft. - Second Floor; 37,734 Cu. Ft.

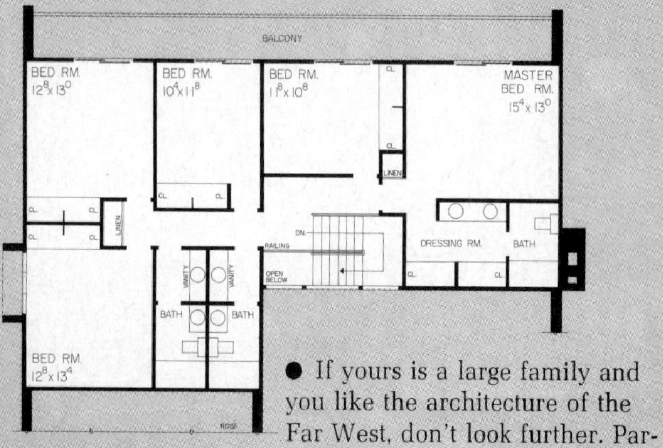

● If yours is a large family and you like the architecture of the Far West, don't look further. Particularly if you envision building on a modest sized lot. Projecting the garage to the front contributes to the drama of this two-story. Its stucco exterior is beautifully enhanced by the clay tiles of the varying roof surfaces.

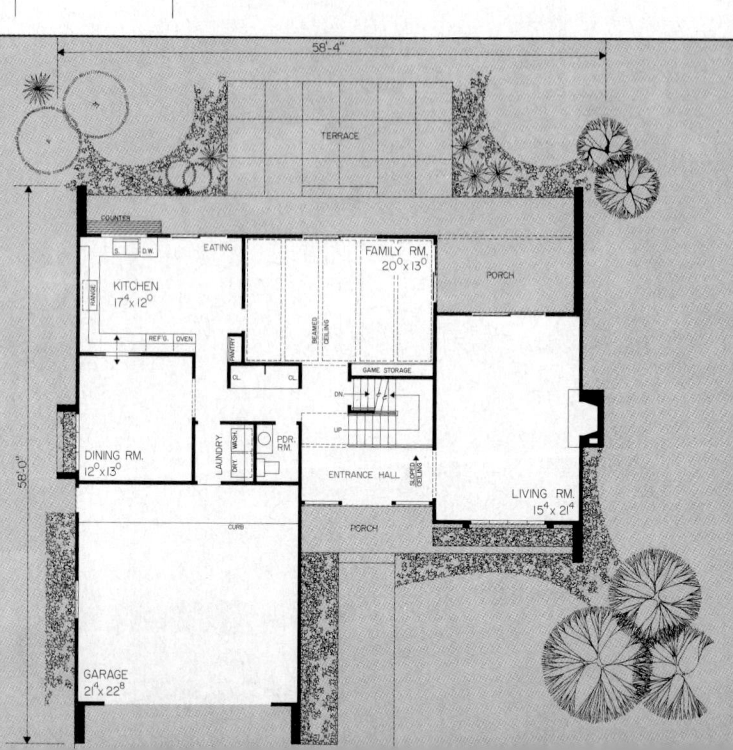

Design T22517

1,767 Sq. Ft. - First Floor
1,094 Sq. Ft. - Second Floor
50,256 Cu. Ft.

● Wherever built - north, east, south, or west - this home will surely command all the attention it deserves. And little wonder with such a well-designed exterior and such an outstanding interior. List your favorite features.

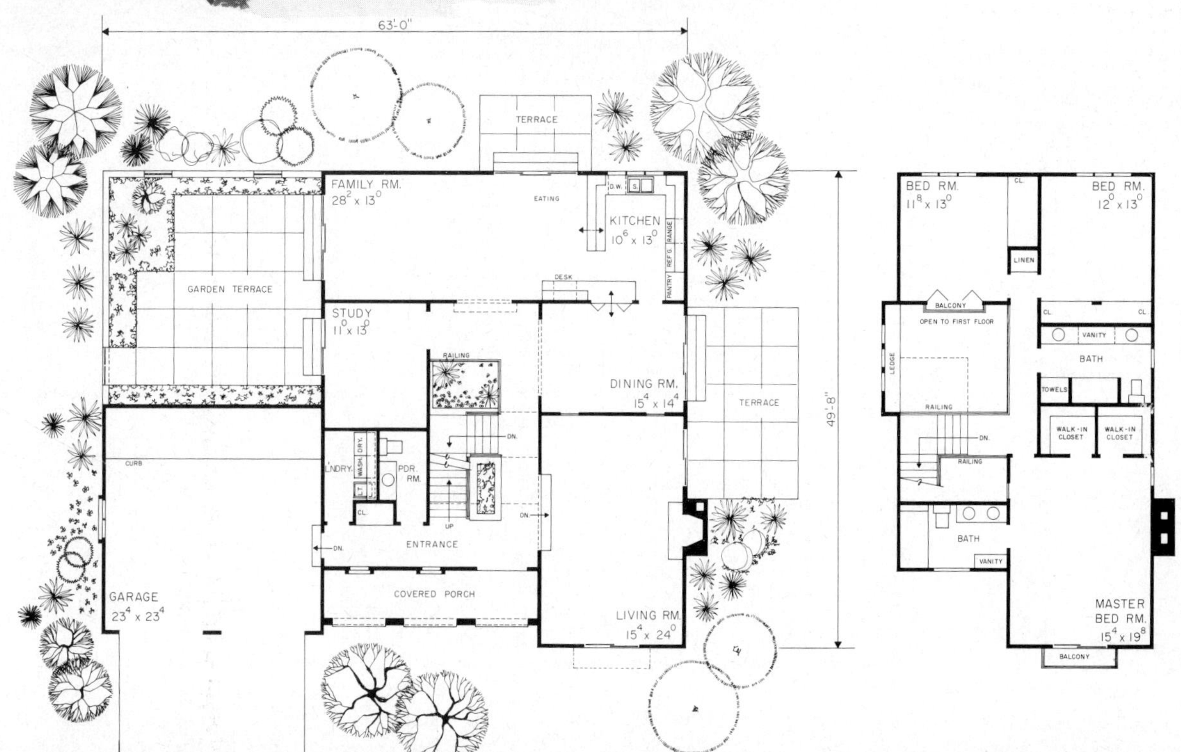

Design T22176

1,485 Sq. Ft. - First Floor
1,175 Sq. Ft. - Second Floor
41,646 Cu. Ft.

● This Georgian adaptation will serve your family well. It will be the soundest investment you'll make in your lifetime and provide your family with wonderful living.

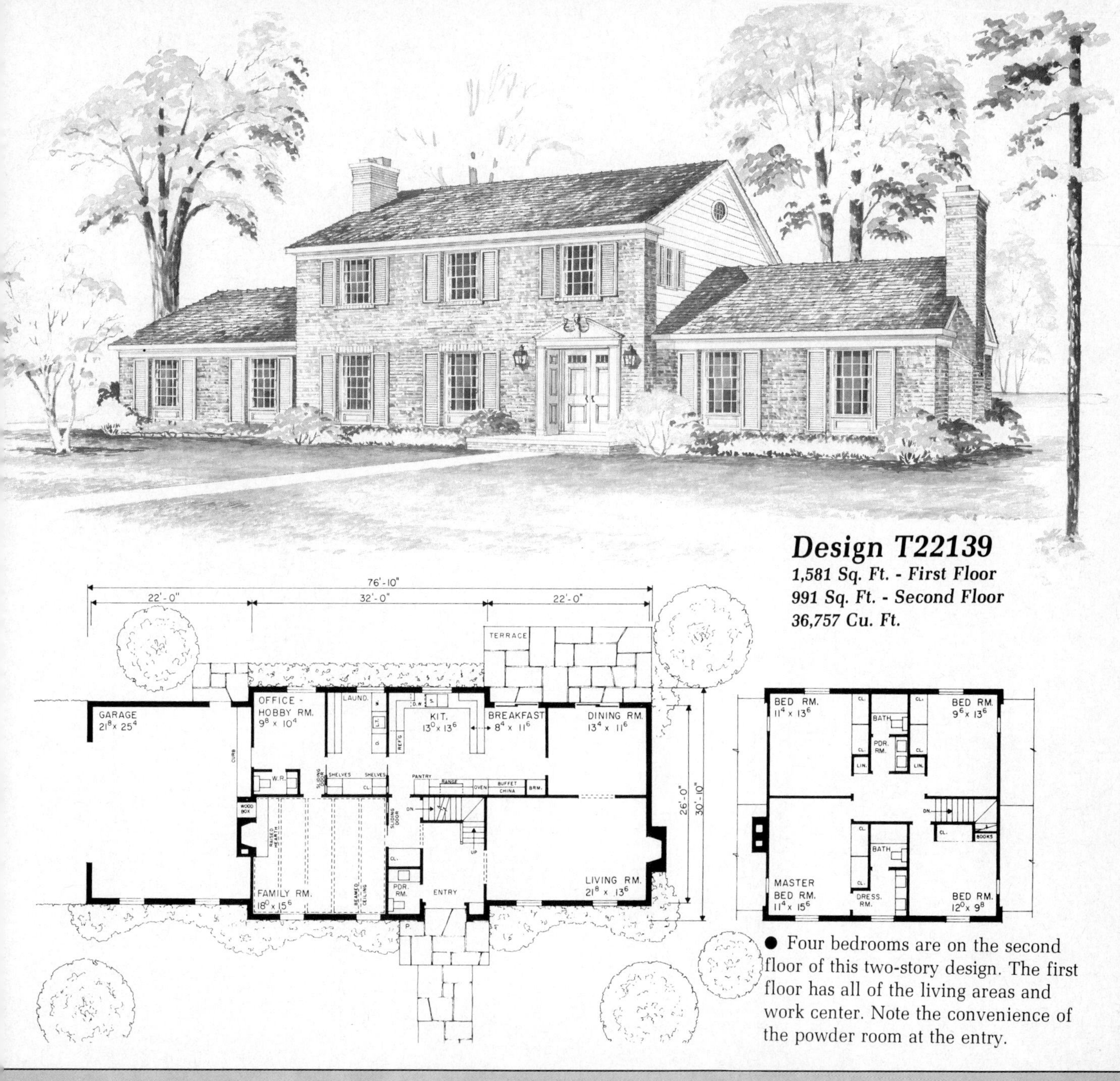

Design T22139

1,581 Sq. Ft. - First Floor
991 Sq. Ft. - Second Floor
36,757 Cu. Ft.

● Four bedrooms are on the second floor of this two-story design. The first floor has all of the living areas and work center. Note the convenience of the powder room at the entry.

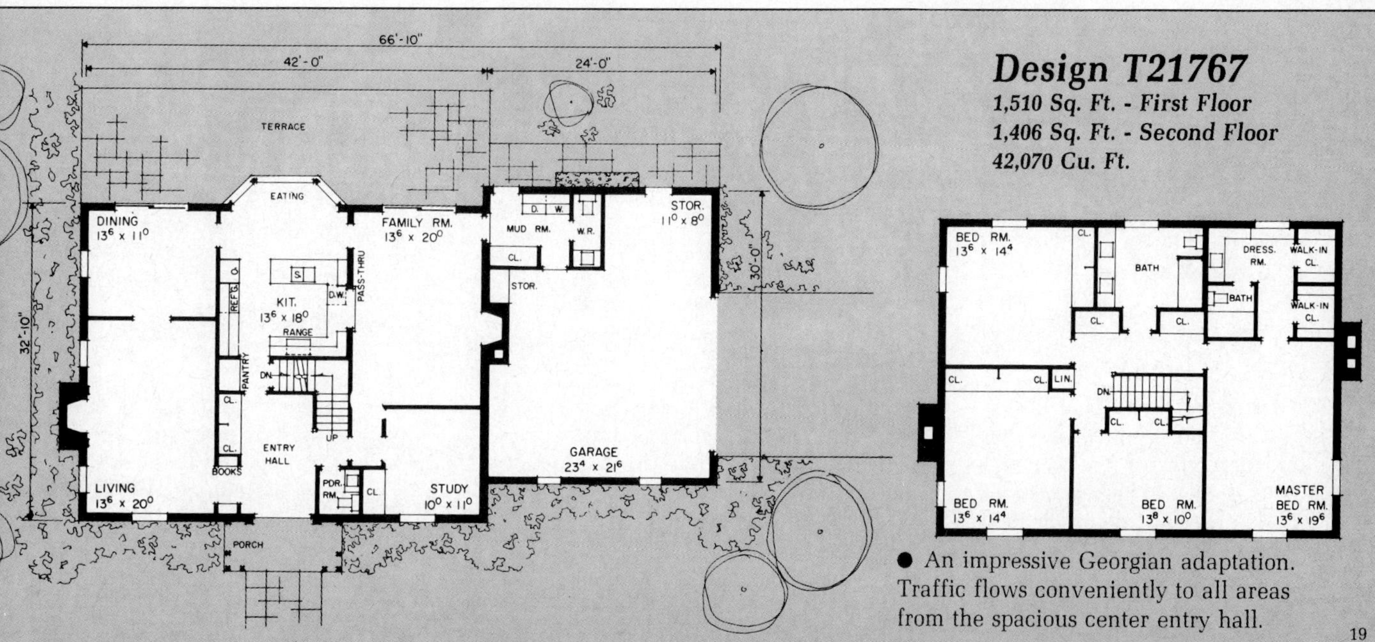

Design T21767

1,510 Sq. Ft. - First Floor
1,406 Sq. Ft. - Second Floor
42,070 Cu. Ft.

● An impressive Georgian adaptation. Traffic flows conveniently to all areas from the spacious center entry hall.

Design T21887

1,518 Sq. Ft. - First Floor
1,144 Sq. Ft. - Second Floor
40,108 Cu. Ft.

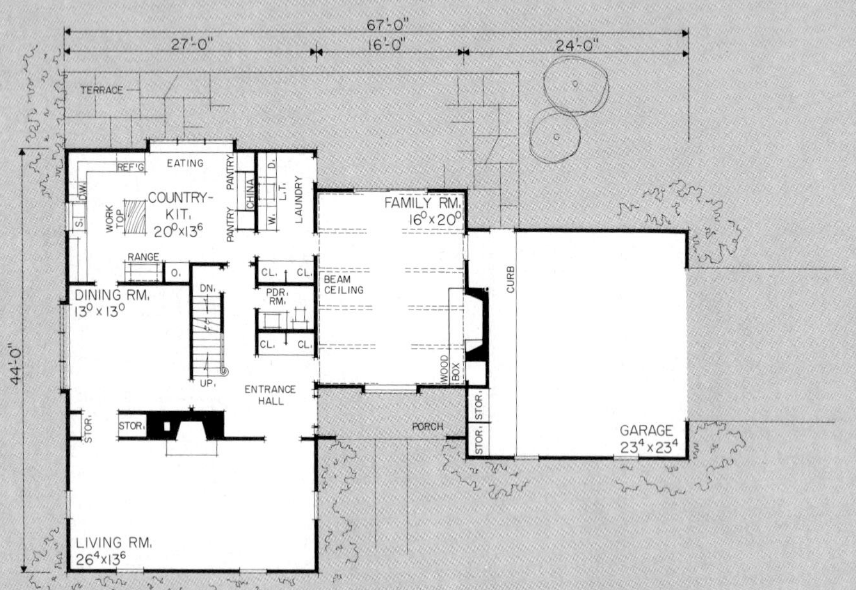

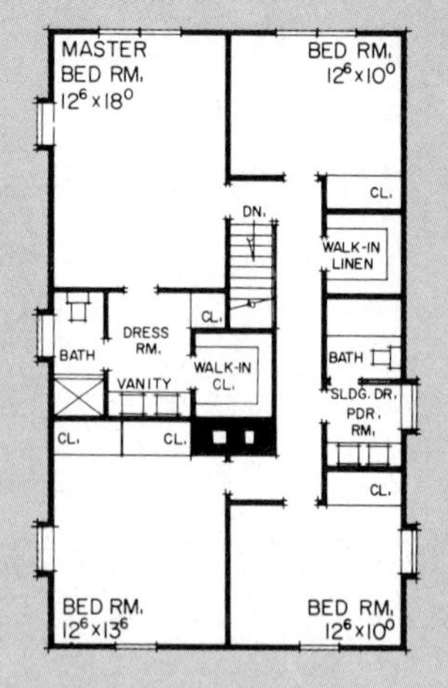

● This Gambrel roof Colonial is steeped in history. And well it should be, for its pleasing proportions are a delight to the eye. The various roof planes, the window treatment, and the rambling nature of the entire house revive a picture of rural New England. The covered porch protects the front door which opens into a spacious entrance hall. Traffic then flows in an orderly fashion to the end living room, the separate dining room, the cozy family room, and to the spacious country-kitchen. There is a first floor laundry, plenty of coat closets, and a handy powder room. Two fireplaces enliven the decor of the living areas. Upstairs there is an exceptional master bedroom layout, and abundant storage. Note the walk-in closets.

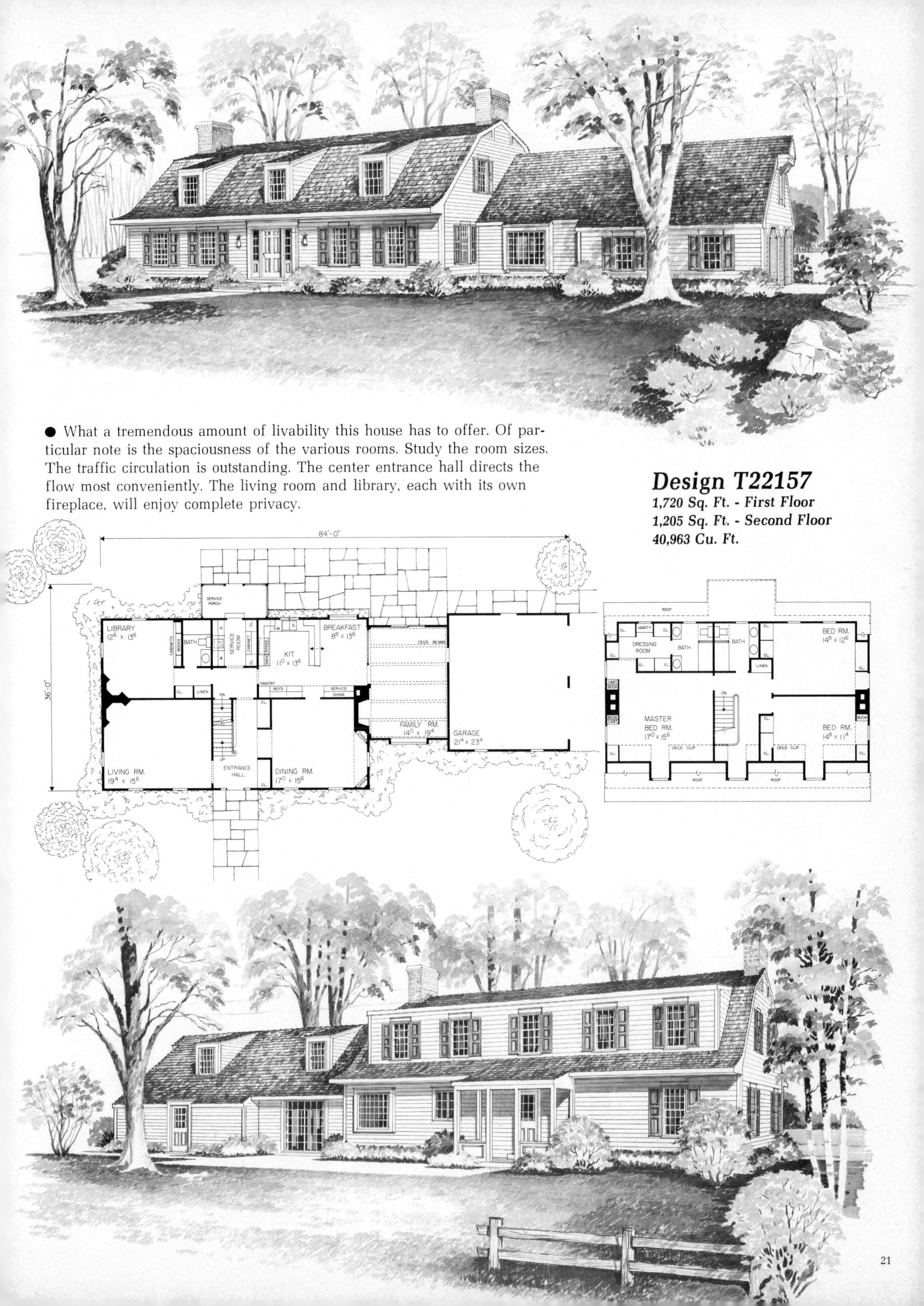

● What a tremendous amount of livability this house has to offer. Of particular note is the spaciousness of the various rooms. Study the room sizes. The traffic circulation is outstanding. The center entrance hall directs the flow most conveniently. The living room and library, each with its own fireplace, will enjoy complete privacy.

Design T22157

1,720 Sq. Ft. - First Floor
1,205 Sq. Ft. - Second Floor
40,963 Cu. Ft.

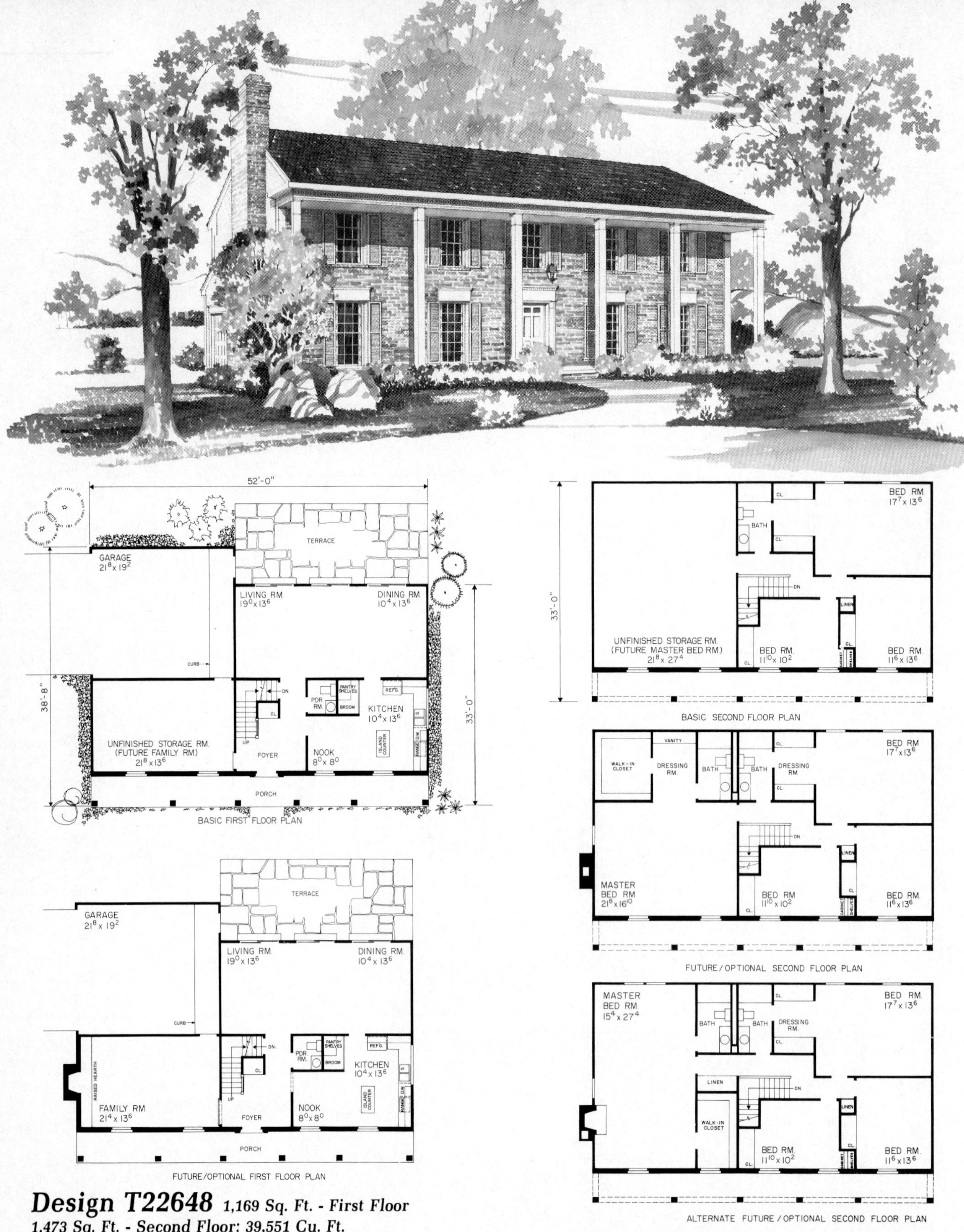

Design T22648 *1,169 Sq. Ft. - First Floor 1,473 Sq. Ft. - Second Floor; 39,551 Cu. Ft.*

● If you are looking for a house to fit your present family, but also need one when it is full grown, then this is the design for you. This house appears large, but until the two unfinished rooms (one upstairs and one on the first floor), are completed it is an economical house. Later development of these rooms conserves initial construction expense. A major economy has been realized because the basic structural work is already standing. From the outside, onlookers will never know that there are unfinished rooms inside. The exterior appeal is outstanding with its two-story pillars extending from the overhanging roof and its rows of windows which cover the length of the facade. The rear elevation features three sets of sliding glass doors.

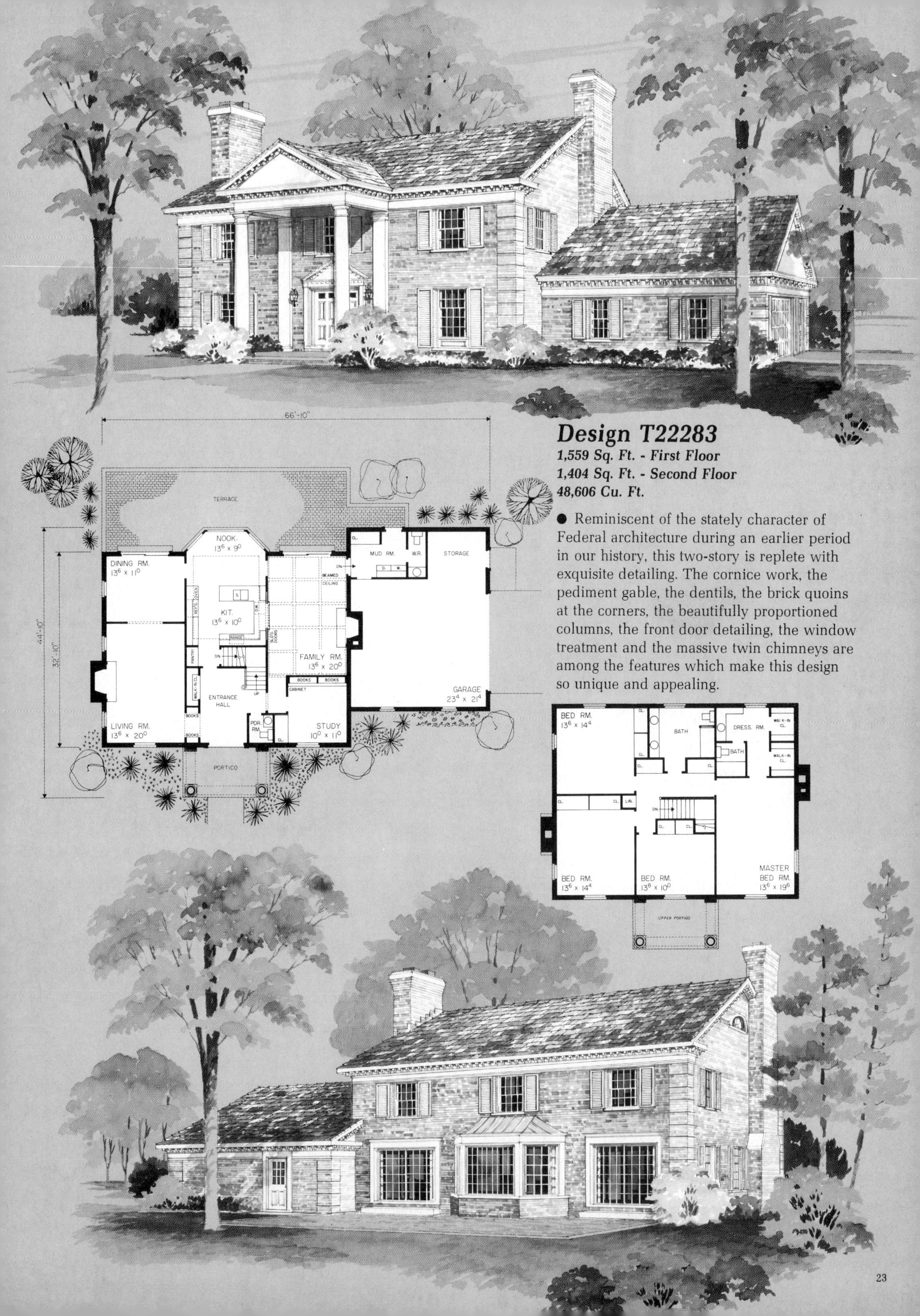

Design T22283

1,559 Sq. Ft. - First Floor
1,404 Sq. Ft. - Second Floor
48,606 Cu. Ft.

● Reminiscent of the stately character of Federal architecture during an earlier period in our history, this two-story is replete with exquisite detailing. The cornice work, the pediment gable, the dentils, the brick quoins at the corners, the beautifully proportioned columns, the front door detailing, the window treatment and the massive twin chimneys are among the features which make this design so unique and appealing.

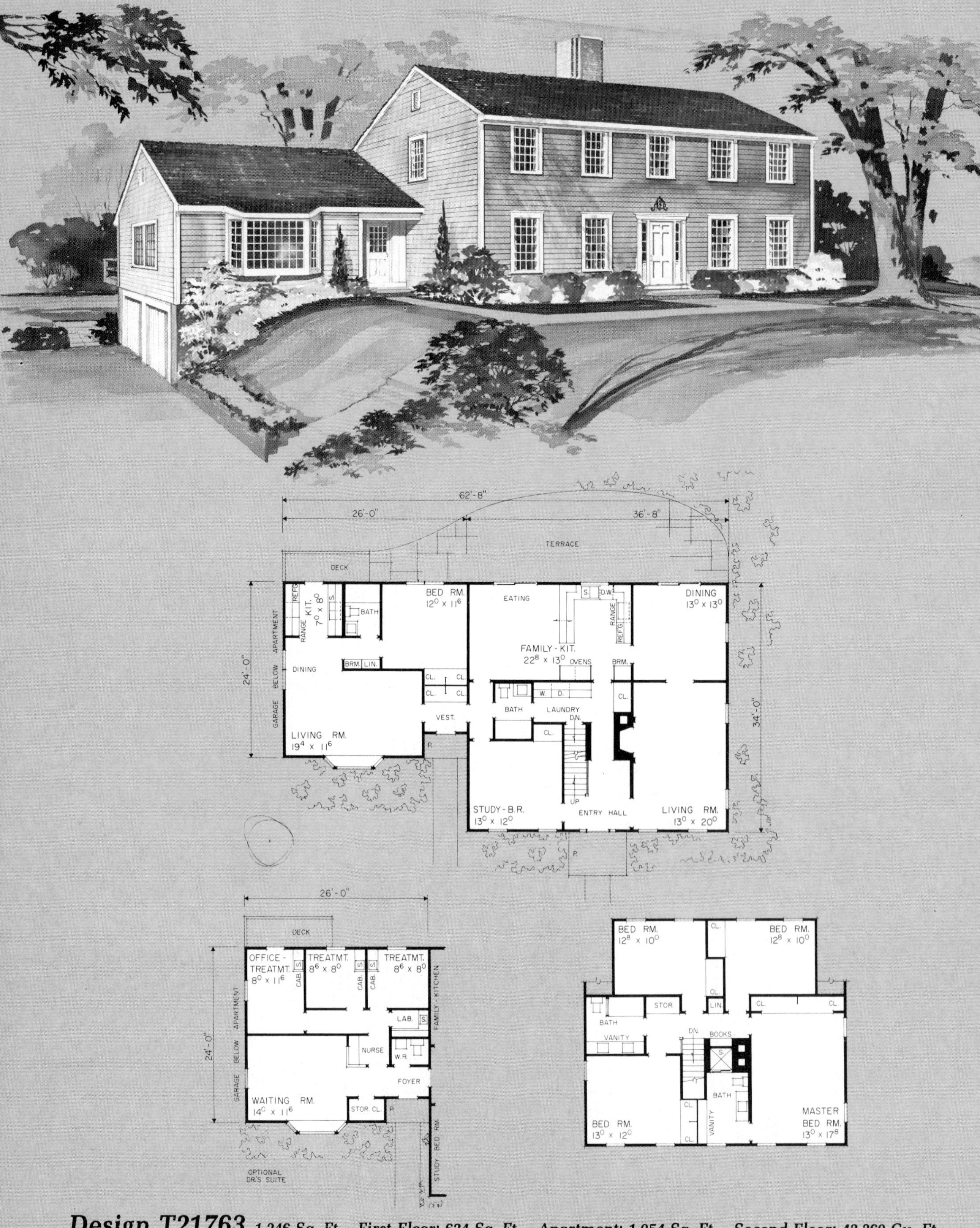

Design T21763 *1,246 Sq. Ft. - First Floor; 624 Sq. Ft. - Apartment; 1,054 Sq. Ft. - Second Floor; 42,260 Cu. Ft.*

● A charming New England Salt Box designed to satisfy the needs of the large family, plus provide facilities for a live-in relative! Many houses can be a problem in adapting to the living requirements of an in-residence relative. But, not this one. Your family will have all the space it needs, while your relative will enjoy all his or her privacy and independence. This apartment area may also be adapted to function as a doctor's suite.

Design T22610 ***1,505 Sq. Ft. - First Floor; 1,344 Sq. Ft. - Second Floor; 45,028 Cu. Ft.***

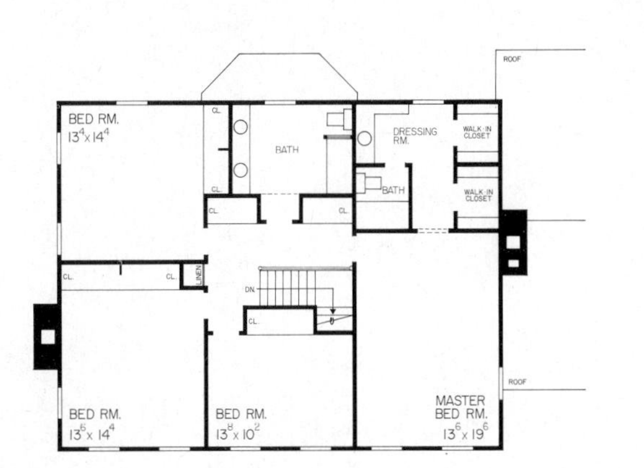

● This full two-story traditional will be worthy of note wherever built. It strongly recalls images of a New England of yesteryear. And well it might; for the window treatment is delightful. The front entrance detail is inviting. The narrow horizontal siding and the corner boards are appealing as are the two massive chimneys. The center entrance hall is large with a handy powder room nearby. The study has built-in bookshelves and offers a full measure of privacy. The interior kitchen has a pass-thru to the family room and enjoys all that natural light from the bay window of the nook. A beamed ceiling, fireplace and sliding glass doors are features of the family room. The mud room highlights a closet, laundry equipment and an extra wash room. Study the upstairs with those four bedrooms, two baths and plenty of closets. An excellent arrangement for all.

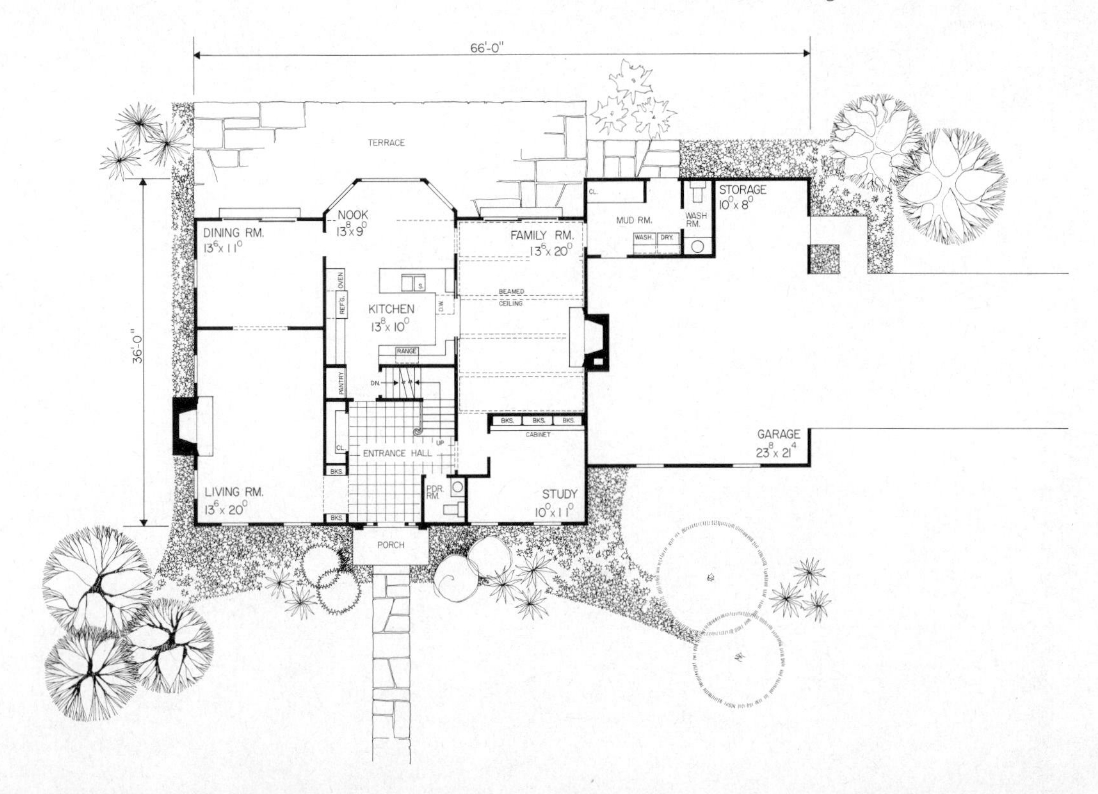

Design T22276 1,273 Sq. Ft. - First Floor
1,323 Sq. Ft. - Second Floor; 40,450 Cu. Ft.

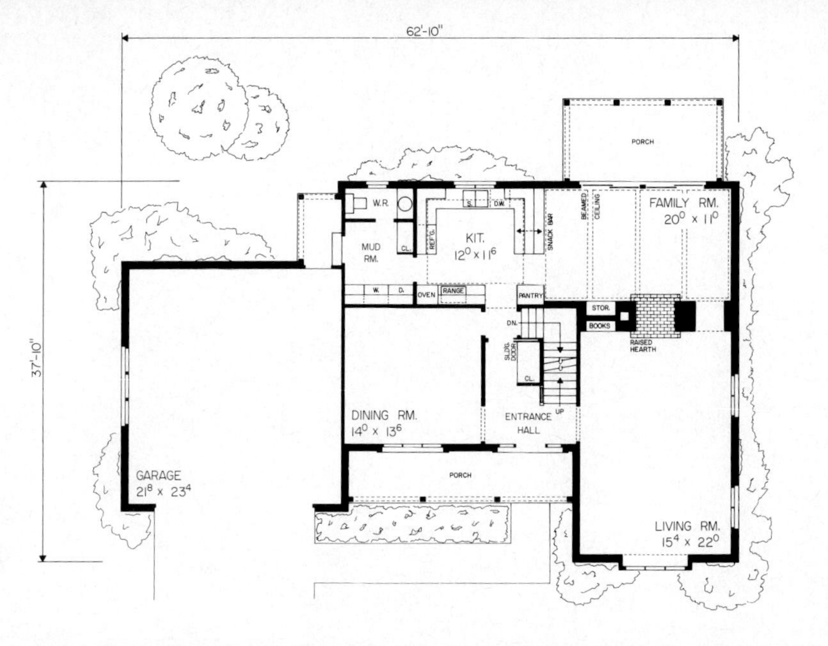

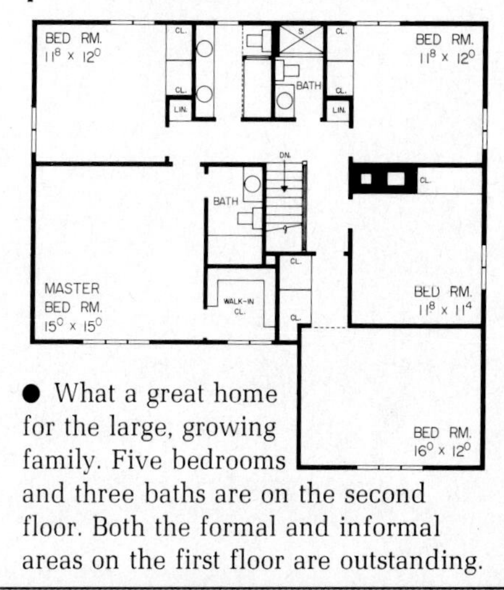

● What a great home for the large, growing family. Five bedrooms and three baths are on the second floor. Both the formal and informal areas on the first floor are outstanding.

Design T22141 1,490 Sq. Ft. - First Floor
1,474 Sq. Ft. - Second Floor; 50,711 Cu. Ft.

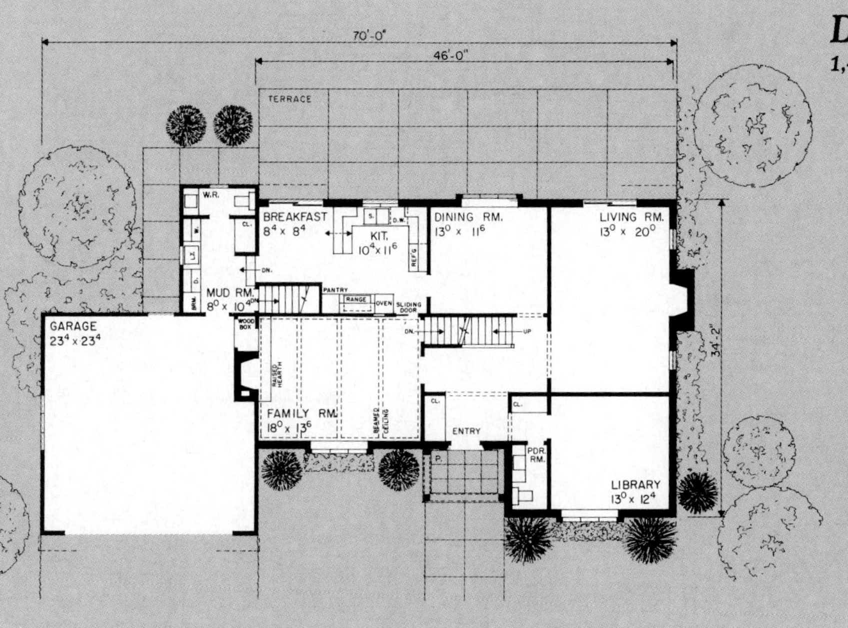

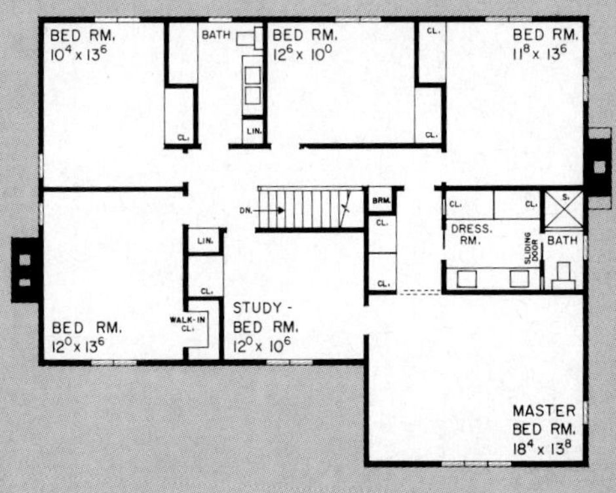

● Imagine, six bedrooms on the second floor. The first floor houses the living areas: family room, living room, dining areas plus a library.

Design T22577 1,718 Sq. Ft. - First Floor
1,147 Sq. Ft. - Second Floor; 42,843 Cu. Ft.

● The exterior of this Tudor has interesting roof planes, delightful window treatment and recessed front entrance. The master suite with sitting room is one of the highlights of the interior.

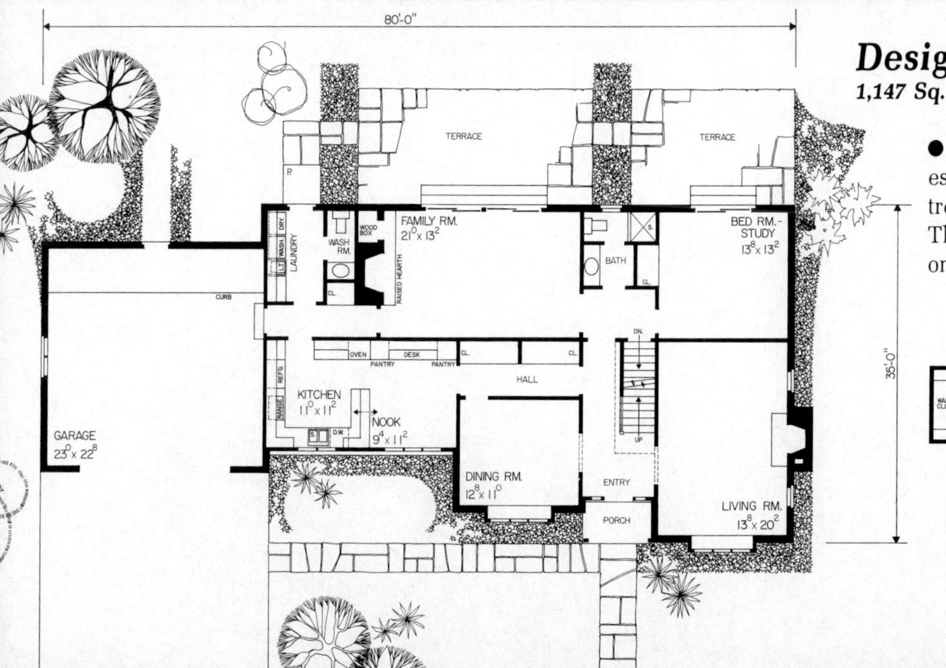

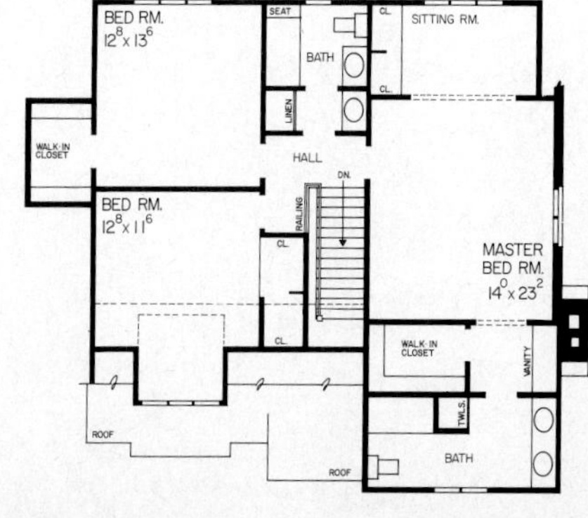

Design T22823

1,370 Sq. Ft. - First Floor
927 Sq. Ft. - Second Floor
34,860 Cu. Ft.

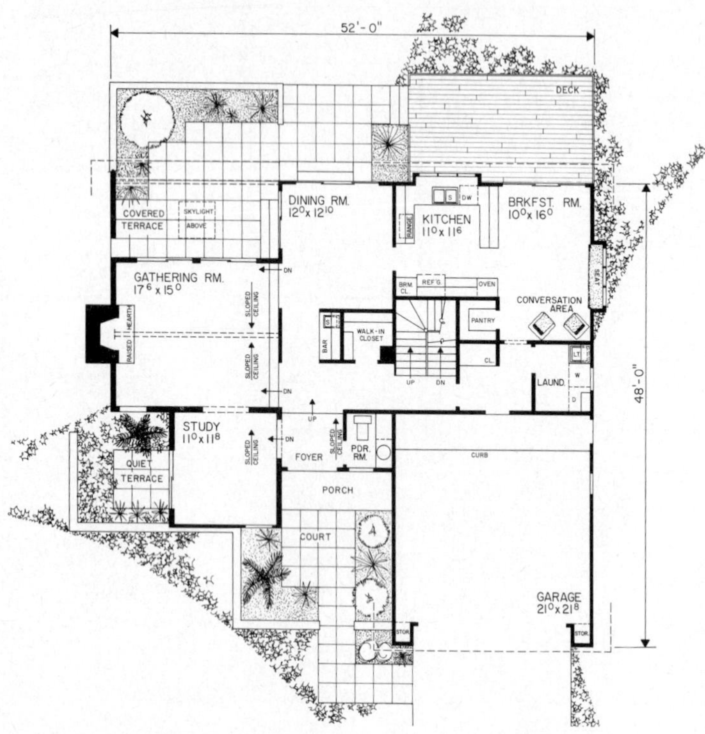

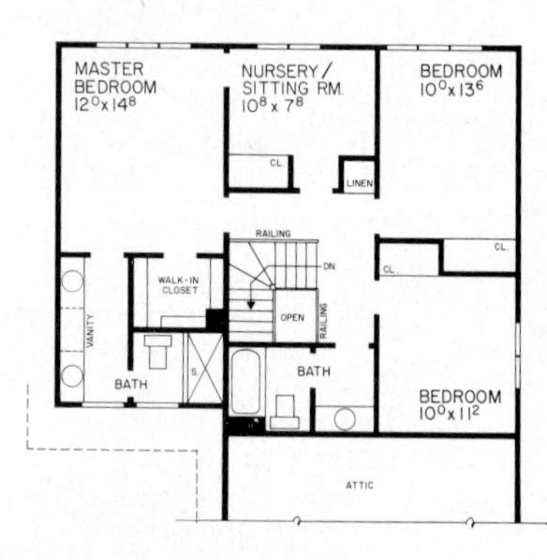

● The street view of this contemporary design features a small courtyard entrance as well as a private terrace off the study. Inside the livability will be outstanding. This design features spacious first floor activity areas that flow smoothly into each other. In the gathering room a raised hearth fireplace creates a dramatic focal point. An adjacent covered terrace, featuring a skylight, is ideal for outdoor dining and could be screened in later for an additional room.

1½-Story Designs

An Optimum Return On Investment

Design T22174

1,506 Sq. Ft. - First Floor
1,156 Sq. Ft. - Second Floor
37,360 Cu. Ft.

● Your building budget could hardly buy more charm, or greater livability. The appeal of the exterior is wrapped up in a myriad of design features. They include: the interesting roof lines; the effective use of brick and horizontal siding; the delightful window treatment; the covered front porch; the chimney and dove-cote detailing. The livability of the interior is represented by a long list of convenient living features. There is a formal area consisting of a living room with fireplace and dining room. The family room has a raised hearth fireplace, wood box and beamed ceiling. Also on the first floor is a kitchen, laundry and bedroom with adjacent bath. Three bedrooms, lounge and two baths upstairs plus plenty of closets and bulk storage over garage. Don't overlook the sliding glass doors, the breakfast area and the basement. An excellent plan.

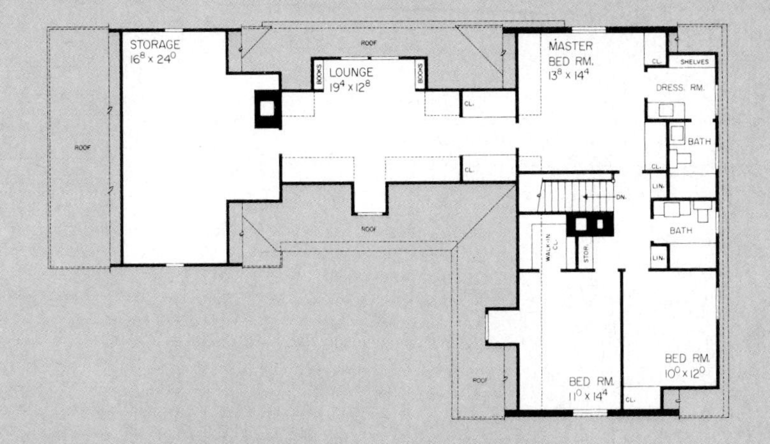

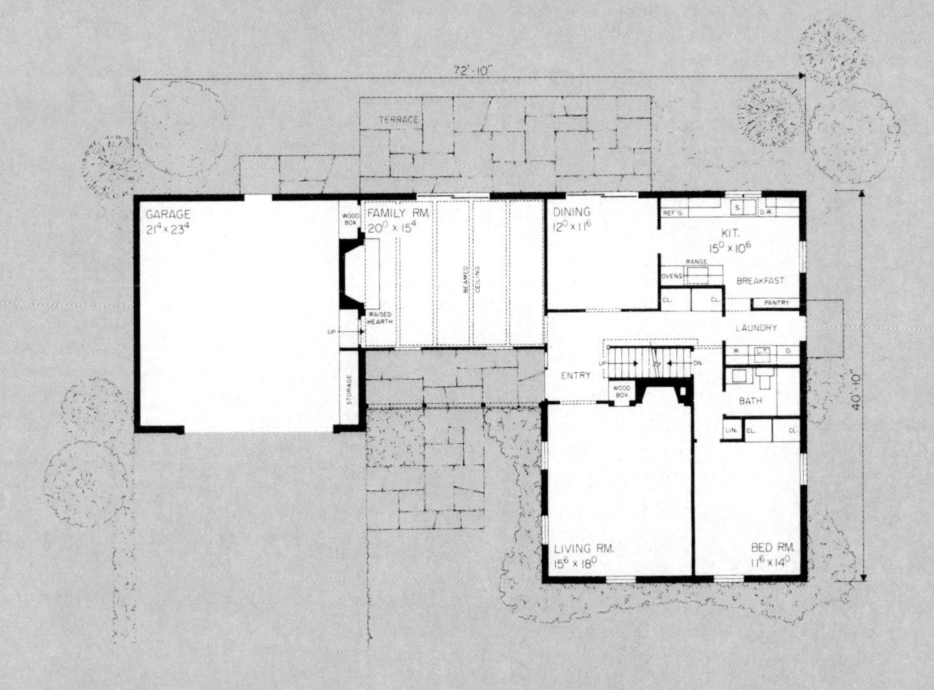

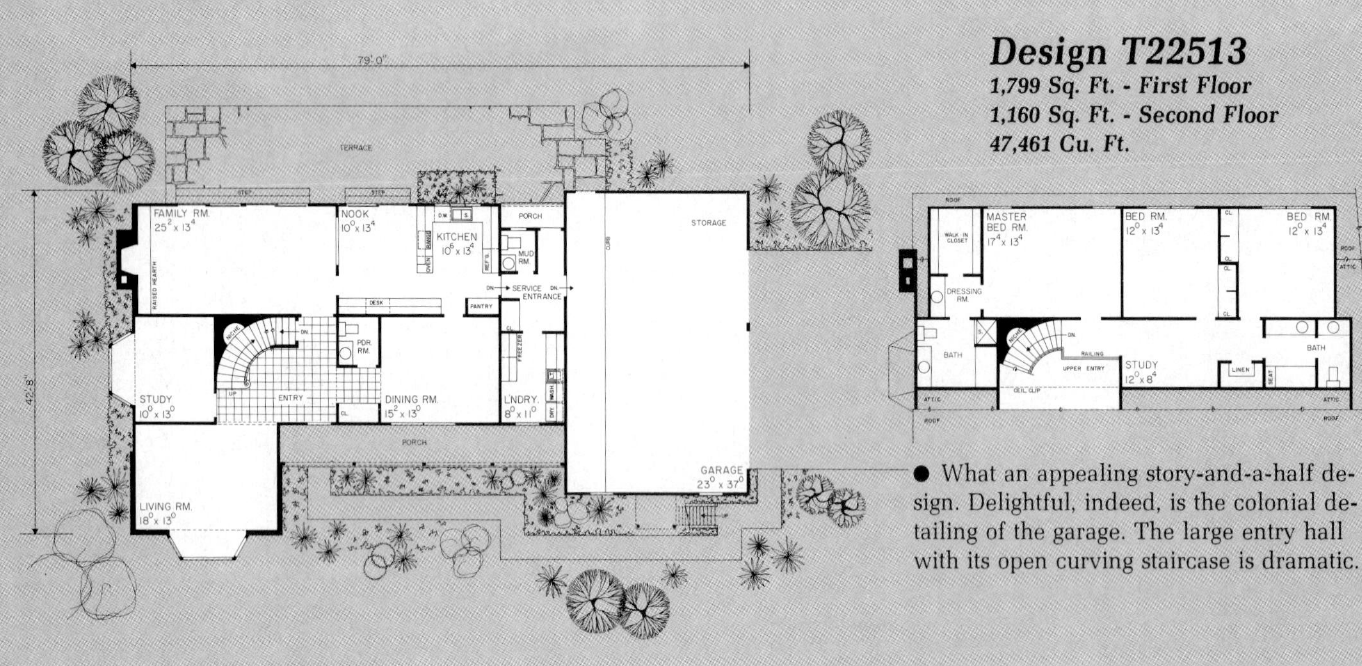

Design T22513

1,799 Sq. Ft. - First Floor
1,160 Sq. Ft. - Second Floor
47,461 Cu. Ft.

● What an appealing story-and-a-half design. Delightful, indeed, is the colonial detailing of the garage. The large entry hall with its open curving staircase is dramatic.

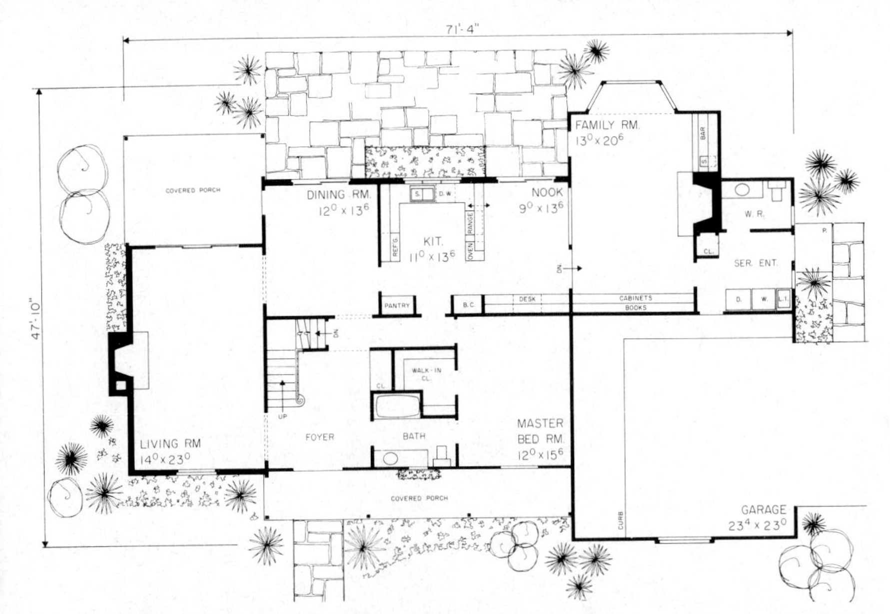

Design T22500

1,851 Sq. Ft. - First Floor
762 Sq. Ft. - Second Floor
43,052 Cu. Ft.

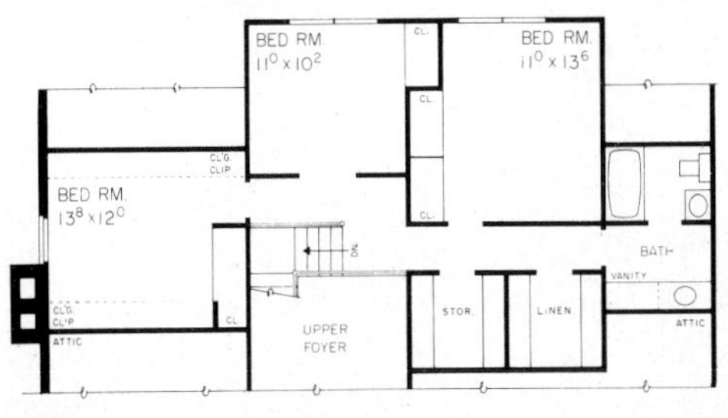

● The large family will enjoy the wonderful living patterns offered by this charming home. Don't miss the covered rear porch and the many features of the family room.

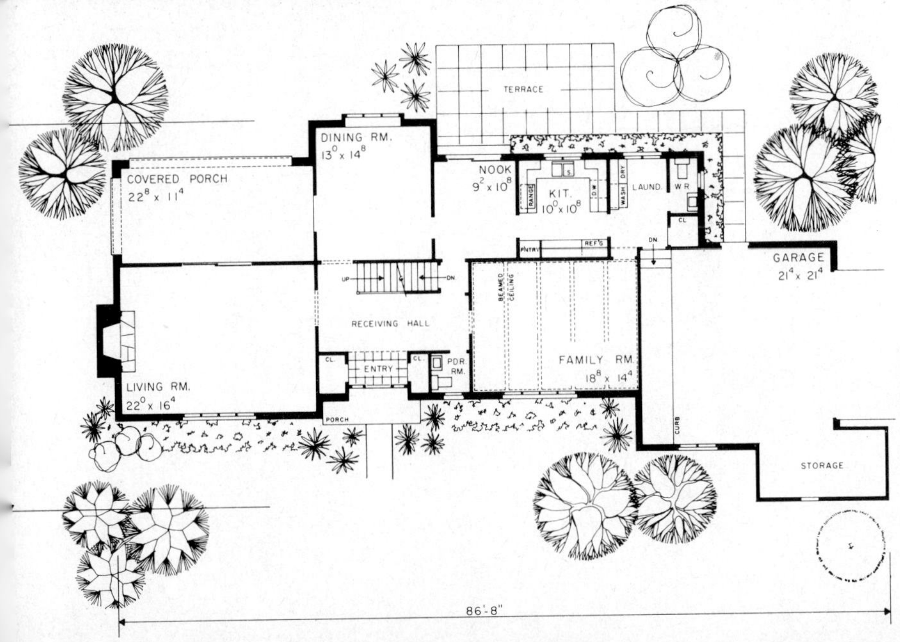

Design T22338

1,505 Sq. Ft. - First Floor
1,219 Sq. Ft. - Second Floor
38,878 Cu. Ft.

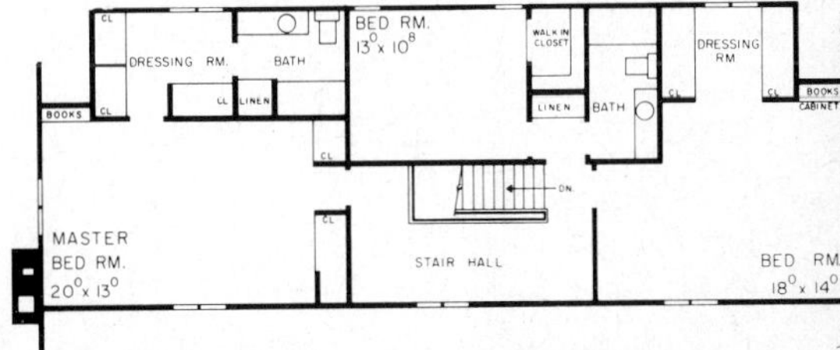

● A spacious receiving hall is a fine setting for the welcoming of guests. Here traffic flows effectively to all areas of the plan. Outstanding livability throughout the entire plan.

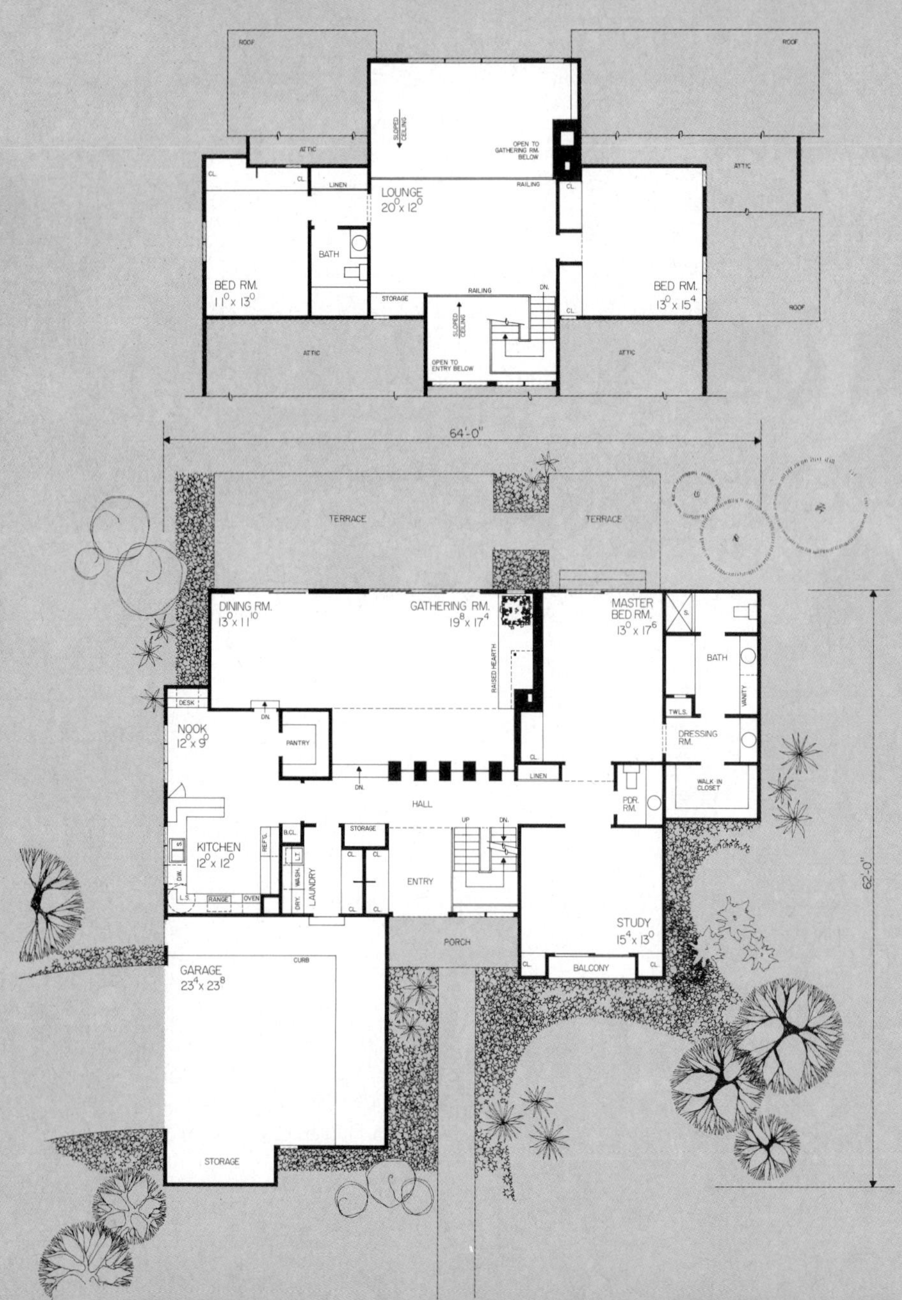

Design T22708

2,108 Sq. Ft. - First Floor
824 Sq. Ft. - Second Floor
52,170 Cu. Ft.

● Here is a one-and-a-half story home whose exterior is distinctive. It has a contemporary feeling, yet it retains some of the fine design features and proportions of traditional exteriors. Inside the appealing double front doors there is livability galore. The sunken rear living-dining area is delightfully spacious and is looked down into from the second floor lounge. The open end fireplace, with its raised hearth and planter, is another focal point. The master bedroom features a fine compartmented bath with both shower and tub. The study is just a couple steps away. The U-shaped kitchen is outstanding. Notice the pantry and laundry. Upstairs provides children with their own sleeping, studying and TV quarters. Absolutely a great design! Study all the fine details closely with your family.

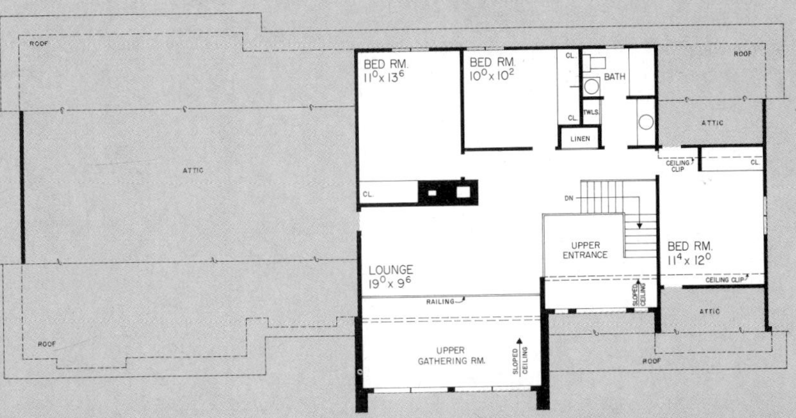

Design T22782

2,060 Sq. Ft. - First Floor
897 Sq. Ft. - Second Floor
47,750 Cu. Ft.

● What makes this such a distinctive four bedroom design? Let's list some of the features. This plan includes great formal and informal living for the family at home or when entertaining guests. The formal gathering room and informal family room share a dramatic raised-hearth fireplace. Other features of the sunken gathering room include: high, sloped ceilings, built-in planter and sliding glass doors to the front entrance court. The kitchen has a snack bar, many built-ins, a pass-thru to dining room and easy access to the large laundry/washroom. The master bedroom suite is located on the main level for added privacy and convenience. There's even a study with a built-in bar. The upper level has three more bedrooms, a bath and a lounge looking down into the gathering room.

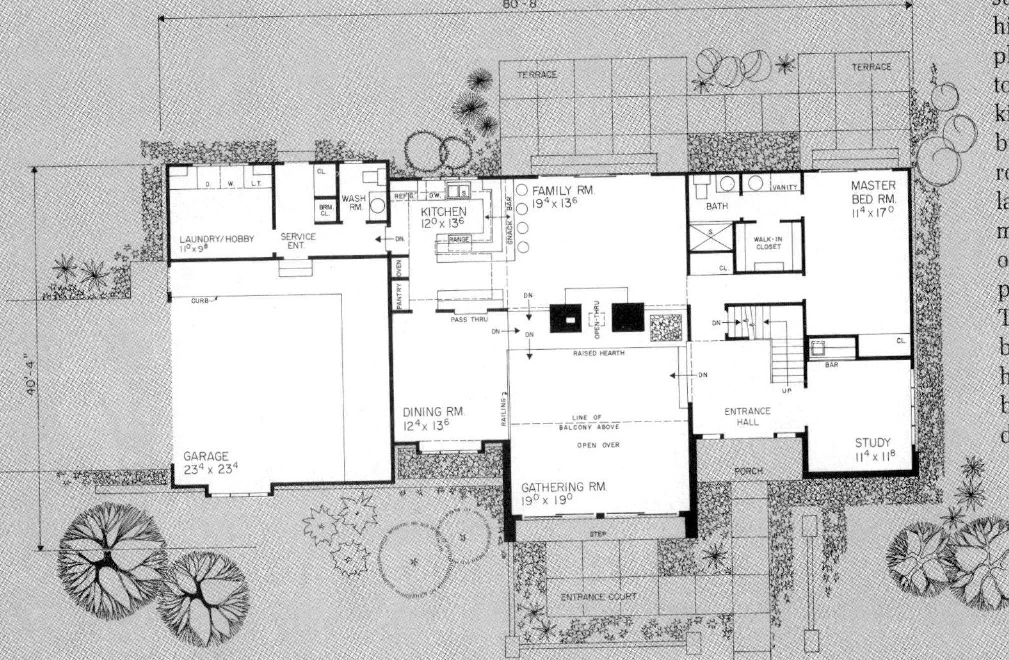

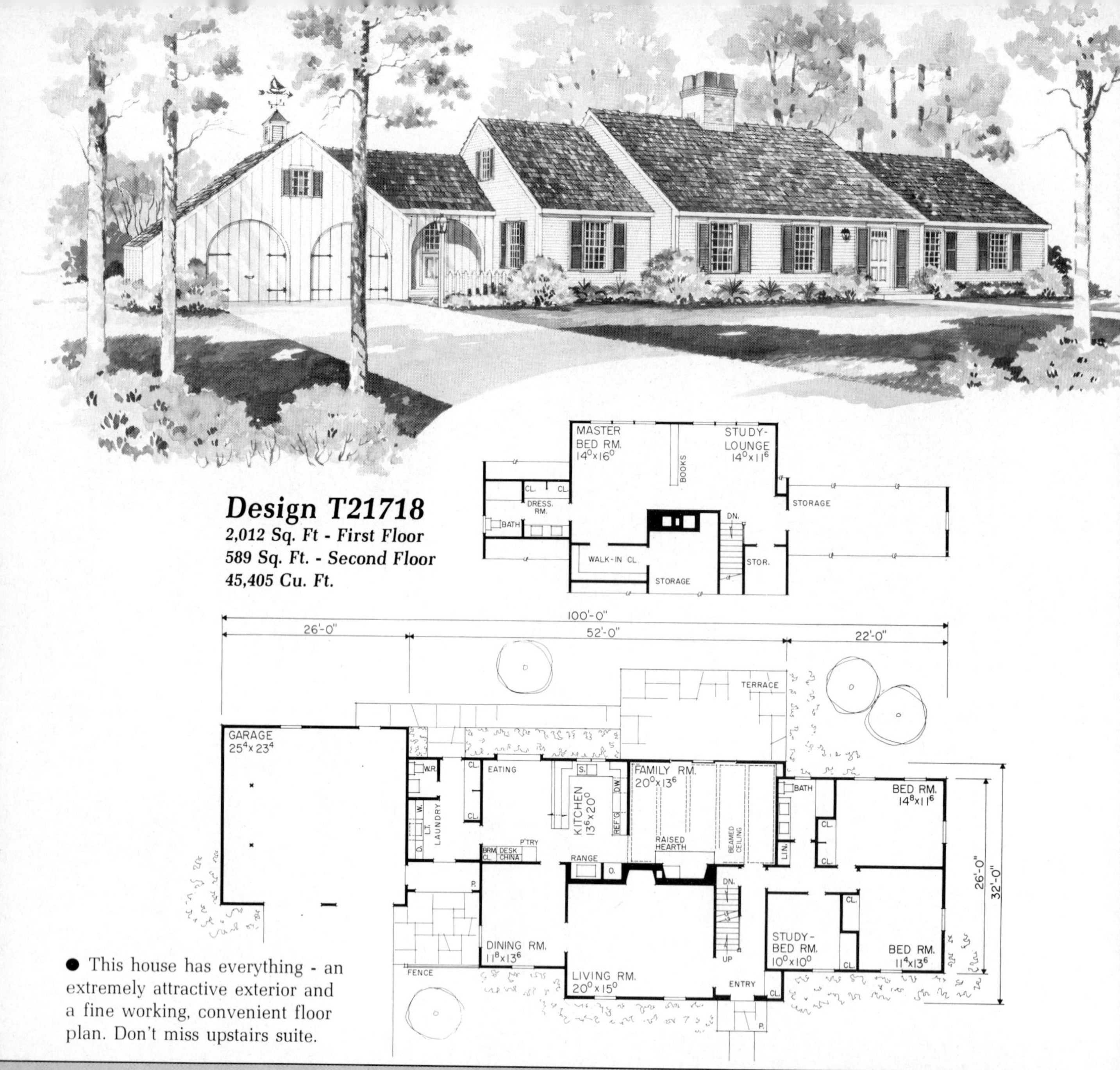

Design T21718

2,012 Sq. Ft - First Floor
589 Sq. Ft. - Second Floor
45,405 Cu. Ft.

● This house has everything - an extremely attractive exterior and a fine working, convenient floor plan. Don't miss upstairs suite.

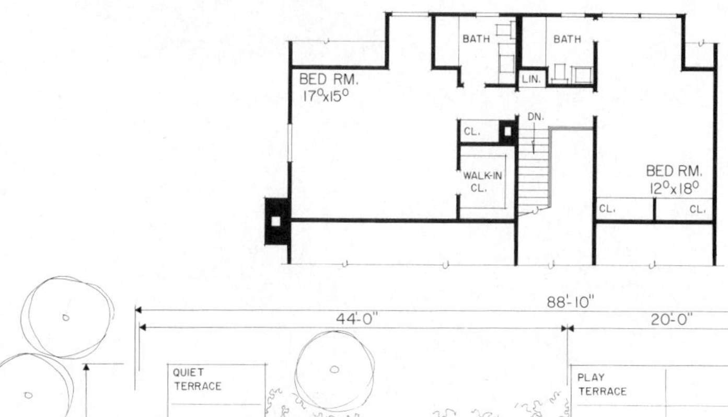

Design T21794

2,122 Sq. Ft. - First Floor
802 Sq. Ft. - Second Floor
37,931 Cu. Ft.

● The inviting warmth of this delightful story-and-a-half home catches the eye of even the most casual observer. Imagine, four big bedrooms! Formal and informal living can be enjoyed throughout this charming plan. Two fireplaces. One has a raised hearth and an adjacent wood box. A very private, formal dining room for those very special occasions. A U-shaped kitchen with pass-thru to family room. Note the two distinct rear terraces.

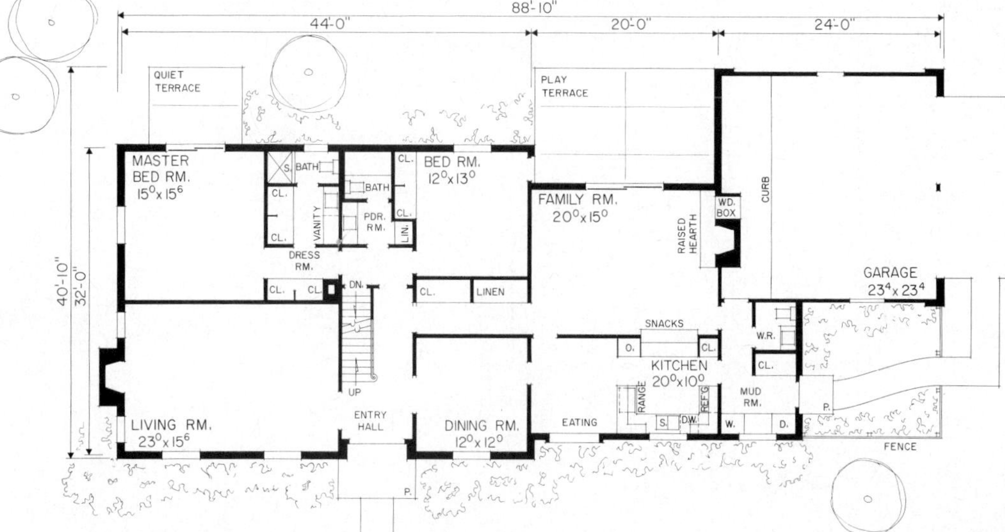

Design T21987

1,632 Sq. Ft. - First Floor
980 Sq. Ft. - Second Floor
35,712 Cu. Ft.

● The comforts of home will surely be endless and enduring when experienced and enjoyed in this Colonial adaptation. What's your favorite feature?

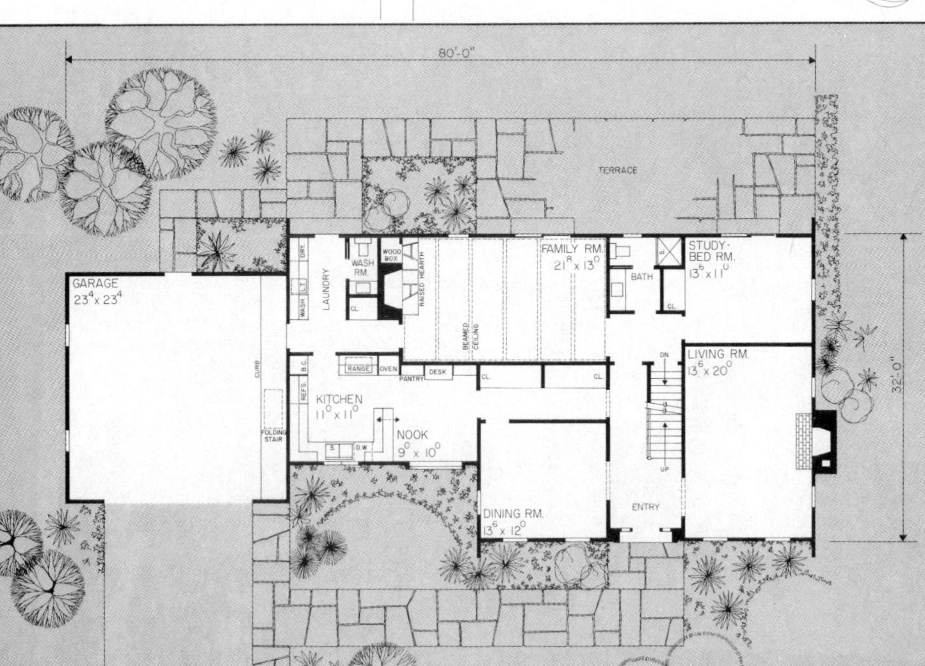

Design T22396

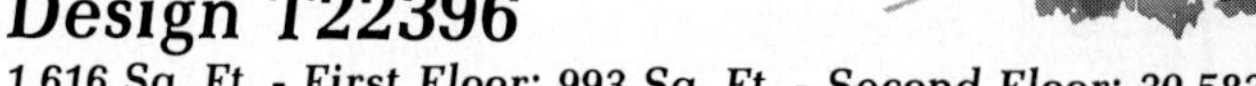

1,616 Sq. Ft. - First Floor; 993 Sq. Ft. - Second Floor; 30,583 Cu. Ft.

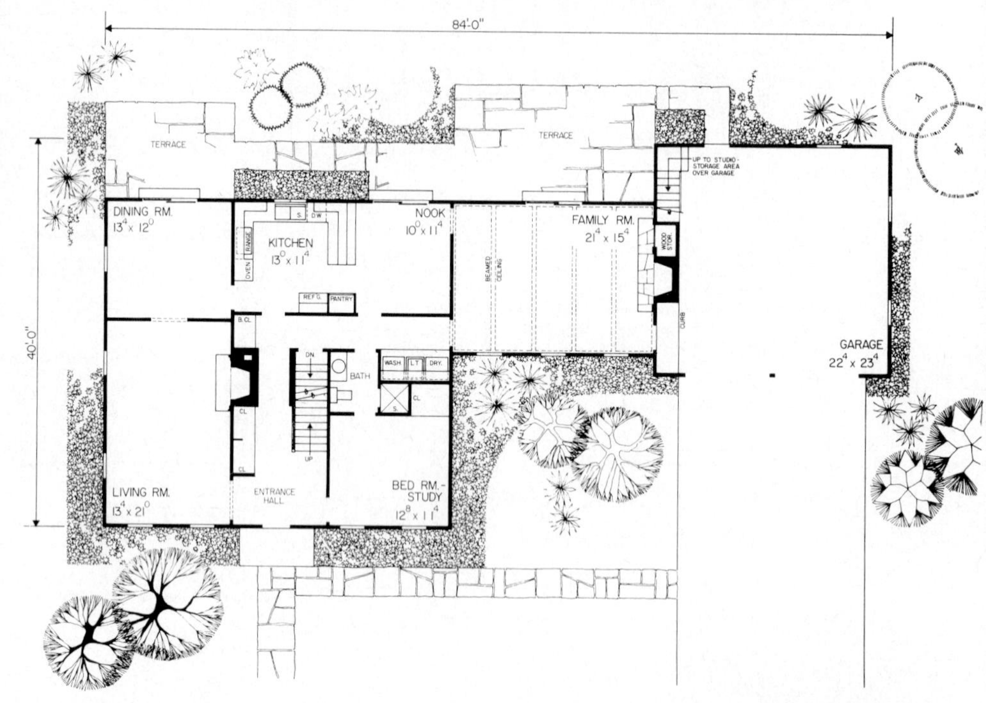

● Another picturesque facade right from the pages of our Colonial heritage. The authentic features are many. Note the centered front door with its flanking shutters, the evenly spaced dormers, and the centered chimney. The window detailing, the horizontal siding and the carriage lamps are pleasing highlights. Inside, there is exceptional livability. Observe the spacious living areas, the flexible dining facilities, the fine bedroom and bath potential. Don't miss the stairs to area over the garage.

Design T22650

1,451 Sq. Ft. - First Floor
1,091 Sq. Ft. - Second Floor; 43,555 Cu. Ft.

● The rear view of this design is just as appealing as the front. The dormers and the covered porch with pillars is a charming way to introduce this house to the on-lookers. Inside, the appeal is also outstanding. Note the size (18 x 25) of the gathering room which is open to the dining room. Kitchen-nook area is very spacious and features an island range, built-in desk and more. It is a great convenience having the laundry in the service area which is close to the kitchen. Imagine, a fireplace in both the gathering room and the master bedroom! Make special note of the front and rear service entrances.

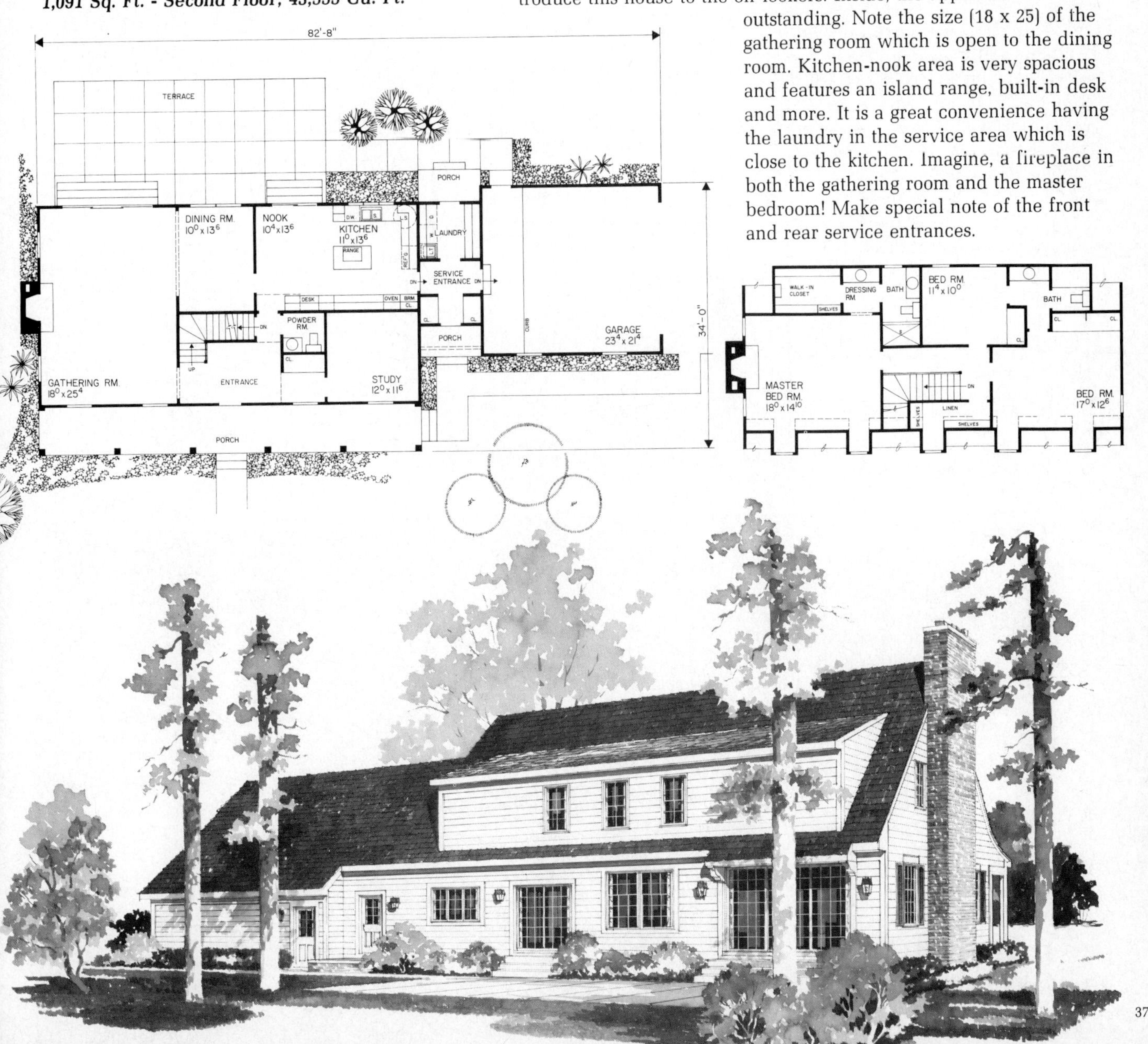

● A versatile plan, wrapped in a pleasing traditional facade, to cater to the demands of even the most active of families. There is plenty of living space for both formal and informal activities. With two bedrooms upstairs and two down, sleeping accommodations are excellently planned to serve all.

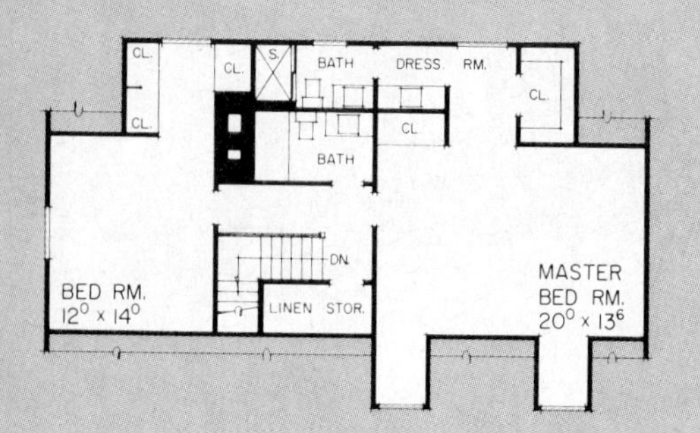

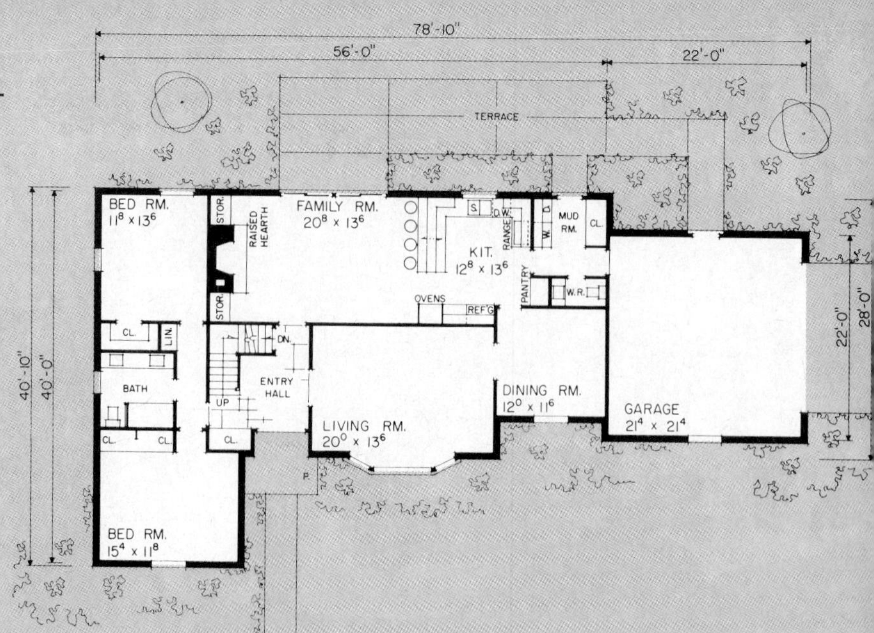

● A great plan! The large family will find its living requirements satisfied admirably all throughout those active years of growing up. This would make a fine expansible house. The upstairs may be finished off as the size of the family increases and budget permits. Complete living requirements can be obtained on the first floor.

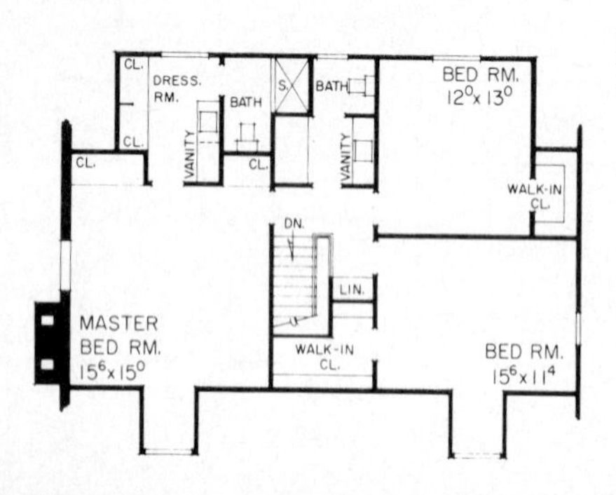

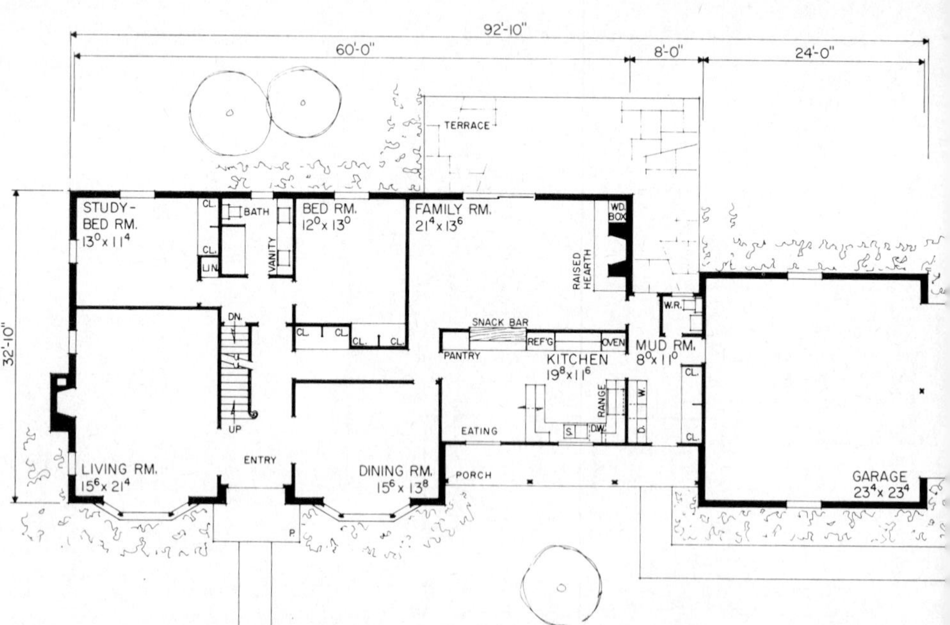

● A study of the first and second floors of this charming design will reveal that nothing has been omitted to assure convenient living. List your family's living requirements and then observe how this house will proceed to satisfy them. Features galore.

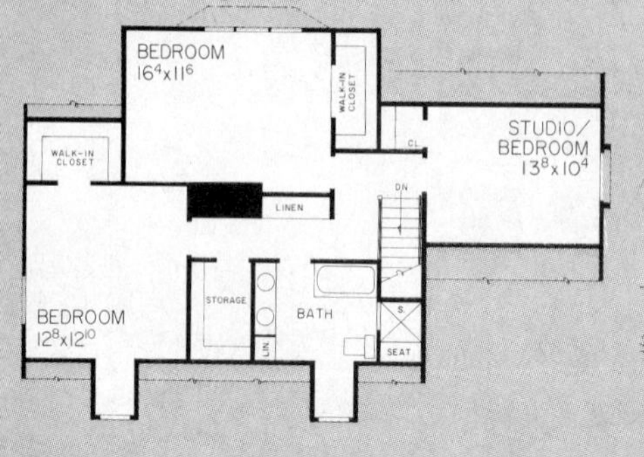

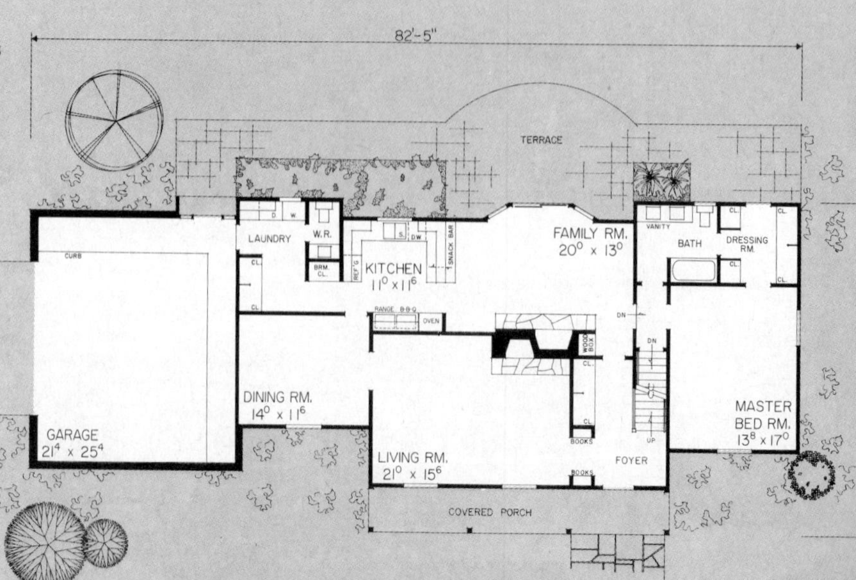

Design T21790 *1,782 Sq. Ft. - First Floor; 920 Sq. Ft. - Second Floor; 37,359 Cu. Ft.*

Design T21793 *1,986 Sq. Ft. - First Floor; 944 Sq. Ft. - Second Floor; 35,800 Cu. Ft.*

Design T21736 *1,618 Sq. Ft. - First Floor; 952 Sq. Ft. - Second Floor; 34,106 Cu. Ft.*

Design T22278

1,804 Sq. Ft. - First Floor
939 Sq. Ft. - Second Floor
44,274 Cu. Ft.

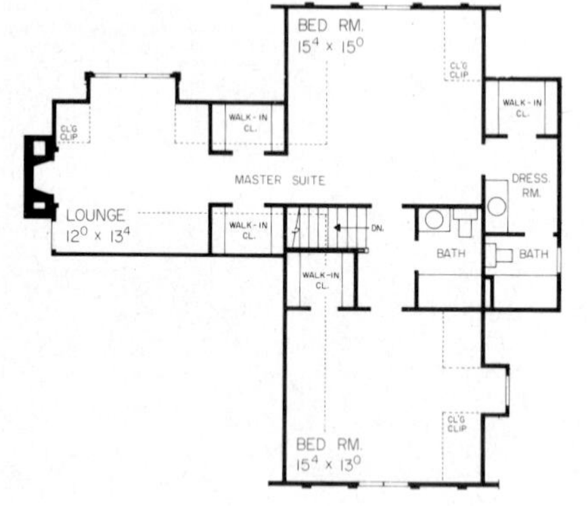

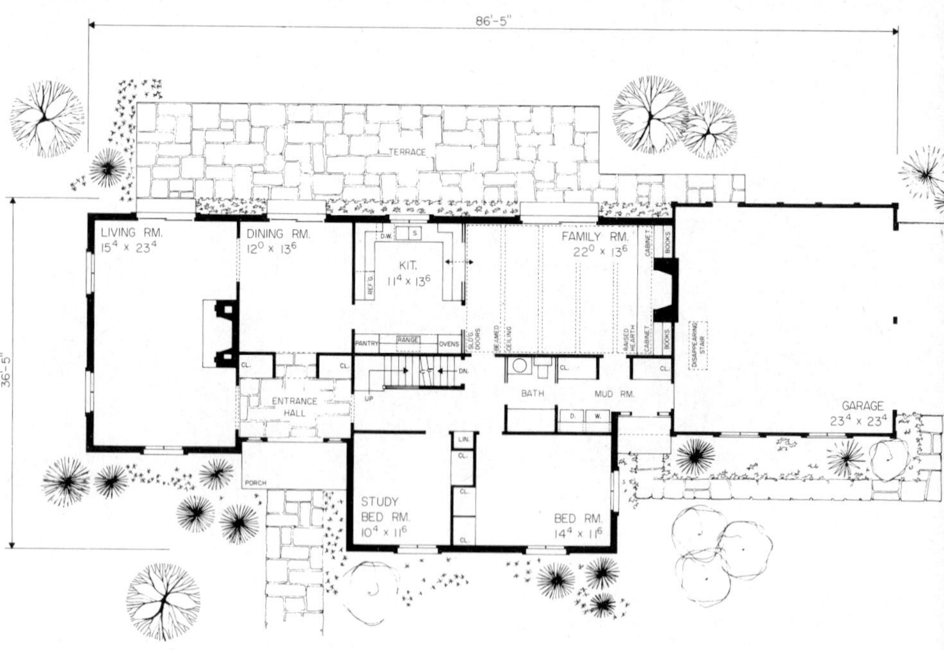

● The Tudor charm is characterized in each of these three one-and-a-half story designs. Study each of them for its own special features.

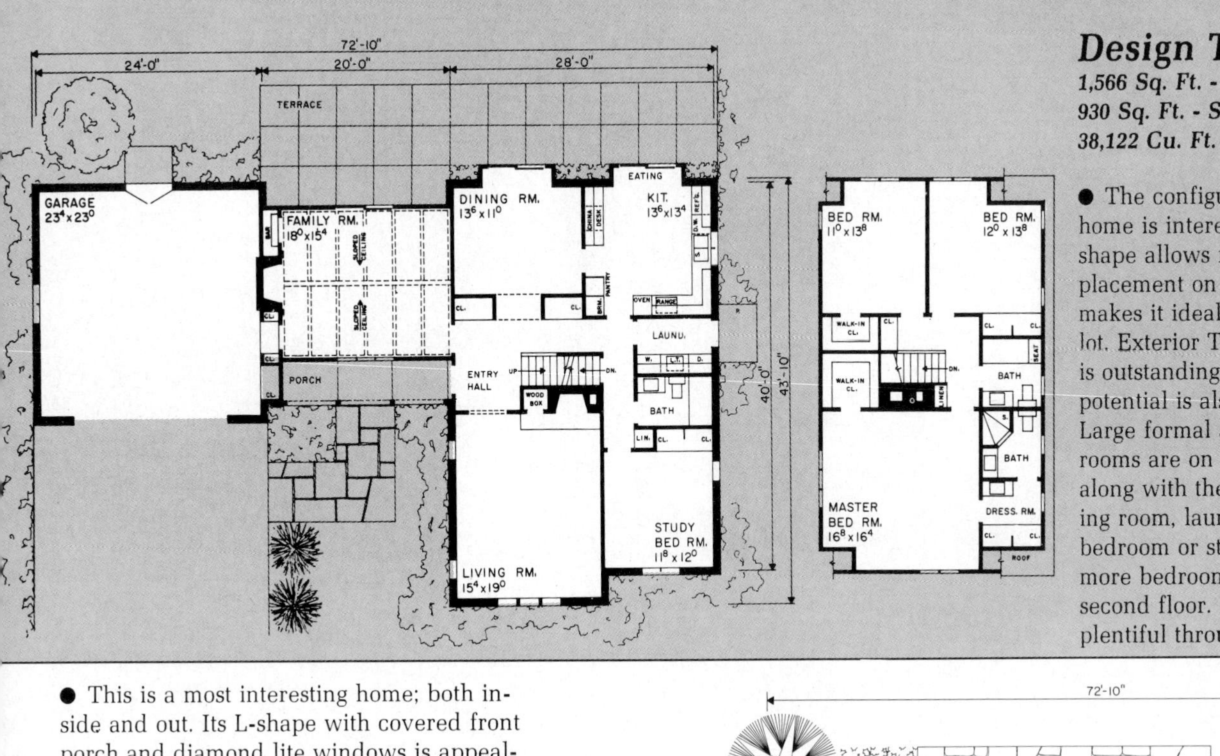

Design T22126

1,566 Sq. Ft. - First Floor
930 Sq. Ft. - Second Floor
38,122 Cu. Ft.

● The configuration of this home is interesting. Its L-shape allows for flexible placement on your lot which makes it ideal for a corner lot. Exterior Tudor detailing is outstanding. Interior living potential is also excellent. Large formal and informal rooms are on the first floor along with the kitchen, dining room, laundry and spare bedroom or study. Three more bedrooms are on the second floor. Closets are plentiful throughout.

● This is a most interesting home; both inside and out. Its L-shape with covered front porch and diamond lite windows is appealing. Its floor plan with extra bedroom, lounge and storage room is exceptional.

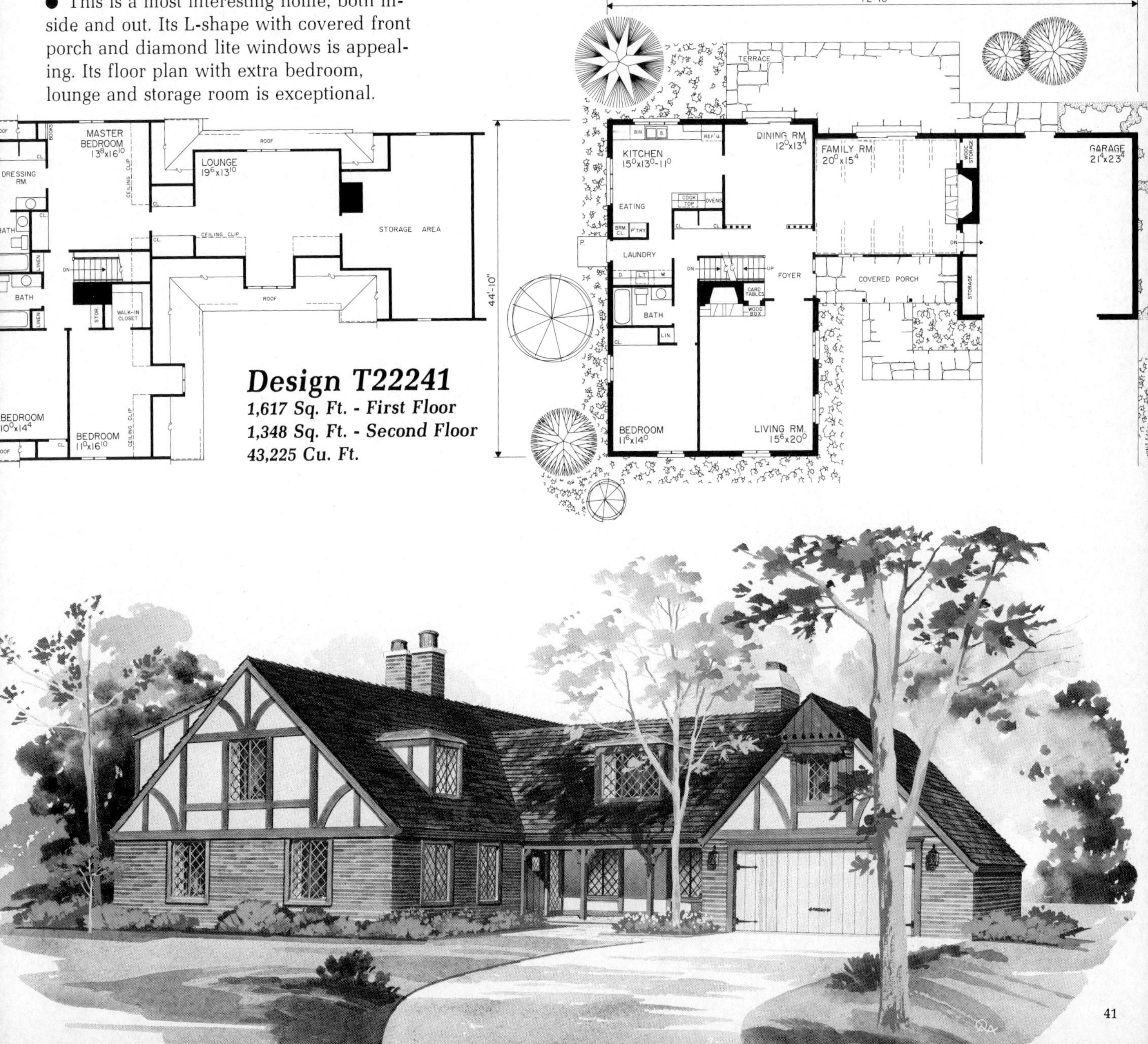

Design T22241

1,617 Sq. Ft. - First Floor
1,348 Sq. Ft. - Second Floor
43,225 Cu. Ft.

Design T22780

2,006 Sq. Ft. - First Floor
718 Sq. Ft. - Second Floor; 42,110 Cu. Ft.

● This 1½-story contemporary has more fine features than one can imagine. The livability is outstanding and can be appreciated by the whole family. Note the fine indoor-outdoor living relationships.

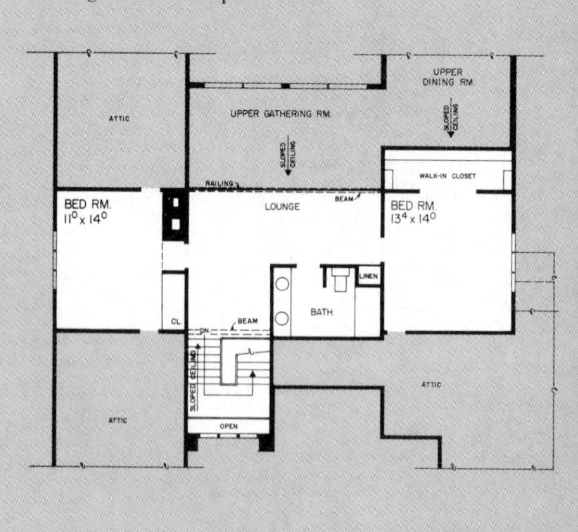

Design T22772

1,579 Sq. Ft. - First Floor
1,240 Sq. Ft. - Second Floor; 39,460 Cu. Ft.

● This four-bedroom two-story contemporary design is sure to suit your growing family needs. The rear U-shaped kitchen, flanked by the family and dining rooms, will be very efficient to the busy homemaker. Parents will enjoy all the convenience of the master bedroom suite.

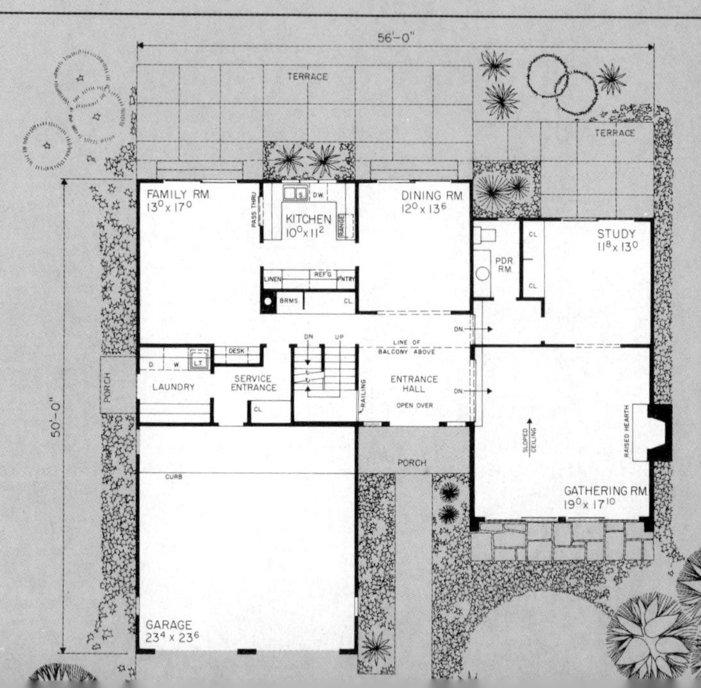

Design T22771

2,087 Sq. Ft. - First Floor
816 Sq. Ft. - Second Floor; 53,285 Cu. Ft.

● This design will provide an abundance of livability for your family. The second floor is highlighted by an open lounge which overlooks both the entry and the gathering room below.

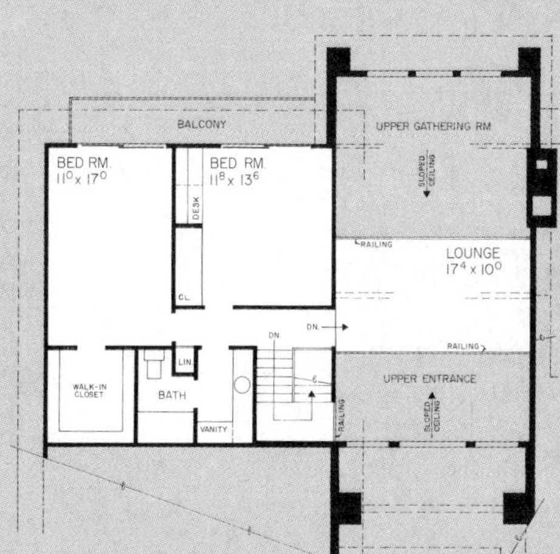

Design T21766 *1,638 Sq. Ft. - First Floor; 1,006 Sq. Ft. - Second Floor; 35,352 Cu. Ft.*

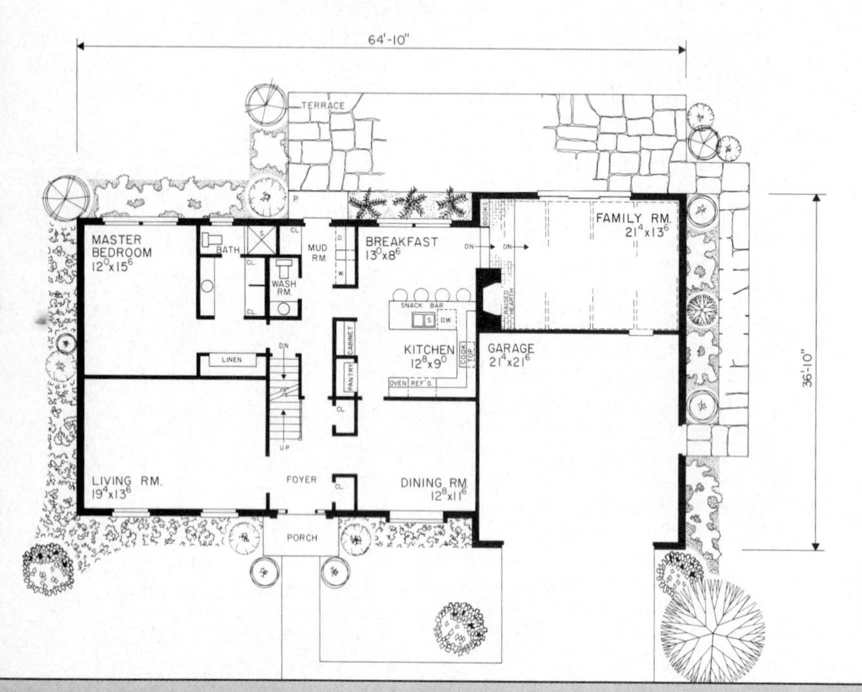

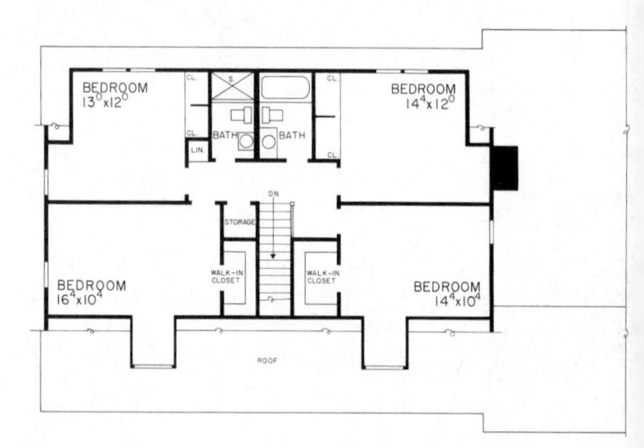

● This cozy home has over 2,600 square feet of livable floor area! And the manner in which this space to put to work to function conveniently for the large family is worth studying. Imagine five bedrooms, three full baths, living, dining and family rooms. Note large kitchen.

Design T21970

1,664 Sq. Ft. - First Floor
1,116 Sq. Ft. - Second Floor
41,912 Cu. Ft.

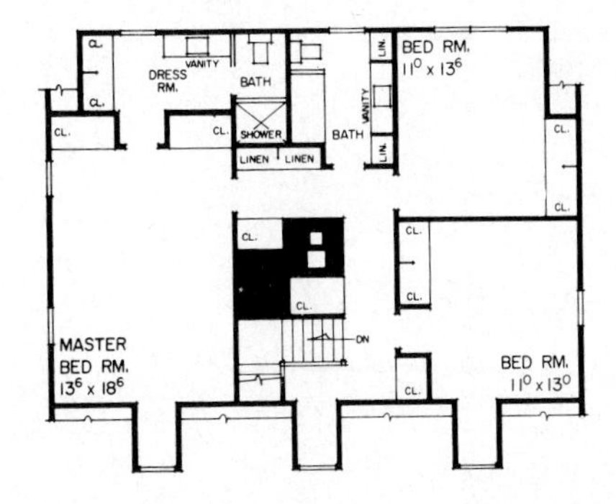

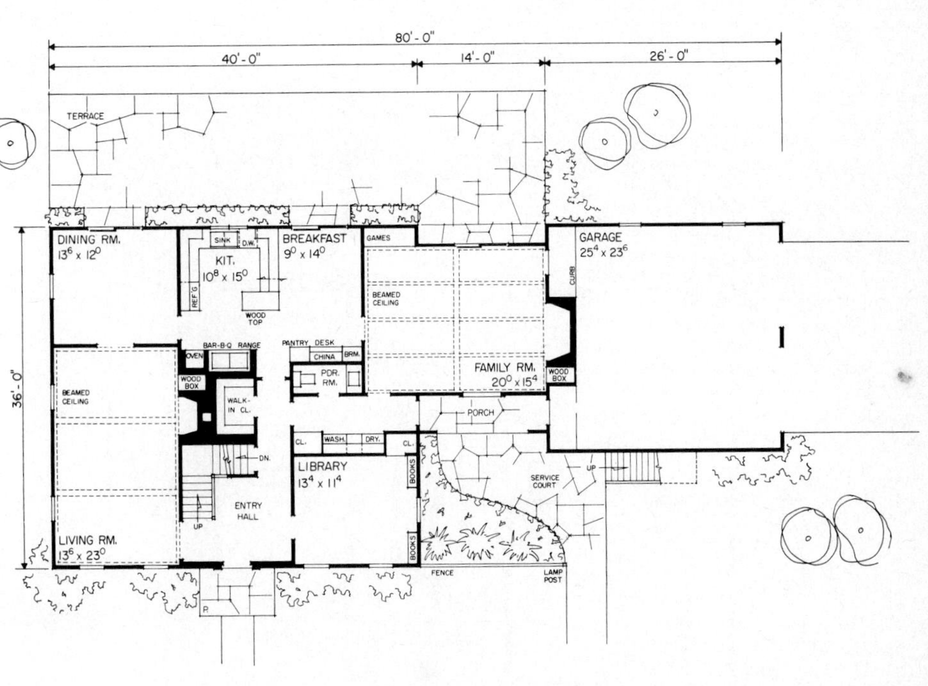

● The prototype of this Colonial house was an integral part of the 18th-Century New England landscape; the updated version is a welcome addition to any suburban scene.

Design T21747 *1,690 Sq. Ft. - First Floor*

1,060 Sq. Ft. - Second Floor; 38,424 Cu. Ft.

● This one-and-a-half story design has everything that any family could want, or need, in a new home. Two fireplaces! One in each of the front living areas. Note the efficient planning of the kitchen area. It is adjacent to the breakfast and dining rooms plus the mud room with wash room. Three bedrooms are on the second floor.

88'-10"
24'-0" 12'-0" 52'-0"
TERRACE
GARAGE 23⁴ x 23⁴
EATING
DINING RM. 13⁴ x 12⁰
STUDY-BED RM. 13⁰ x 11⁴
KIT. 18⁸ x 13⁶
MUD RM.
SEAT PANTRY
RANGE DESK
PDR. RM.
DISAPR. STAIR TO LOFT
WOOD BOX
RAISED HEARTH
BEAMED CEILING
FAMILY RM. 20⁸ x 13⁶
ENTRY HALL
LIVING RM. 20⁸ x 13⁶
24'-0" 10'-0" 28'-0"

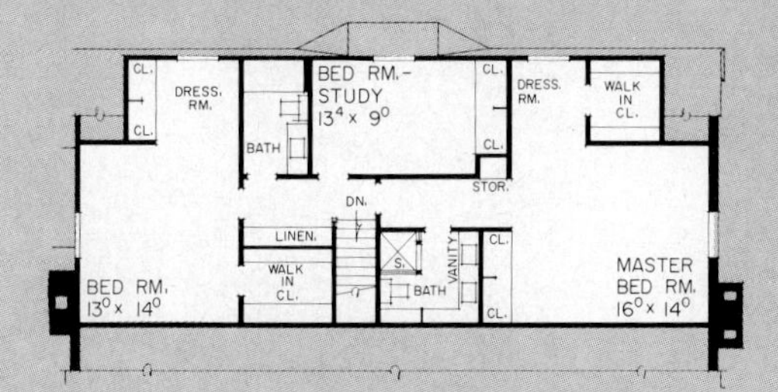

Design T22884 *1,855 Sq. Ft. - First Floor*
837 Sq. Ft. - Second Floor; 51,305 Cu. Ft.

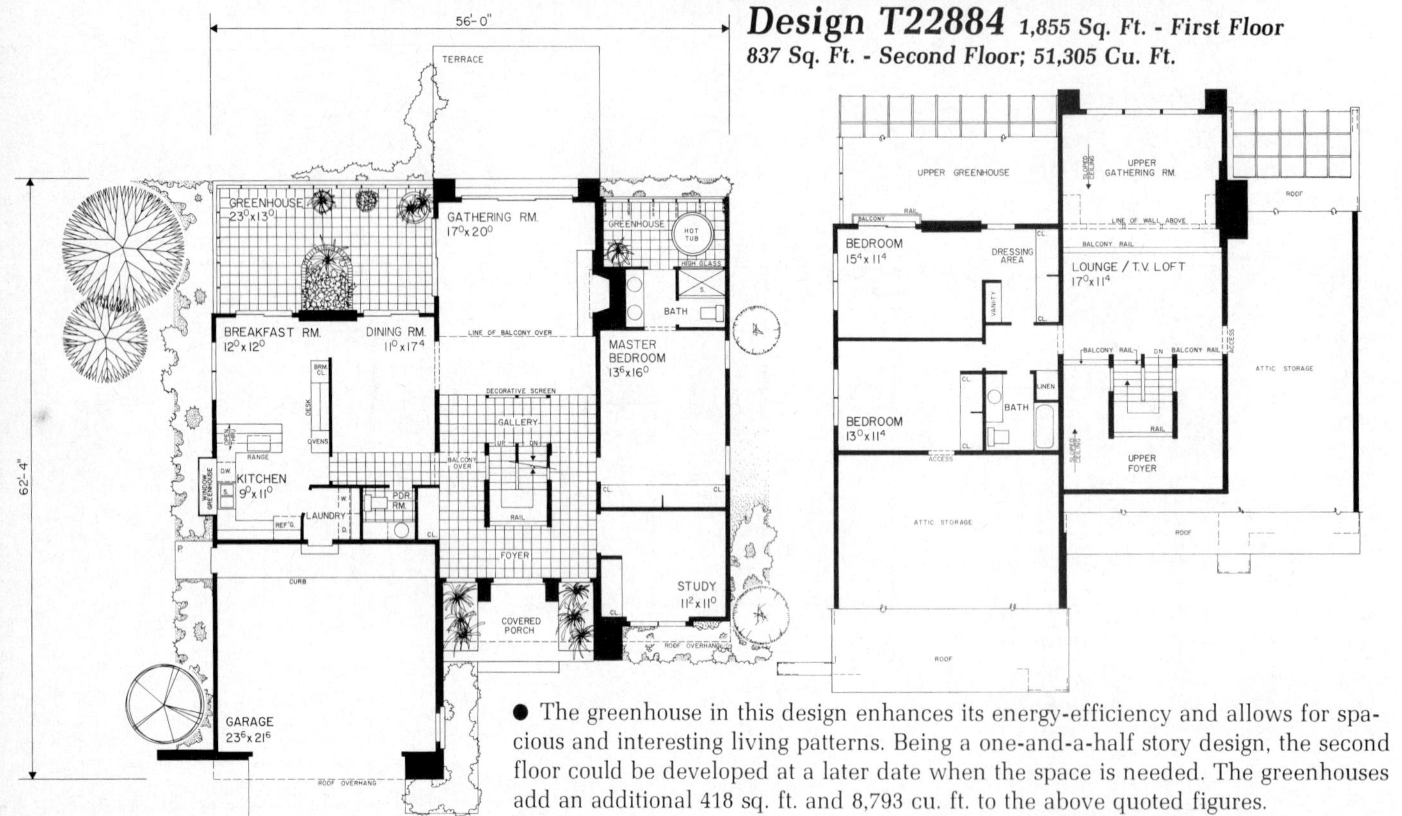

● The greenhouse in this design enhances its energy-efficiency and allows for spacious and interesting living patterns. Being a one-and-a-half story design, the second floor could be developed at a later date when the space is needed. The greenhouses add an additional 418 sq. ft. and 8,793 cu. ft. to the above quoted figures.

One-Story Homes
For Family Living From 1791 Sq. Ft.

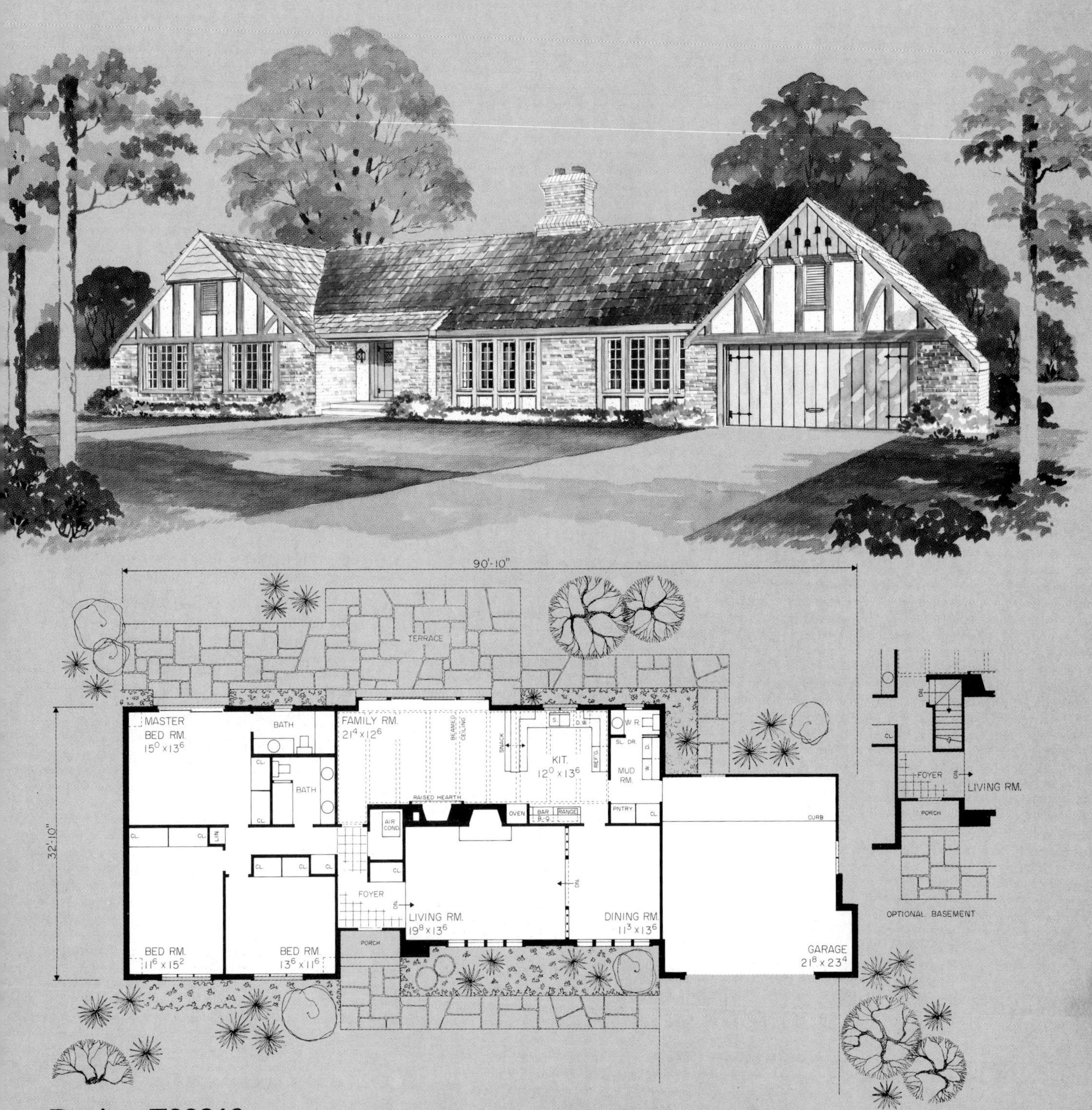

Design T22318 *2,029 Sq. Ft.; 31,021 Cu. Ft.*

● Warmth and charm are characteristics of the Tudor adaptations. This modest sized home, with its twin front-facing gabled roofs, represents a great investment. While it will be an exciting and refreshing addition to any neighborhood, its appeal will never grow old. The covered front entrance opens to the center foyer. Traffic patterns flow in an orderly and efficient manner to the three main zones — the formal dining zone, the sleeping zone and the informal living zone. The sunken living room with its fireplace is separated from the dining room by an attractive trellis divider. A second fireplace along with beamed ceiling and sliding glass doors highlight the family room. Note snack bar, mud room, cooking facilities, two full baths and optional basement.

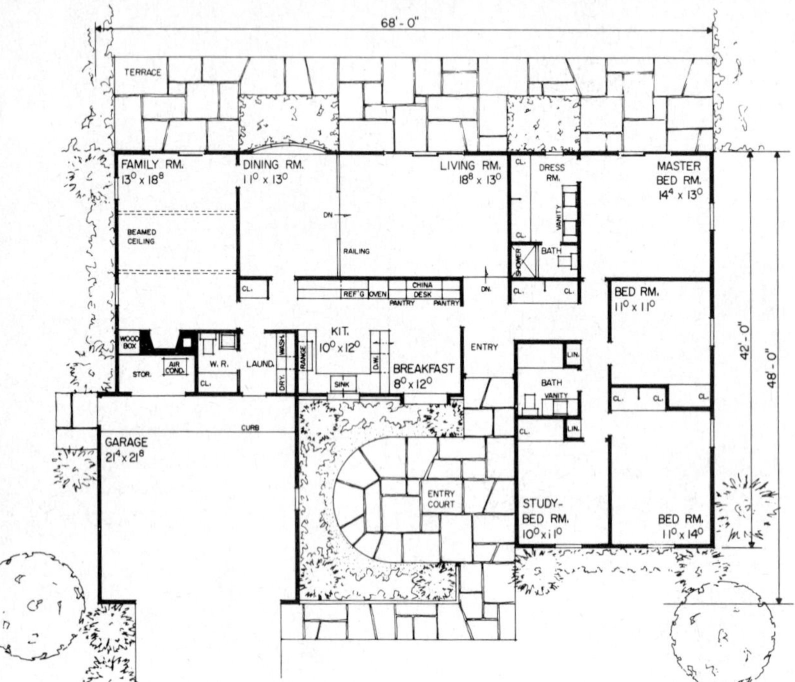

Design T21950

2,076 Sq. Ft.; 27,520 Cu. Ft.

● If you were to count the various reasons that will surely cause excitement over the prospect of moving into this home, you would certainly be able to compile a long list. You might head your list with the grace and charm of the front exterior. You'd certainly have to comment on the delightful entry court, the picket fence and lamp post, and the recessed front entrance. Comments about the interior obviously would begin with the listing of such features as: spaciousness galore; sunken living room; separate dining room; beamed ceiling family room; excellent kitchen with pass-thru to breakfast room; two full baths, plus wash room, etc.

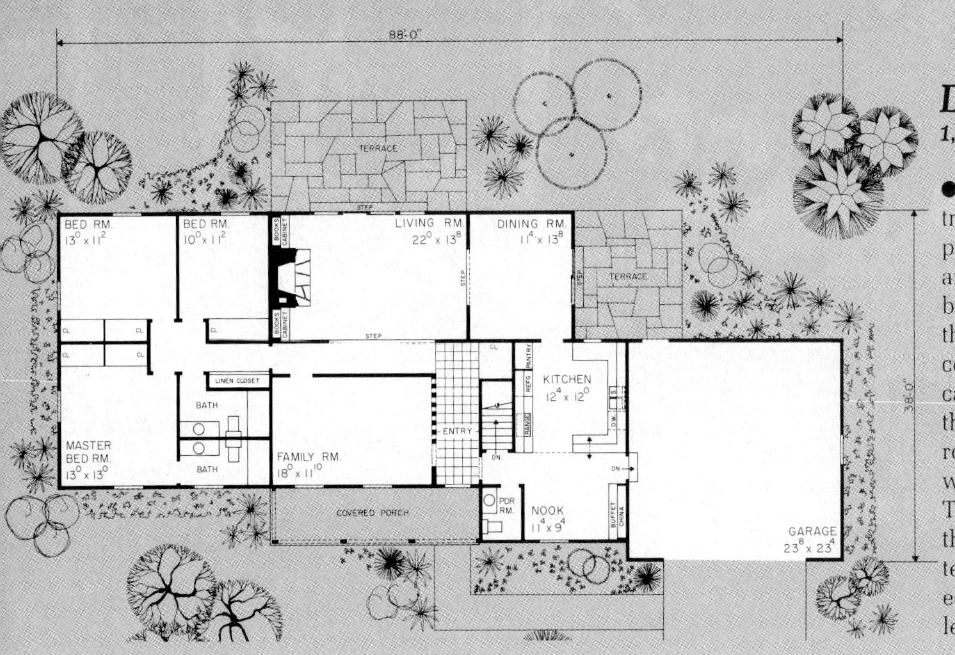

Design T22360

1,936 Sq. Ft.; 37,026 Cu. Ft.

● The charming characteristics of this traditional one-story are many. Fine proportion and pleasing lines assure a long and rewarding study. A list of them may begin with the fine window treatment, the covered front porch with its stolid columns, the raised panelled door, the carriage lamp, the horizontal siding, and the cupola. Inside, the family's everyday routine will enjoy all the facilities which will surely guarantee pleasurable living. The formal rear sunken living room and the dining room function with their own terraces. A 3½ foot high wall with turned wood posts on top separate the excellent family room from the entry hall.

Design T22867

2,388 Sq. Ft.; 49,535 Cu. Ft.

● A live-in relative would be very comfortable in this home. This design features a self-contained suite (473 sq. ft.) consisting of a bedroom, bath, living room and kitchenette with dining area. This suite is nestled behind the garage away from the main areas of the house. The rest of this traditional one-story house faced with fieldstone and vertical wood siding is also very livable. One whole wing houses the four family bedrooms and bath facilities. The center of the plan has a front U-shaped kitchen and breakfast room. Formal dining room and large gathering room will enjoy the view of the backyard. The large rear covered porch will receive much use.

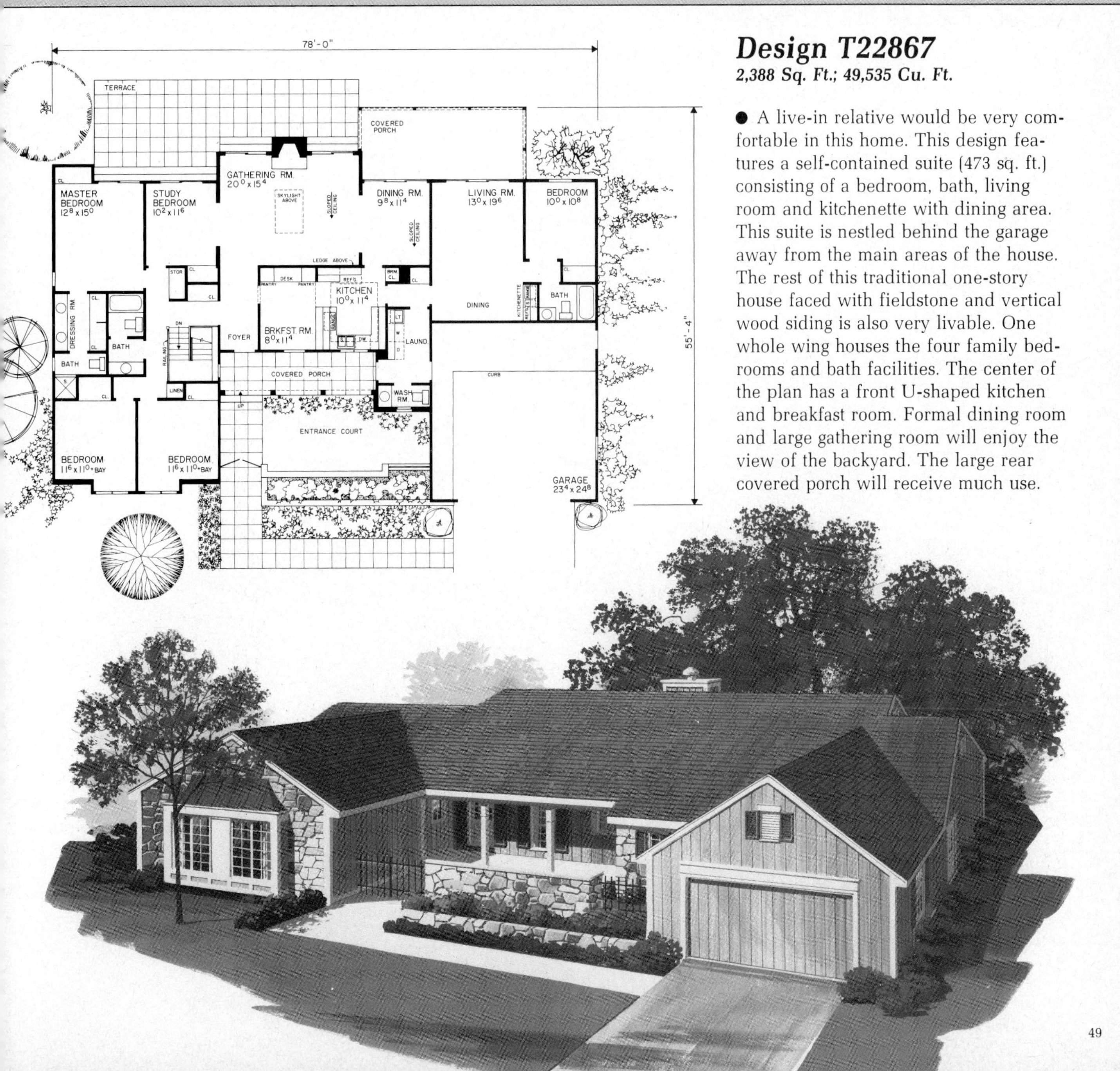

Design T22523

2,055 Sq. Ft.; 43,702 Cu. Ft.

● You'll want the investment in your new home to be one of the soundest you'll ever make. And certainly the best way to do this is to make sure your new home has unexcelled exterior appeal and outstanding interior livability. For those who like refreshing contemporary lines, this design will rate at the top. The wide overhanging roof, the brick masses, the glass areas, the raised planters, and the covered front entrance highlight the facade. As for the interior, all the elements are present to assure fine living patterns. Consider the room relationships and how they function with one another. Note how they relate to the outdoors.

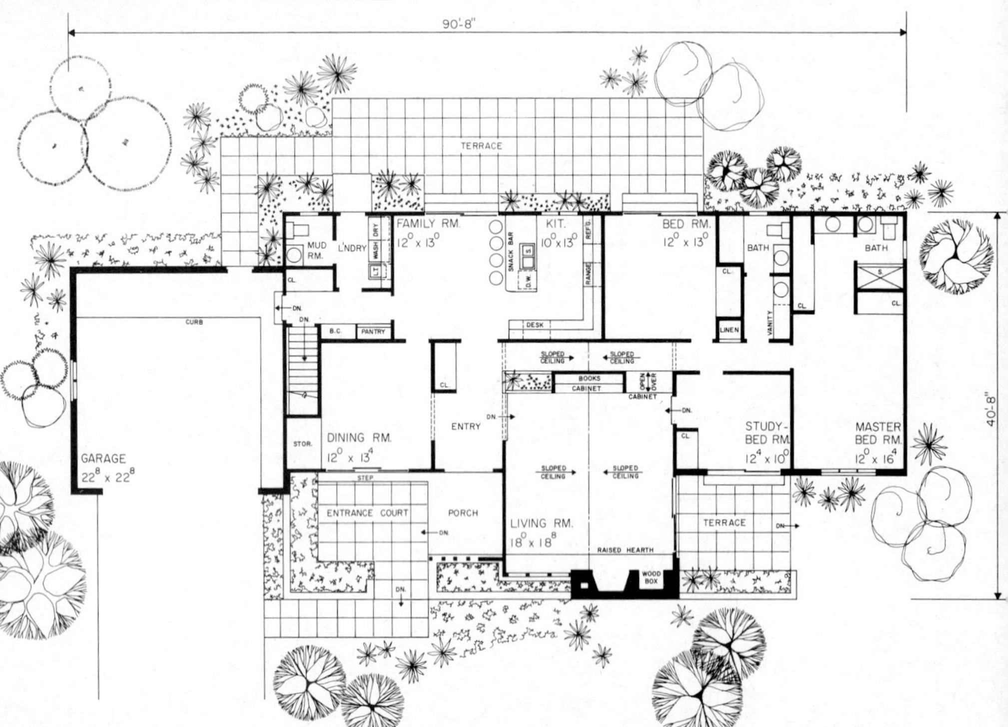

Design T21111

2,248 Sq. Ft.; 18,678 Cu. Ft.

● "Great", will be just the word to characterize the ownership of this home. The trim hip-roof with its wide overhang, the massiveness of the vertical brick piers, and the extension of the brick wall to form a front court are but a few of the features. Among the other features include the four bedrooms, two full baths and extra wash room, a spacious L-shaped living and dining area, a dramatic family room and a mud room.

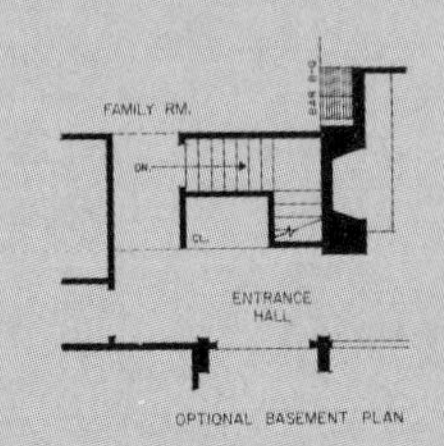

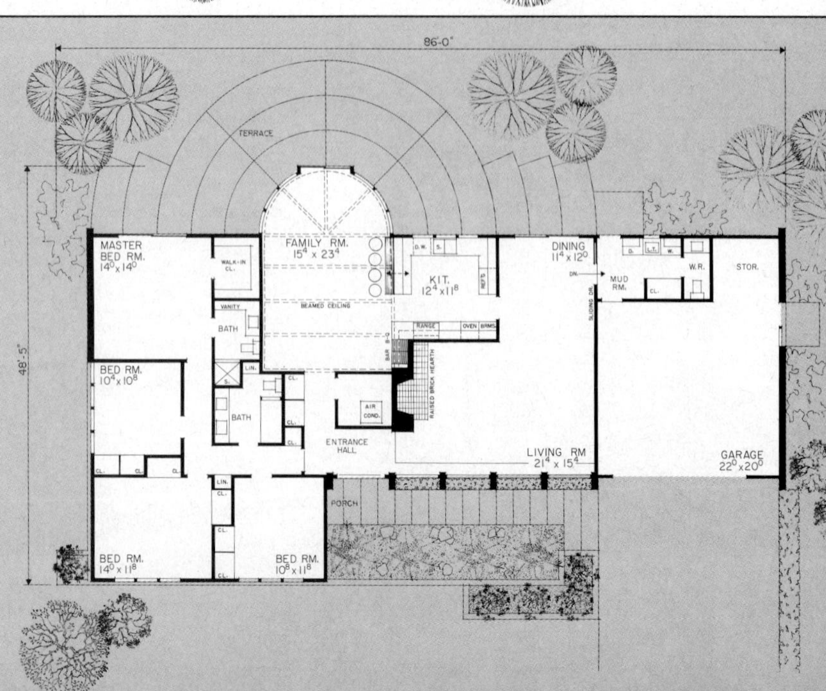

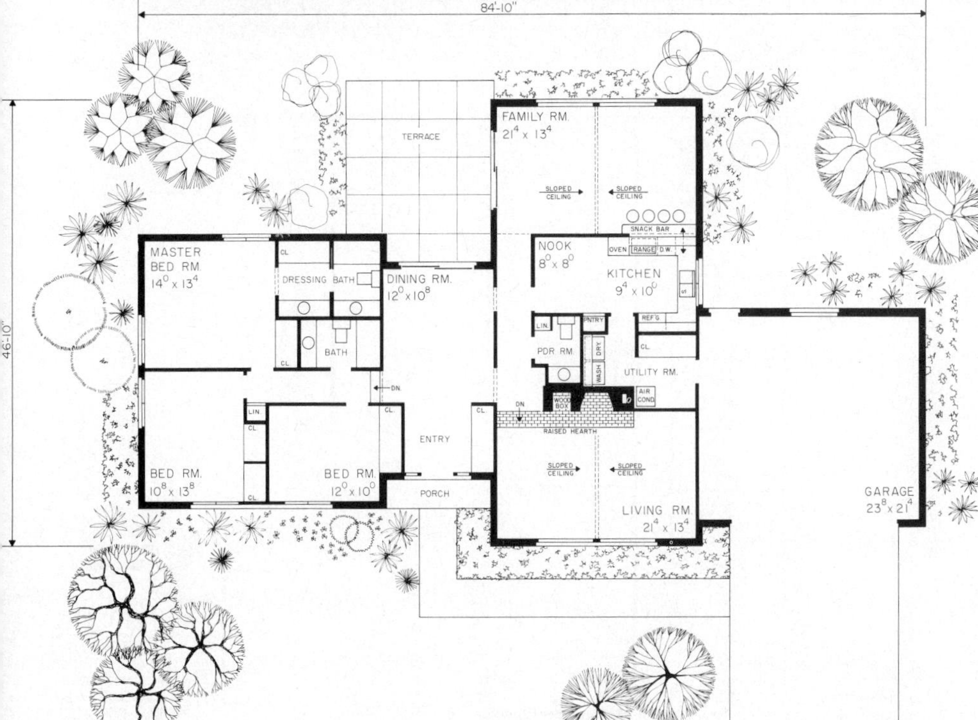

Design T22359

2,078 Sq. Ft.; 22,400 Cu. Ft.

● The low-pitched, wide-overhanging roof with its exposed beams, acts as a visor for the dramatic glass gable end of the projecting living room. This will be an exceedingly pleasant room with its sunken floor, sloped ceiling, large glass area, and raised hearth fireplace. At the rear of this living rectangle is the family room. This room also has a sloped ceiling and a glass gable end. In addition, there is the snack bar and sliding glass doors to the protected terrace. Between these two living areas is the efficient kitchen with its adjacent eating area. The utility room and its laundry equipment is nearby, as is the powder room. A separate dining room acts as the connecting link to the bedroom zone. Note the master bedroom with its dressing room, twin lavatories and two closets.

Design T21026

2,506 Sq. Ft.; 26,313 Cu. Ft.

● When you move into this attractive home you'll find you and your family will begin to experience new dimensions in living. All areas will be forever conscious of the beauty of the out-of-doors. The front entry court provides both the quiet living room and the formal dining room with a delightful view. The functional terraces will expand the horizons of each of the other rooms. While the raised hearth fireplaces of the two living areas are major focal points, there are numerous convenient living features which will make everyday living a joy. Some of these features are the mud room, the pantry, the planning desk with china storage above, the snack bar and pass-thru. As noted in the illustration, an optional basement plan is included.

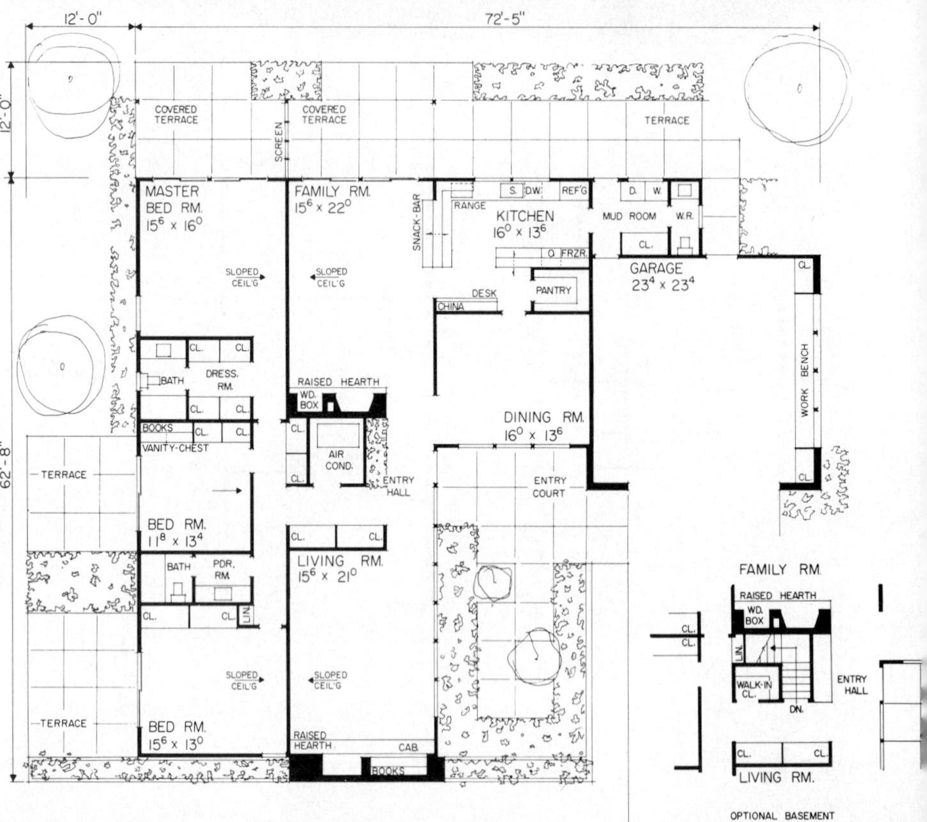

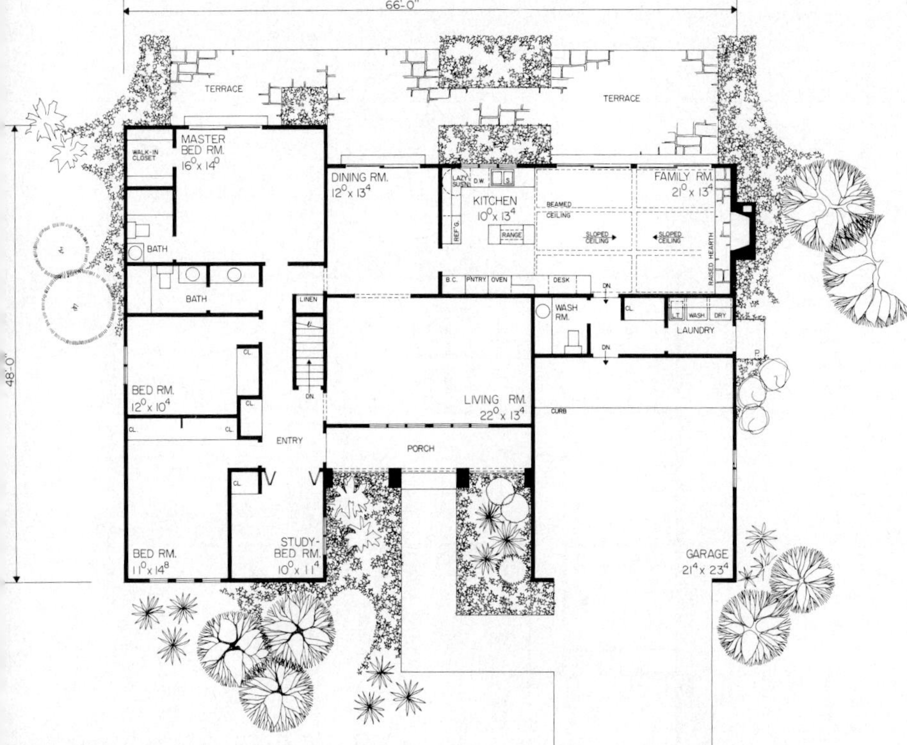

Design T22532

2,112 Sq. Ft.; 42,300 Cu. Ft.

● Here is a refreshing, modified U-shaped contemporary that is long on both looks and livability. The board and batten exterior creates simple lines which are complimented by the low-pitched roof with its wide overhang and exposed rafters. The appeal of the front court is enhanced by the massive stone columns at the edge of the covered porch. A study of the floor plan reveals interestingly different and practical living patterns. The location of the entry hall represents a fine conservation of space for the living areas. The L-shaped formal living-dining zone has access to both front and rear yards. The informal living area is a true family kitchen. Its open planning produces a spacious and cheerful area. Note sloping, beamed ceiling, raised hearth fireplace and sliding glass doors.

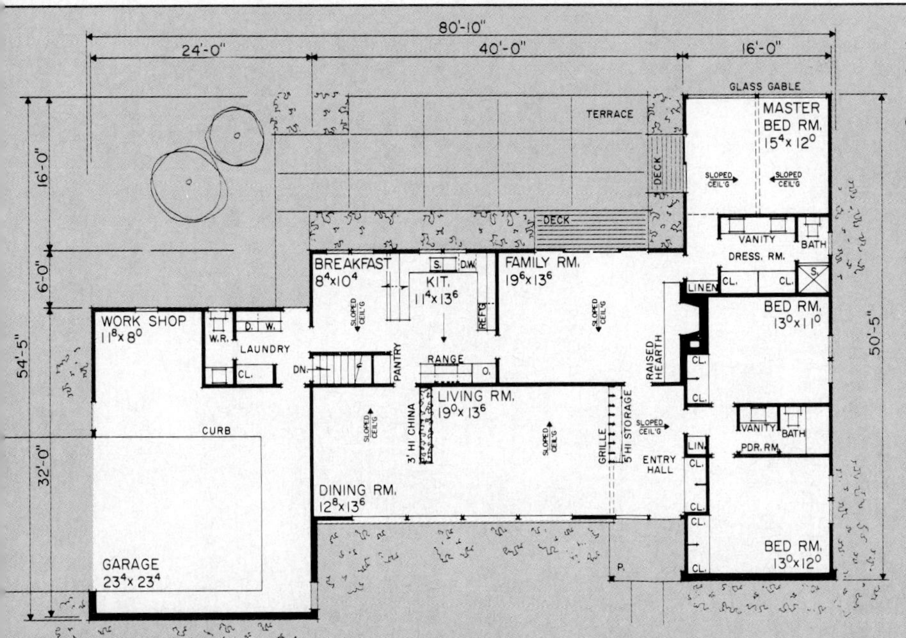

Design T21844

2,047 Sq. Ft.; 32,375 Cu. Ft.

● A sparkling contemporary with all the elements to help assure a lifetime of complete livability. This one-story home is essentially a frame dwelling with two dramatic areas of durable and colorful quarried stone. The low-pitched, wide-overhanging roof provides shelter for the front porch. In addition, it acts as a visor for the large glass areas. The plan is positively outstanding. The informal areas are to the rear of the plan and overlook the rear terrace. The formal, separate dining room and living room are strategically located to the front. The sleeping zone comprises a wing of its own with the master bedroom suite apart from the children's room. Don't miss the extra wash room, laundry and shop. Basement stairs are near this work area.

Design T21989

2,282 Sq. Ft.; 41,831 Cu. Ft.

● High style with a plan as contemporary as today and tomorrow. There is, indeed, a feeling of coziness that emanates from the ground-hugging qualities of this picturesque home. Inside, there is livability galore. There's the sunken living room and the separate dining room to function as the family's formal living area. Then, overlooking the rear yard, there's the informal living area with its beamed ceiling family room, kitchen and adjacent breakfast room.

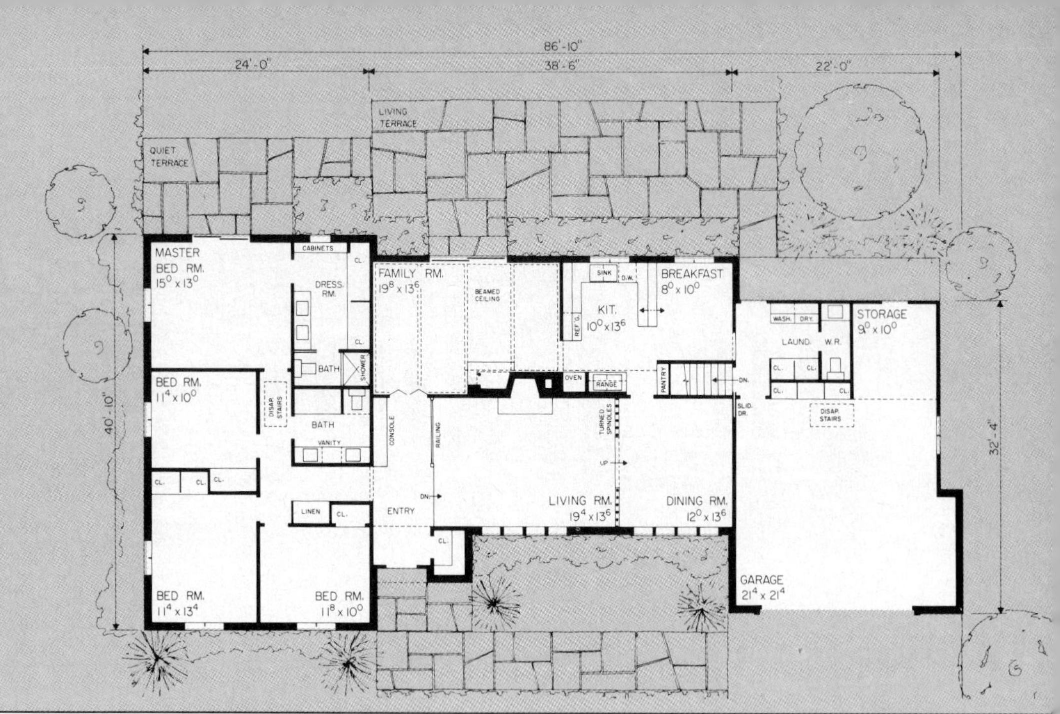

Design T22620

2,048 Sq. Ft.; 42,000 Cu. Ft.

● An enclosed courtyard! That sets this home apart right from the start. There are more unusual features inside. Like the 21' by 15' keeping room . . . complete with a wet bar, built-in bookcase, fireplace/woodbox combination. Plus sliding glass doors leading to the terrace. That's the kind of space you need for family life as well as entertaining! There's a formal dining room, too! And a well-designed kitchen. U-shaped for efficiency, with a built-in oven and range. Plus a separate breakfast room. Around the corner, the first floor laundry. That puts all the work areas together, saving you time and energy. Four large bedrooms grouped together for privacy. Ideal planning throughout.

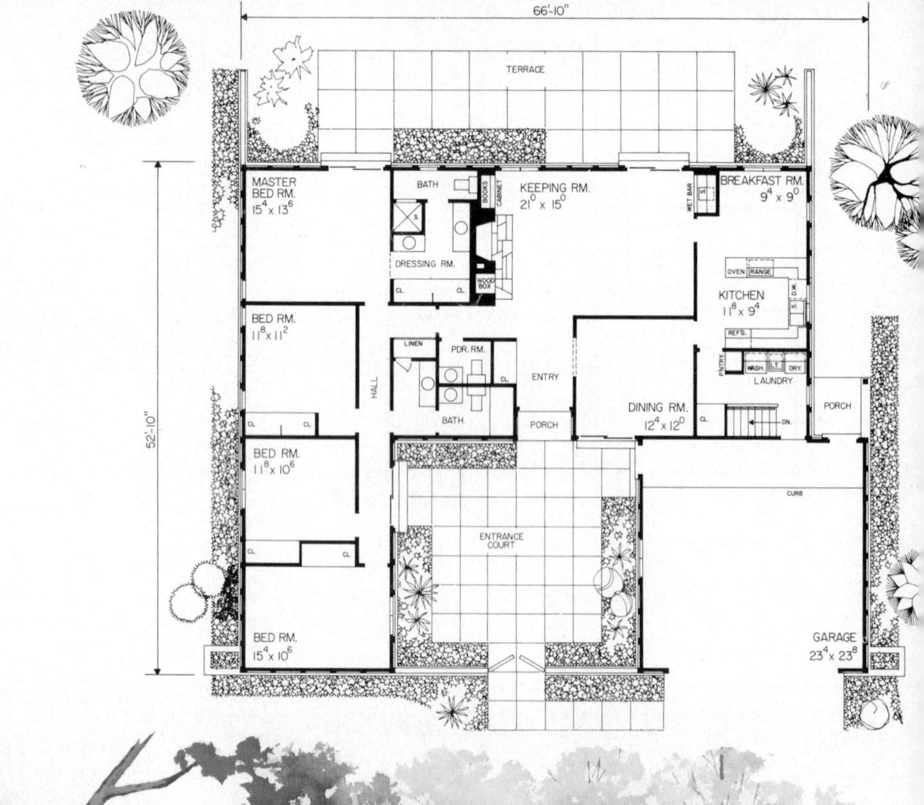

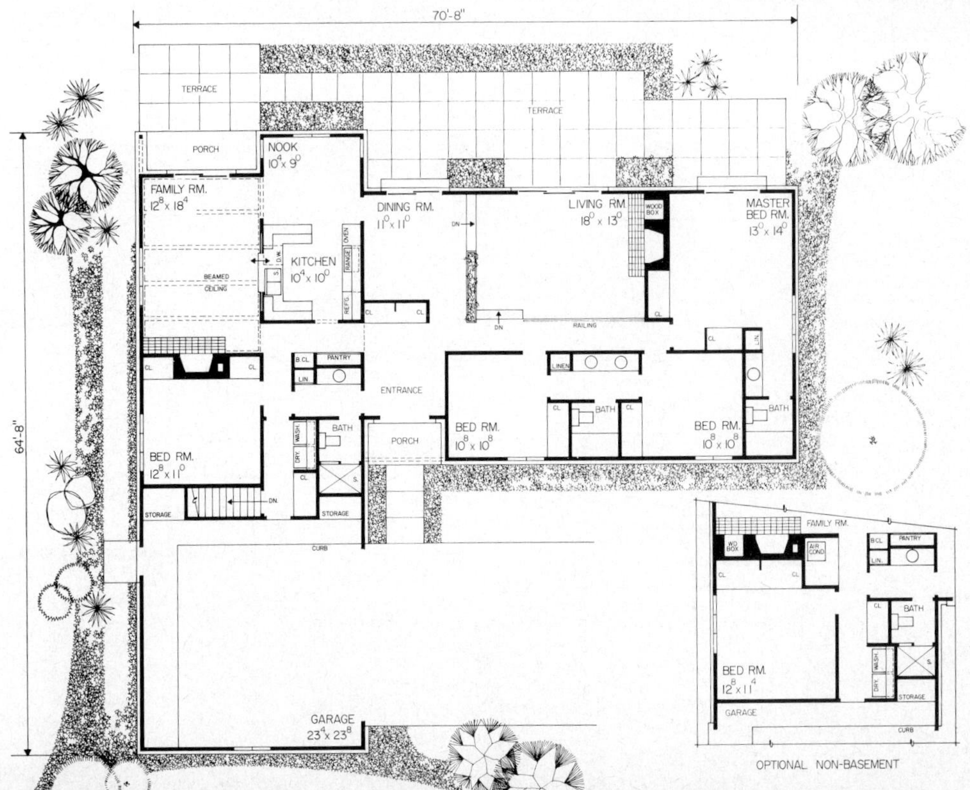

Design T22613

2,132 Sq. Ft.; 38,328 Cu. Ft.

● A classic Tudor! With prominent wood and stucco styling. And unique features throughout. Start with the sunken living room where an attractive railing has replaced the anticipated hallway wall. For more good looks, a traditional fireplace with an attached woodbox and sliding glass doors that open onto the terrace. There's a formal dining room, too, also with access onto the terrace. Together these rooms form a gracious center for entertaining! For casual times, a family room with a beamed ceiling, fireplace and summer porch. And a work-efficient kitchen plus a roomy breakfast nook.

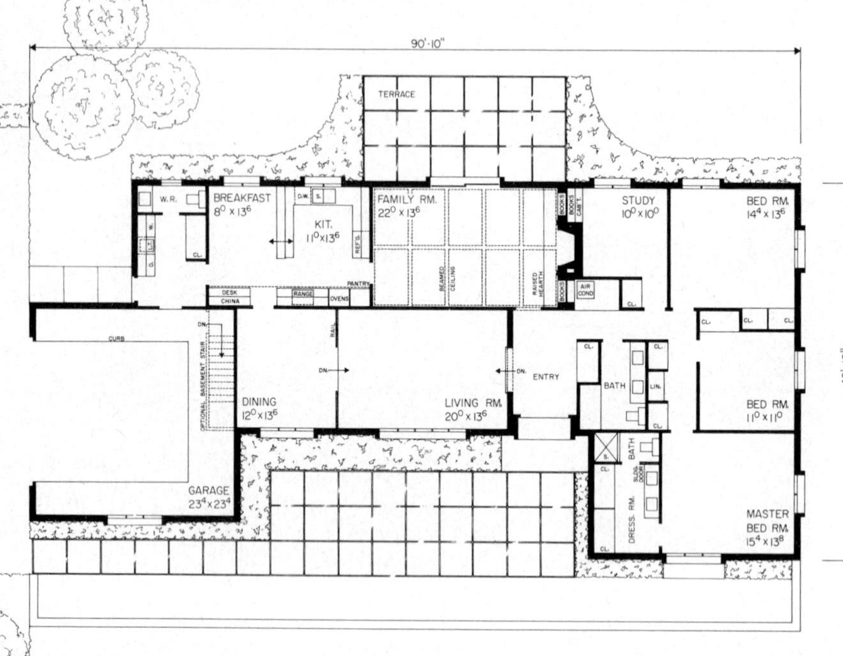

Design T22179

2,439 Sq. Ft.; 33,043 Cu. Ft.

● The formality of this French adaptation is a pleasing picture to behold. Wherever you may choose to build it, this one-story will most assuredly receive the accolades of passers-by. It is the outstanding proportion and the fine detail that make this a home of distinction. What's inside is every bit as delightful as what is outside. Your family will enjoy its three sizable bedrooms. The study will be a favorite haven for those who wish a period of peace and quiet. The sunken living room and the informal family room offer two large areas for family living. For eating there is the breakfast and separate dining room. Two baths and extra wash room serve the family well.

Design T21054

2,080 Sq. Ft.; 43,406 Cu. Ft.

● Here is a pleasantly formal exterior whose fine floor plan offers the same kind of formal living patterns. The front living room is outstanding. It is large and has a dramatic picture window, fireplace and plenty of wall space for effective and flexible furniture placement. The formal dining room is big and is but a step or two from the outdoor terrace. There is a breakfast room, too. The kitchen and first floor laundry will be efficient. Four bedrooms and two baths are in the sleeping wing. Outstanding livability throughout.

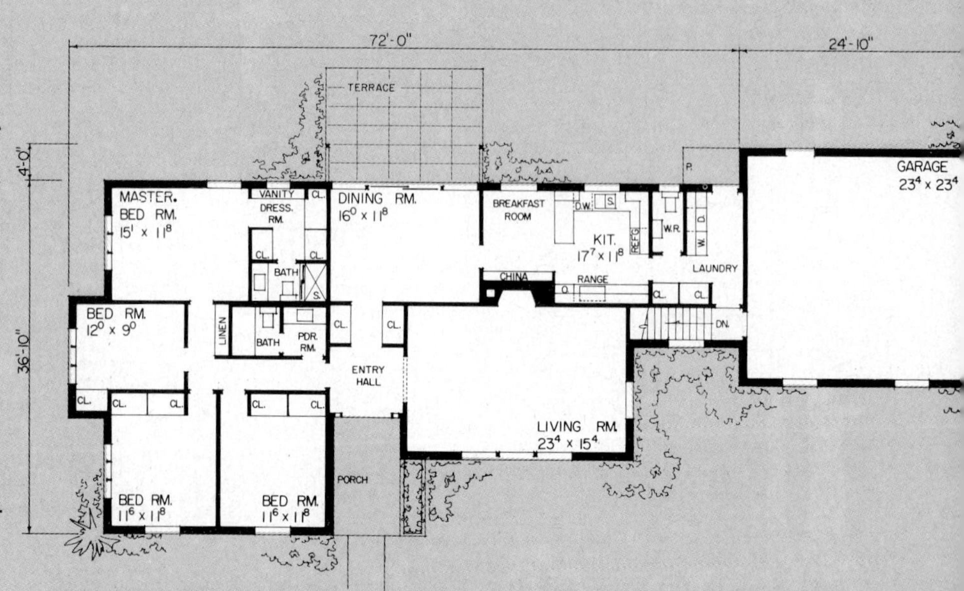

Design T21892

2,036 Sq. Ft.; 26,575 Cu. Ft.

● The romance of French Provincial is captured here by the hip-roof masses, the charm of the window detailing, the brick quoins at the corners, the delicate dentil work at the cornices, the massive centered chimney, and the recessed double front doors. The slightly raised entry court completes the picture. The basic floor plan is a favorite of many. And little wonder, for all areas work well together, while still maintaining a fine degree of separation of functions. The highlight of the interior, perhaps, will be the sunken living room. The family room, with its beamed ceiling, will not be far behind in its popularity. The separate dining room, mud room, efficient kitchen, complete the livability.

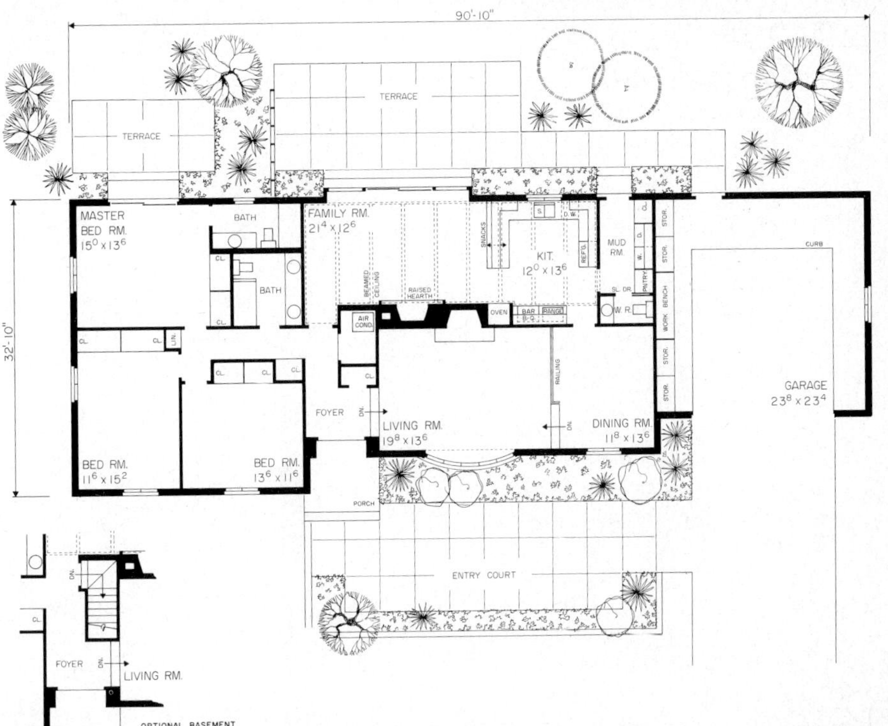

● A spectacular foyer! Fully 21' long, it offers double entry to the heart of this home . . . a 21' by 21' gathering room, complete with sloped ceiling, raised hearth fireplace and sliding glass doors onto the terrace. There's a formal dining room, too. Plus a well-located study . . . insuring space for solitude or undisturbed work. The kitchen features a snack bar and a breakfast nook with sliding doors onto the terrace . . . an arrangement that's sure to make every meal easy and pleasant. For more convenience, a pantry and first-floor laundry. In the master suite, a dressing room with entry to the bath, four closets . . . and sliding doors onto the terrace! Two more bedrooms if you wish to convert the study . . . or one easily large enough for two children, with a dressing area and private entry to the second bath.

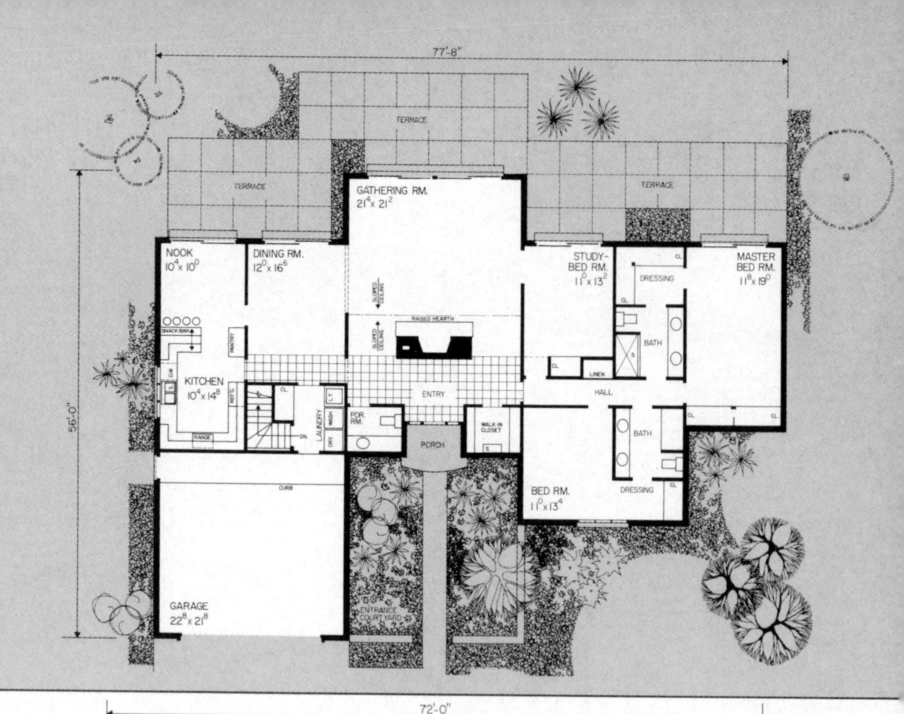

Design T22590

2,380 Sq. Ft.; 26,680 Cu. Ft.

● A large enclosed garden courtyard. A rear terrace. Formal living and dining rooms, plus a family room with a raised hearth fireplace. Three large bedrooms, including a master suite with a dressing room and private bath. These are just some of the outstanding features of this design. This home is designed for easy living, whether you're entertaining with a summer barbecue or a formal dinner party. And it's got the extras you want to help ensure life-long convenience . . . an island range and built-in desk in the kitchen, a first-floor laundry, lots of convenient storage. You will like the strategically placed walk-in closet adjacent to the kitchen.

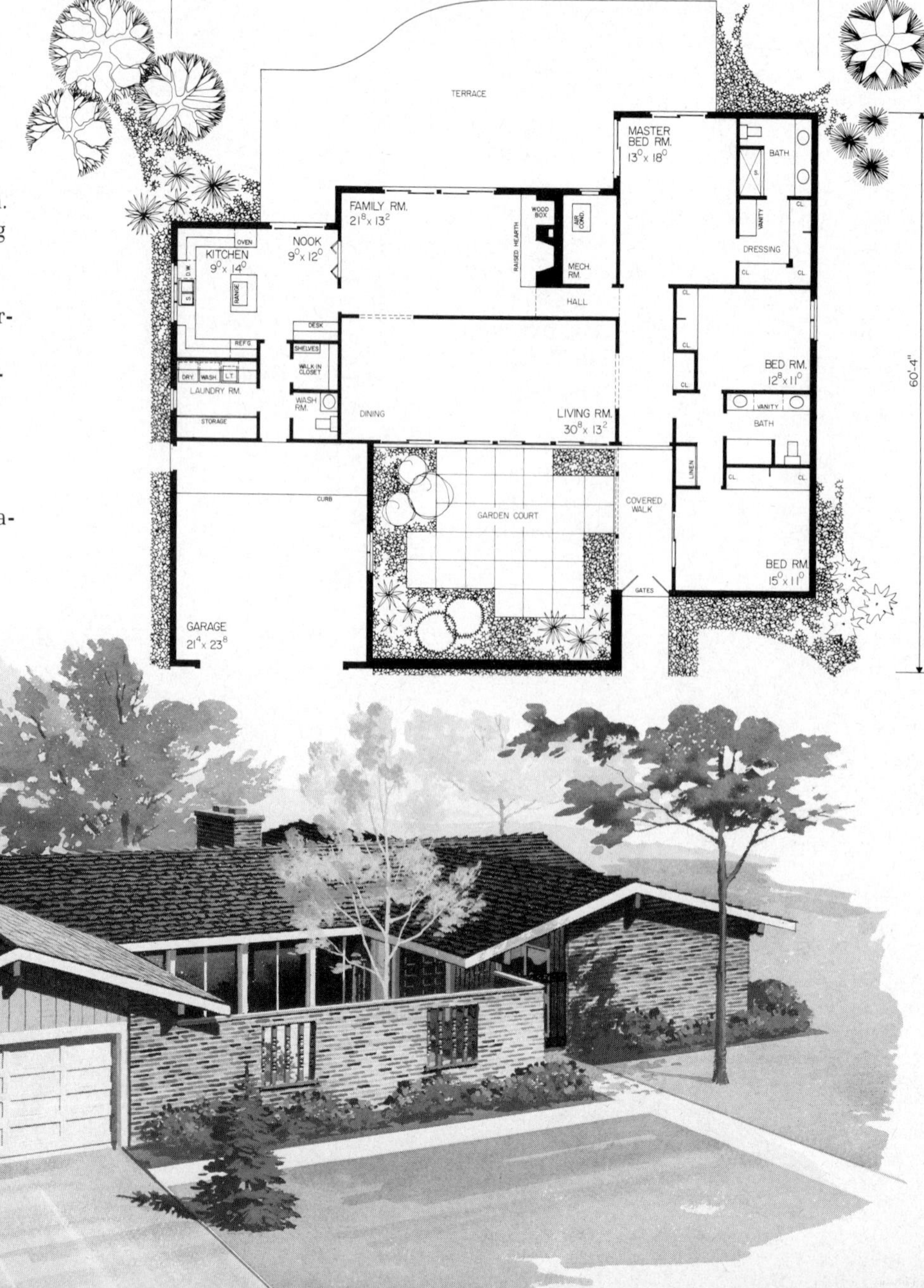

Design T22594 *2,294 Sq. Ft.; 42,120 Cu. Ft.*

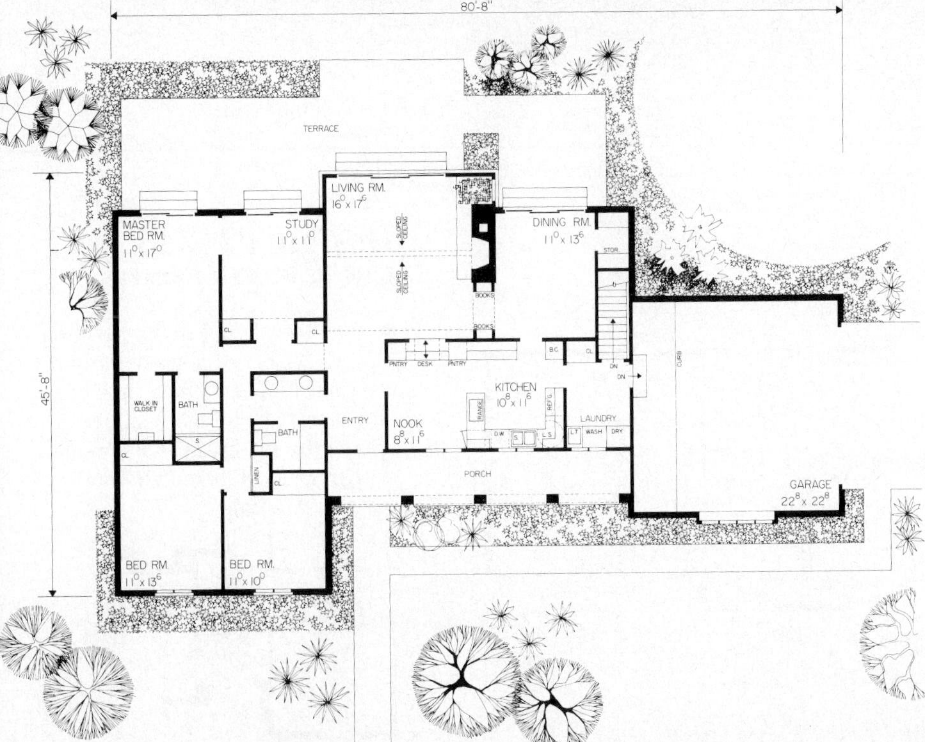

Design T22557

1,955 Sq. Ft.; 43,509 Cu. Ft.

● This eye-catching design with a flavor of the Spanish Southwest will be as interesting to live in as it will be to look at. The character of the exterior is set by the wide overhanging roof with its exposed beams; the massive arched pillars; the arching of the brick over the windows; the panelled door and the horizontal siding that contrasts with the brick. The elegantly large master bedroom/study suite is a focal point of the interior. However, if necessary, the study could become the fourth bedroom. The living and dining rooms are large and are separated by a massive raised hearth fireplace.

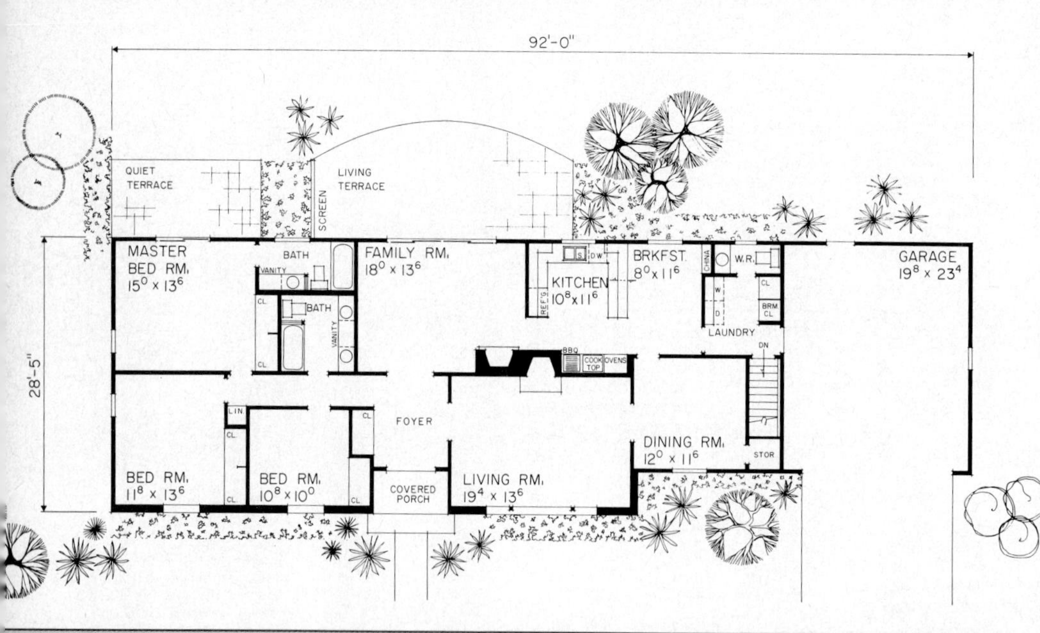

Design T21325

1,942 Sq. Ft.; 35,384 Cu. Ft.

● The large front entry hall permits direct access to the formal living room, the sleeping area and the informal family room. Both of the living areas have a fireplace. When formal dining is the occasion of the evening the separate dining room is but a step from the living room. The U-shaped kitchen is strategically flanked by the family room and the breakfast areas.

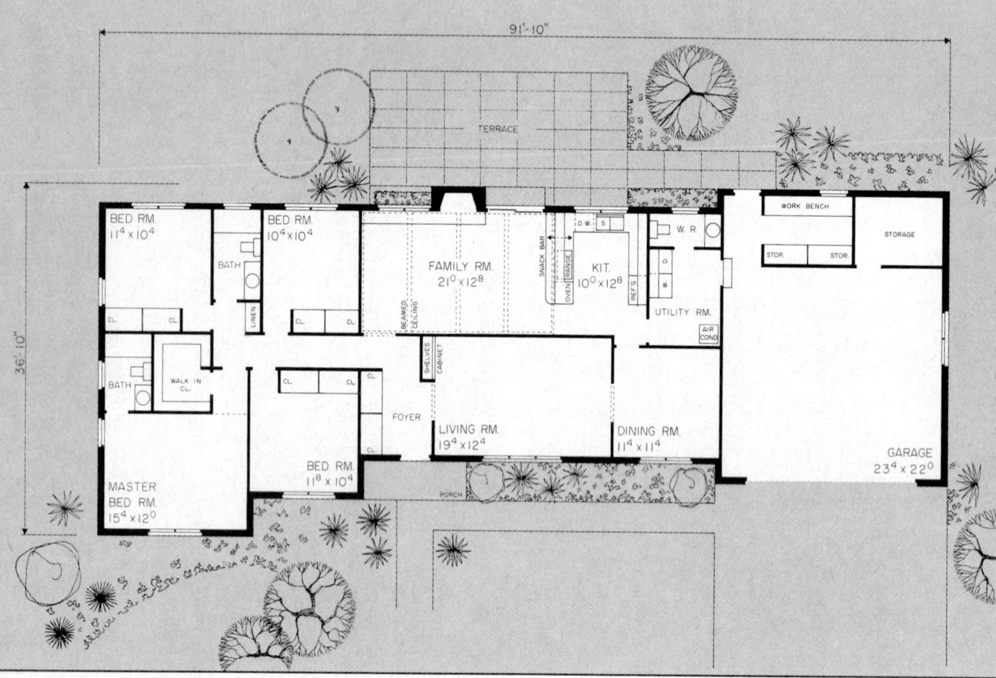

Design T22316

2,000 Sq. Ft.; 25,242 Cu. Ft.

● If you are looking for a four bedroom version of the two other designs on this page, look no further. Here, in essentially the same number of square feet, is a Colonial adaptation for a larger family. The floor planning of this basic design results in excellent zoning. The four bedroom, two-bath sleeping zone comprises a wing of its own directly accessible from the main foyer.

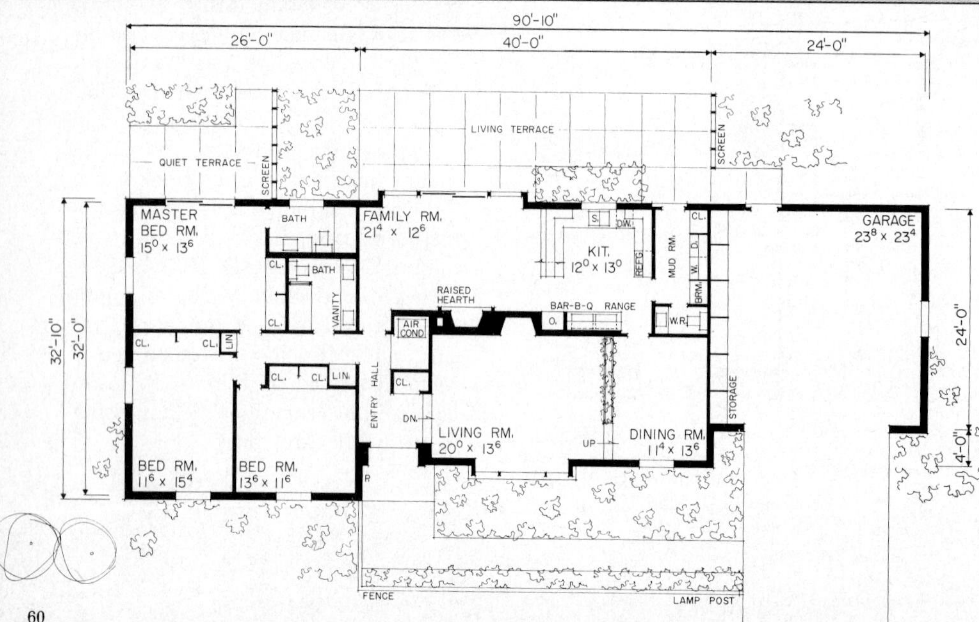

Design T21748

1,986 Sq. Ft.; 23,311 Cu. Ft.

● A sunken living room, two fireplaces, 2½ baths, a rear family room, a formal dining room, a mud room and plenty of storage facilities are among the features of this popular design. Blueprints include optional basement details.

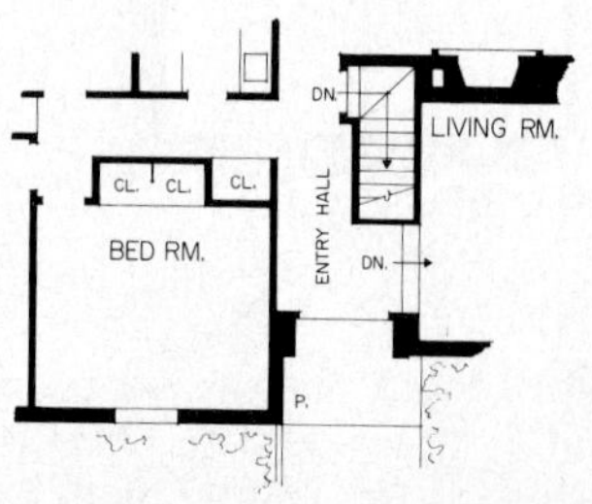

OPTIONAL BASEMENT

Design T22795

1,952 Sq. Ft.; 43,500 Cu. Ft.

● This three-bedroom design leaves no room for improvement. Any size family will find it difficult to surpass the fine qualities that this home offers. Begin with the exterior. A fine contemporary design with open trellis work above the front covered private court, this area is sheltered by a privacy wall extending from the projecting garage. Inside, the floor plan will be just as breathtaking. Begin at the foyer and choose a direction. To the right is the sleeping wing equipped with three bedrooms and two baths. Straight ahead from the foyer is the gathering room with thru-fireplace to the dining room. To the right is the work center. This area includes a breakfast nook, a U-shaped kitchen and laundry.

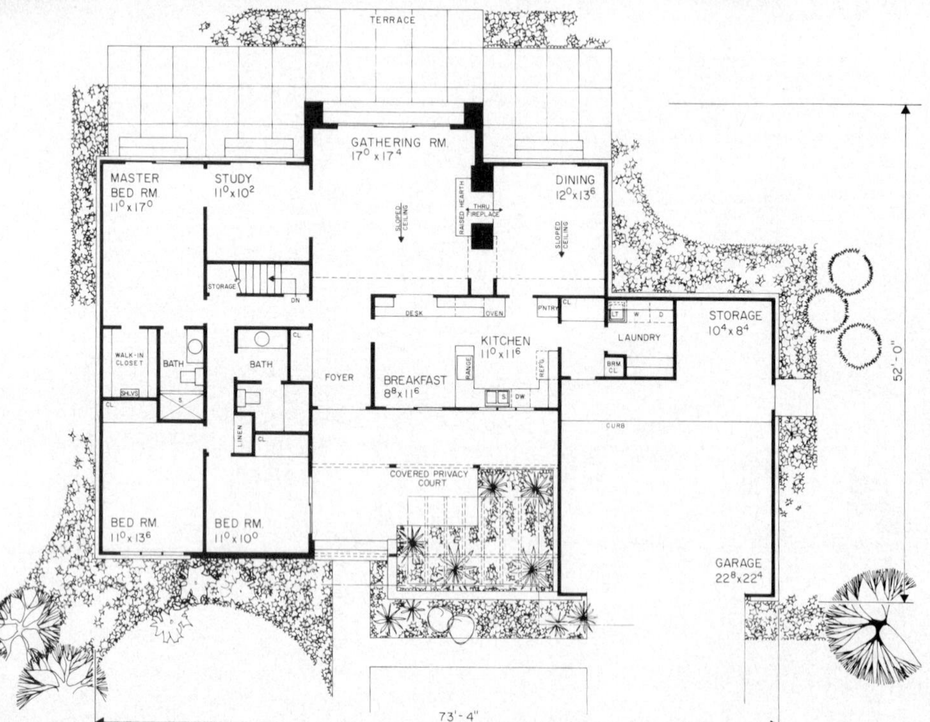

Design T22754

1,844 Sq. Ft.; 26,615 Cu. Ft.

● This really is a most dramatic and refreshing contemporary home. The slope of its wide overhanging roofs is carried right indoors to provide an extra measure of spaciousness. The U-shaped privacy wall of the front entrance area provides an appealing outdoor living spot accessible from the front bedroom. The rectangular floor plan will be economical to build. Notice the efficient use of space and how it all makes its contribution to outstanding livability. The small family will find its living patterns delightful, indeed. Two bedrooms and two full baths comprise the sleeping zone. The open planning of the L-shaped living and dining rooms is most desirable. The thru-fireplace is just a great room divider. The kitchen and breakfast nook function well together. There is laundry and mechanical room nearby.

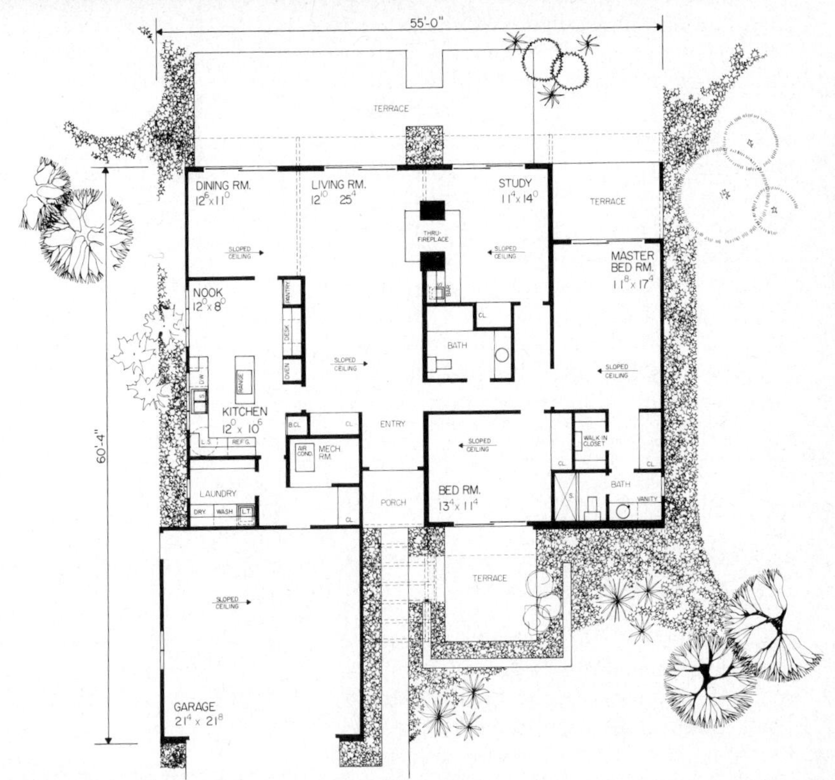

Design T22796

1,828 Sq. Ft.; 39,990 Cu. Ft.

● This home features a front living room with sloped ceiling and sliding glass doors which lead to a front private court. What a delightful way to introduce this design. This bi-nuclear design has a great deal to offer. First - the children's and parent's sleeping quarters are on opposite ends of this house to assure the utmost in privacy. Each area has its own full bath. The interior kitchen is a great idea. It frees up valuable wall space for the living areas exclusive use. There is a snack bar in the kitchen/family room for those very informal meals. Also, a planning desk is in the family room. The dining room is conveniently located near the kitchen plus it has a built-in china cabinet. The laundry area has plenty of storage closets plus the stairs to the basement. This home will surely be a welcome addition to any setting.

Design T22604

1,956 Sq. Ft.; 28,212 Cu. Ft.

● A feature that will set the whole wonderful pattern of true family living will be the 26 foot wide country kitchen. The spacious, L-shaped kitchen has its efficiency enhanced by the island counter work surface. Beamed ceilings, fireplace and sliding glass doors add to the cozy atmosphere of this area. The laundry, dining room and entry hall are but a step or two away. The big keeping room also has a fireplace and can function with the terrace. There are built-in bookshelves and cabinets in the keeping room and more bookshelves in the entry hall. Observe the two baths and three bedrooms in the sleeping wing. Blueprints include details for both basement and non-basement.

Design T22142

2,450 Sq. Ft.; 43,418 Cu. Ft.

● Adaptations of Old England have become increasingly popular in today's building scene. And little wonder; for many of these homes when well-designed have a very distinctive charm. Here is certainly a home which will be like no other in its neighborhood. Its very shape adds an extra measure of uniqueness. And inside, there is all the livability the exterior seems to foretell. The sleeping wing has four bedrooms, two full baths and the laundry room - just where the soiled linen originates. Both formal and informal living areas are ready to serve the active family.

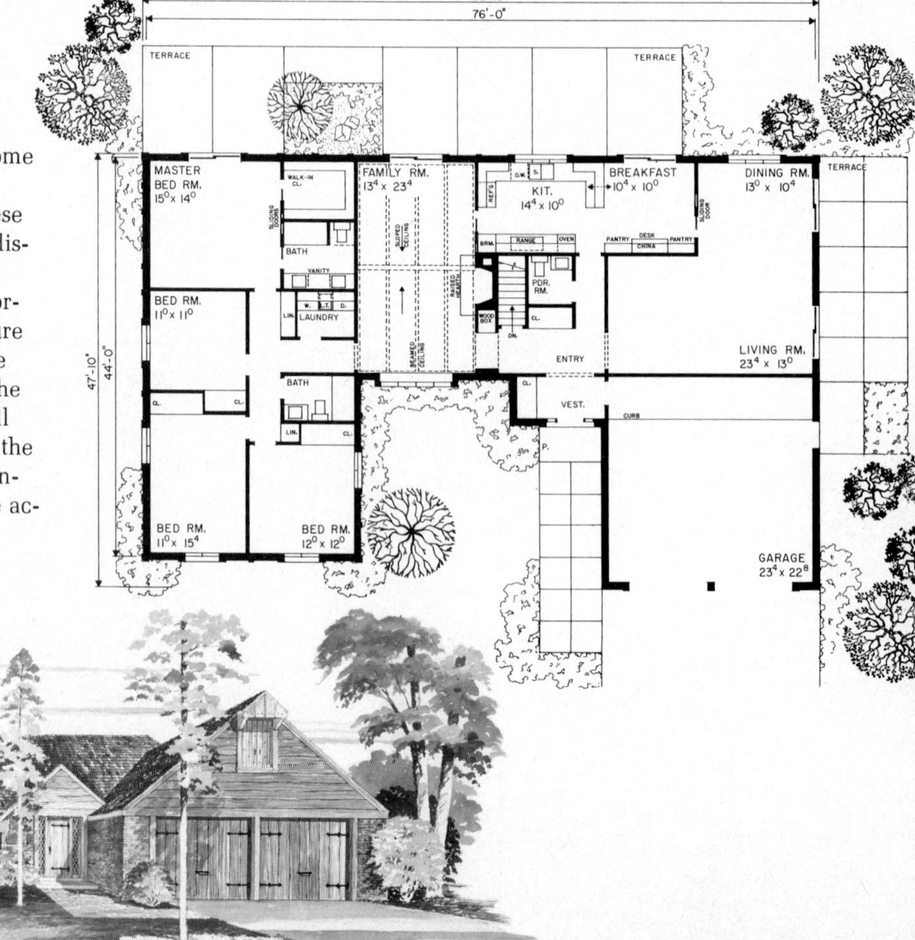

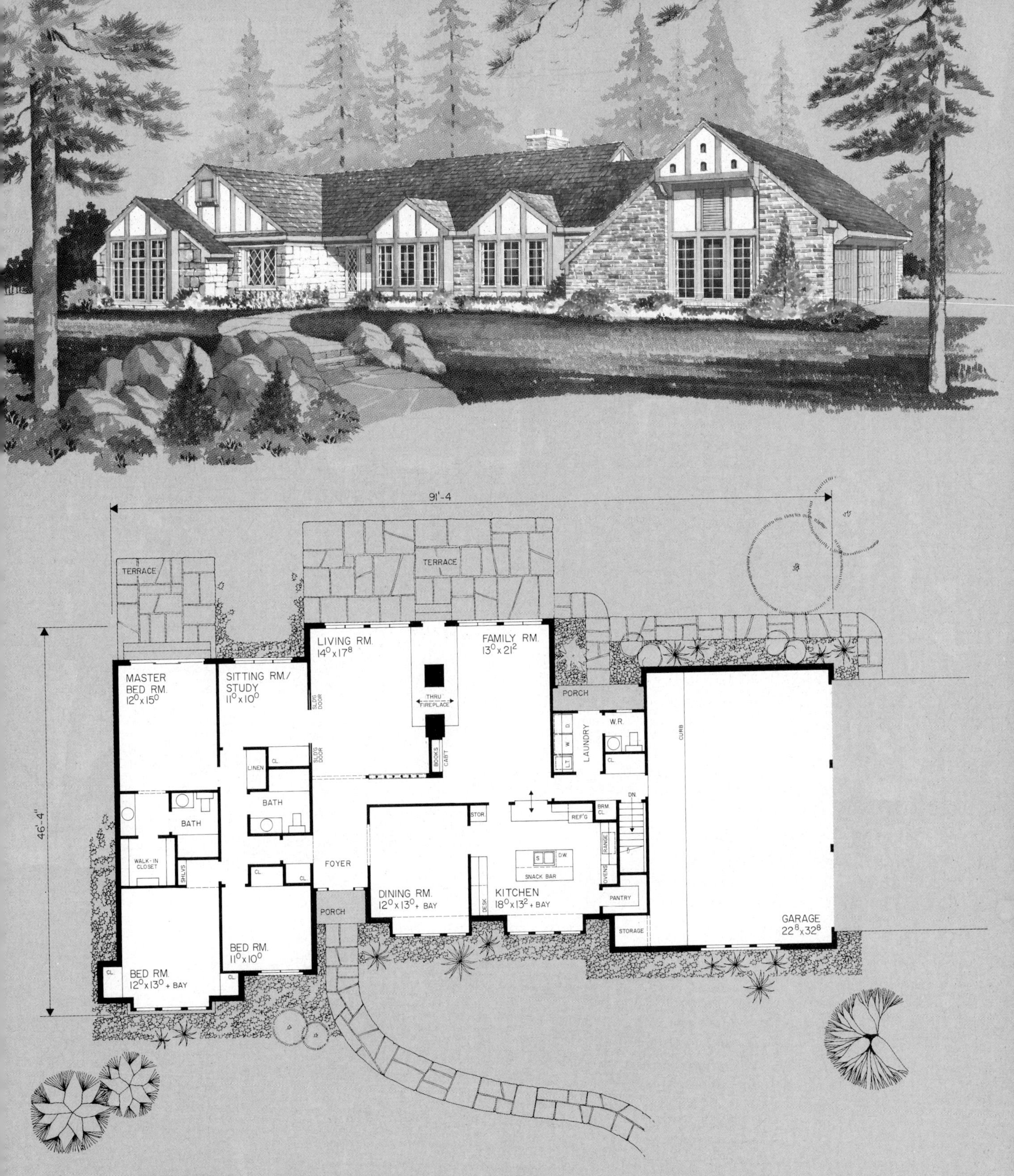

Design T22785 *2,375 Sq. Ft.; 47,805 Cu. Ft.*

● Exceptional Tudor design! Passers-by will surely take a second glance at this fine home wherever it may be located. And the interior is just as pleasing. As one enters the foyer and looks around, the plan will speak for itself in the areas of convenience and efficiency. Cross room traffic will be avoided. There is a hall leading to each of the three bedrooms and study of the sleeping wing and another leading to the living room, family room, kitchen and laundry with wash room. The formal dining room can be entered from both the foyer and the kitchen. Efficiency will surely be the by-word when describing the kitchen. Note the fine features: a built-in desk, pantry, island snack bar with sink and pass-thru to the family room. The fireplace will be enjoyed in the living and family rooms.

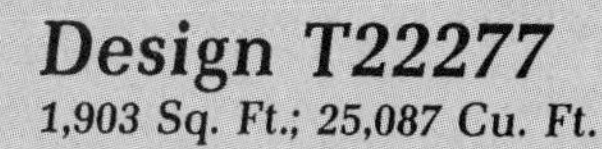

Design T22277

1,903 Sq. Ft.; 25,087 Cu. Ft.

● Tudor design front and center! And what an impact this beautifully proportioned L-shaped home does deliver. Observe the numerous little design features which make this such an attractive home. The half-timber work, the window styling, the front door detailing, the covered porch post brackets and the chimney are all among the delightful highlights. Well-zoned, the dining and living rooms are openly planned for formal dining and living.

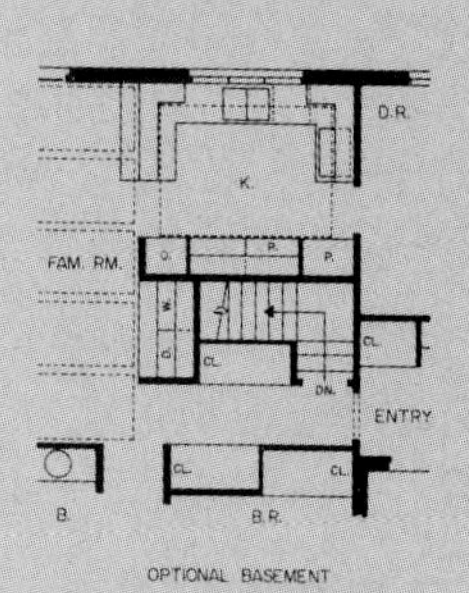

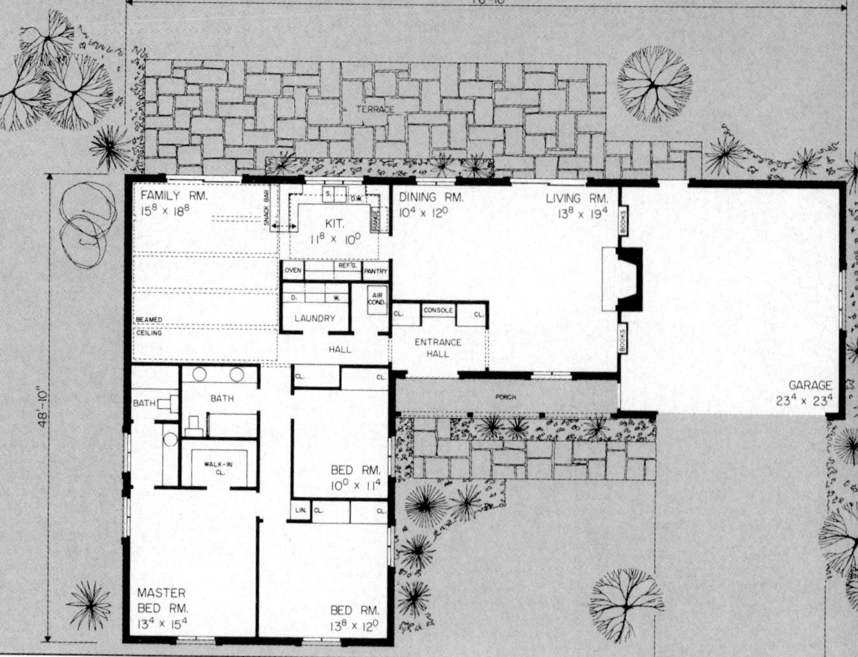

Design T22728

1,825 Sq. Ft.; 38,770 Cu. Ft.

● Your family's new lifestyle will surely flourish in this charming, L-shaped English adaptation. The curving front driveway produces an impressive approach. A covered front porch shelters the centered entry hall which effectively routes traffic to all areas. The fireplace is the focal point of the spacious, formal living and dining area. The kitchen is strategically placed to service the dining room and any informal eating space developed in the family room. In addition to the two full baths of the sleeping area, there is a handy wash room at the entrance from the garage. A complete, first floor laundry is nearby and has direct access to the yard. Sliding glass doors permit easy movement to the outdoor terrace and side porch. Don't overlook the basement and its potential for the development of additional livability and/or storage.

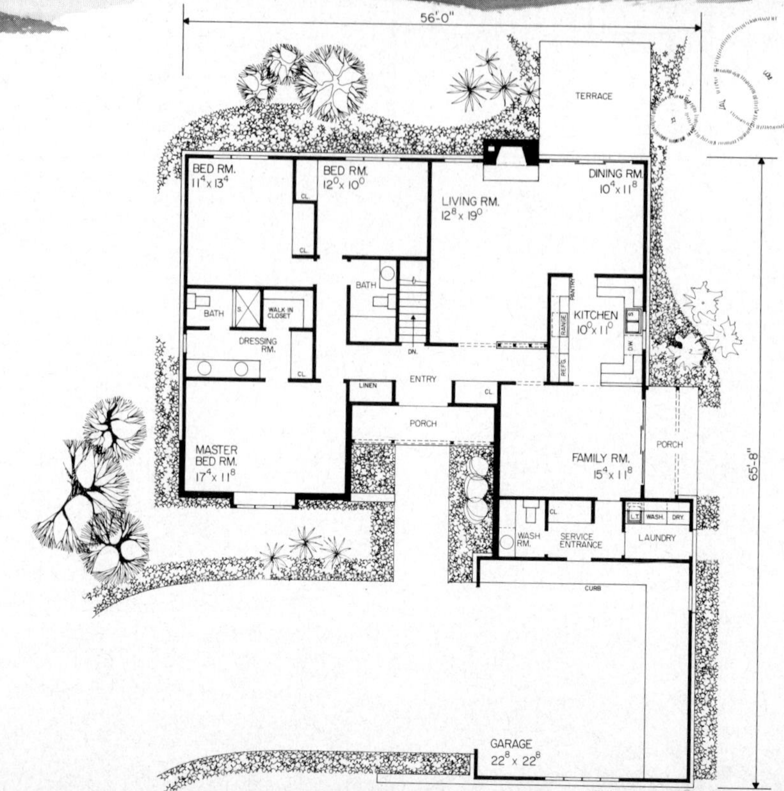

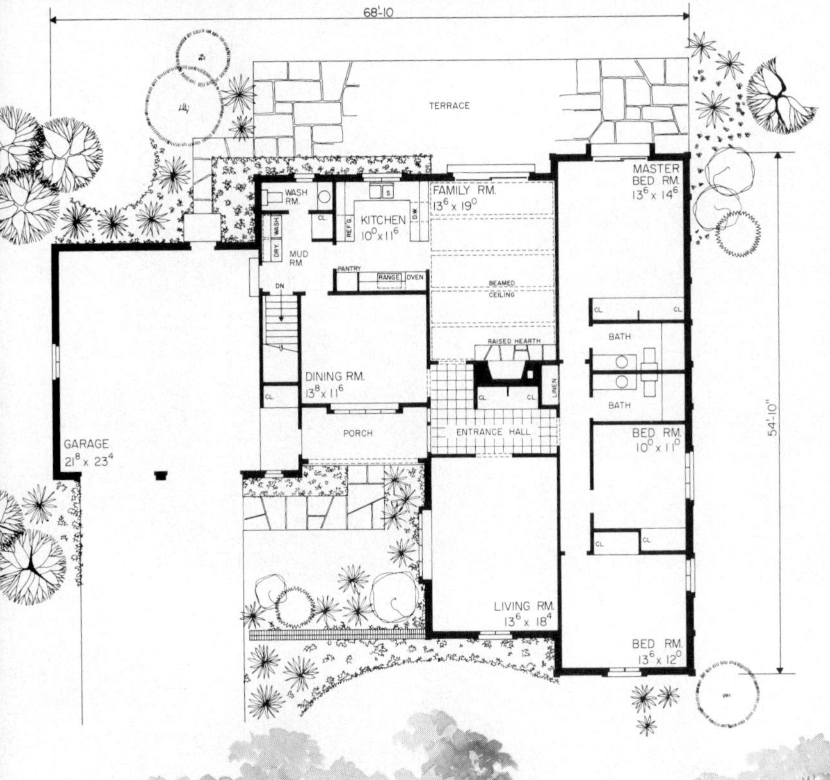

Design T22374

1,919 Sq. Ft.; 39,542 Cu. Ft.

● This English adaptation will never grow old. There is, indeed, much here to please the eye for many a year to come. The wavy-edged siding contrasts pleasingly with the diagonal pattern of brick below. The diamond lites of the windows create their own special effect. The projecting brick wall creates a pleasant court outside the covered front porch. The floor plan is well-zoned with the three bedrooms and two baths comprising a distinct sleeping wing. Flanking the entrance hall is the formal living room and the informal, multi-purpose family room. The large dining room is strategically located. The mud room area is adjacent to the extra wash room and the stairs to the basement.

Design T22737

1,796 Sq. Ft.; 43,240 Cu. Ft.

● You will be able to build this distinctive, modified U-shaped one-story home on a relatively narrow site. But, then, if you so wished, with the help of your architect and builder you may want to locate the garage to the side of the house. Inside, the living potential is just great. The interior U-shaped kitchen handily services the dining and family rooms and nook. A rear covered porch functions ideally with the family room while the formal living room has its own terrace. Three bedrooms and two baths highlight the sleeping zone (or make it two bedrooms and a study). Notice the strategic location of the wash room, laundry, two storage closets and the basement stairs.

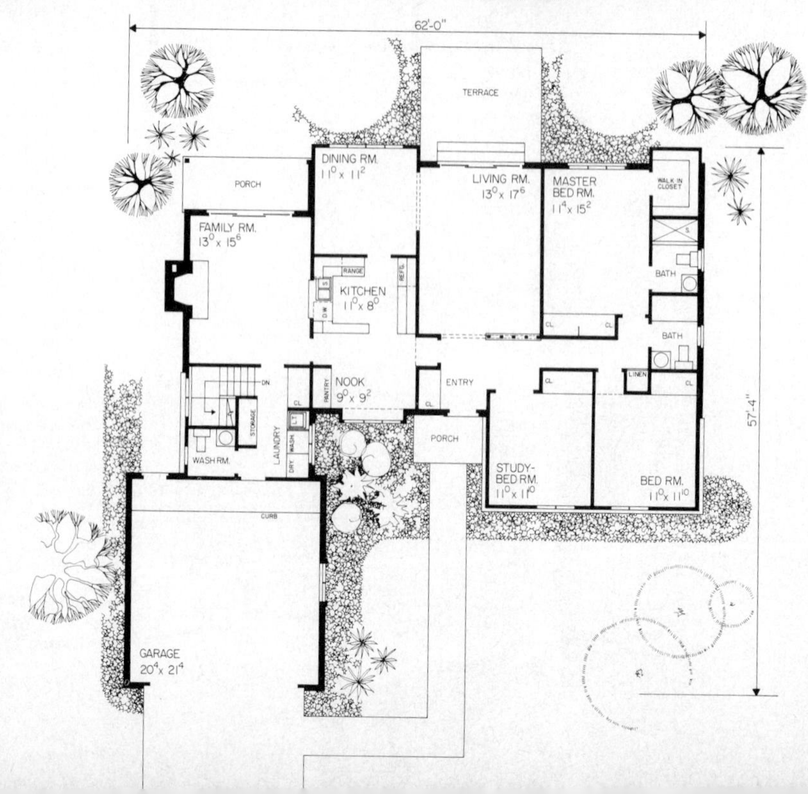

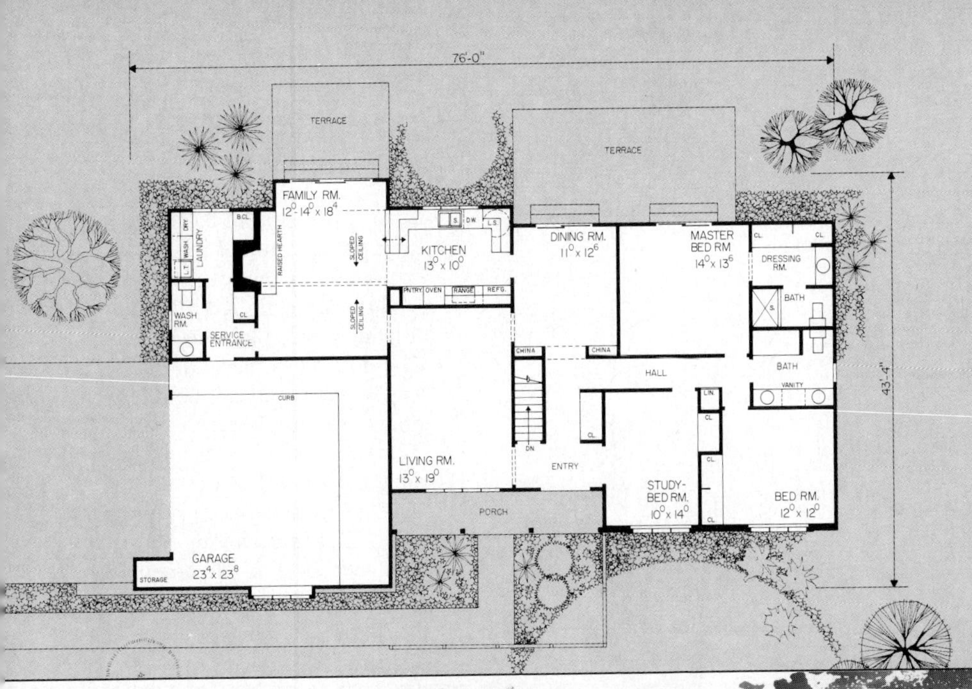

Design T22742

1,907 Sq. Ft.; 38,950 Cu. Ft.

● Colonial charm is expressed in this one-story design by the vertical siding, the post pillars, the cross fence, paned glass windows and the use of stone. A 19' wide living room, a sloped ceilinged family room with a raised hearth fireplace and its own terrace, a kitchen with many built-ins and a dining room with built-in china cabinets are just some of the highlights. The living terrace is accessible from the dining room and master bedroom. There are two more bedrooms and a full bath in addition to the master bed-room.

Design T22738

1,898 Sq. Ft.; 36,140 Cu. Ft.

● Impressive architectural work is indeed apparent in this three bedroom home. The three foot high entrance court wall, the high pitched roof and the paned glass windows all add to this home's appeal. It is also apparent that the floor plan is very efficient with the side U-shaped kitchen and nook with two pantry closets, the rear dining and gathering rooms and the three (or make it two with a study) bedrooms and two baths of the sleeping wing. Indoor-outdoor living also will be enjoyed in this home with a dining terrace off the nook and a living terrace off the gathering room and master bedroom. Note the fireplace in the gathering room and bay window in dining room.

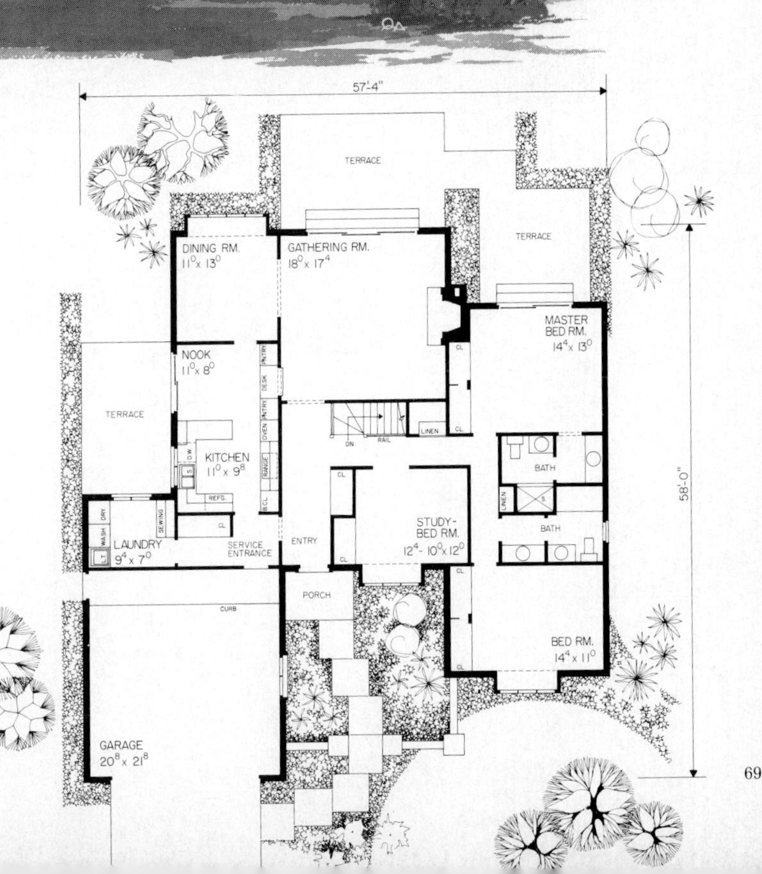

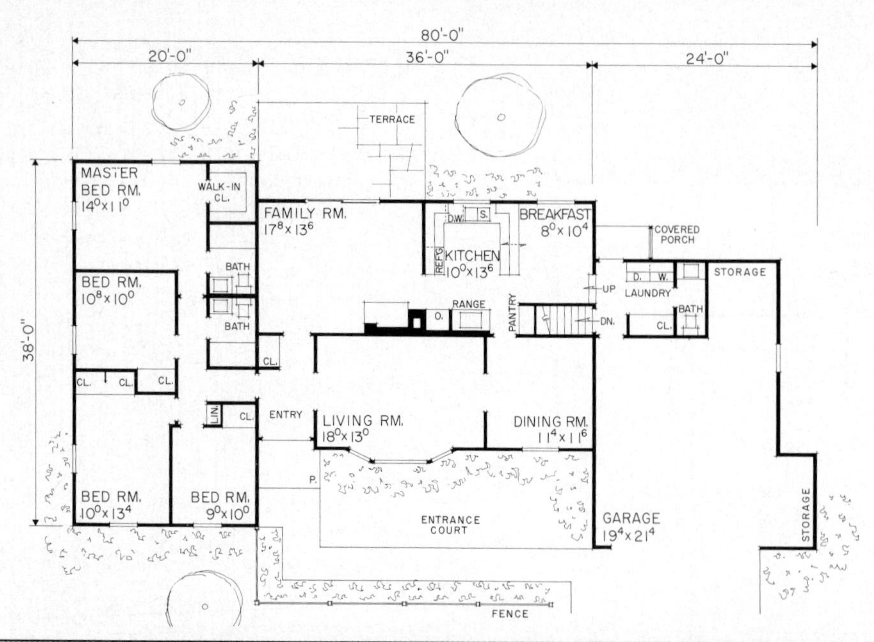

Design T21829

1,800 Sq. Ft.; 32,236 Cu. Ft.

● All the charm of a traditional heritage is wrapped up in this U-shaped home with its narrow, horizontal siding, delightful window treatment and high-pitched roof. The massive center chimney, the bay window and the double front doors are plus features. Inside, the living potential is outstanding. The sleeping wing is self-contained and has four bedrooms and two baths. The large family and living rooms cater to the divergent age groups.

Design T22603

1,949 Sq. Ft.; 41,128 Cu. Ft.

● Surely it would be difficult to beat the appeal of this traditional one-story home. Its slightly modified U-shape with the two front facing gables, the bay window, the covered front porch and the interesting use of exterior materials all add to the exterior charm. Besides, there are three large bedrooms serviced by two full baths and three walk-in closets. The excellent kitchen is flanked by the formal dining room and the informal family room. Don't miss the pantry, the built-in oven and the pass-thru to the snack bar. The handy first floor laundry is strategically located to act as a mud room. The extra wash room is but a few steps away. The sizable living room highlights a fireplace and a picture window. Note the location of the basement stairs.

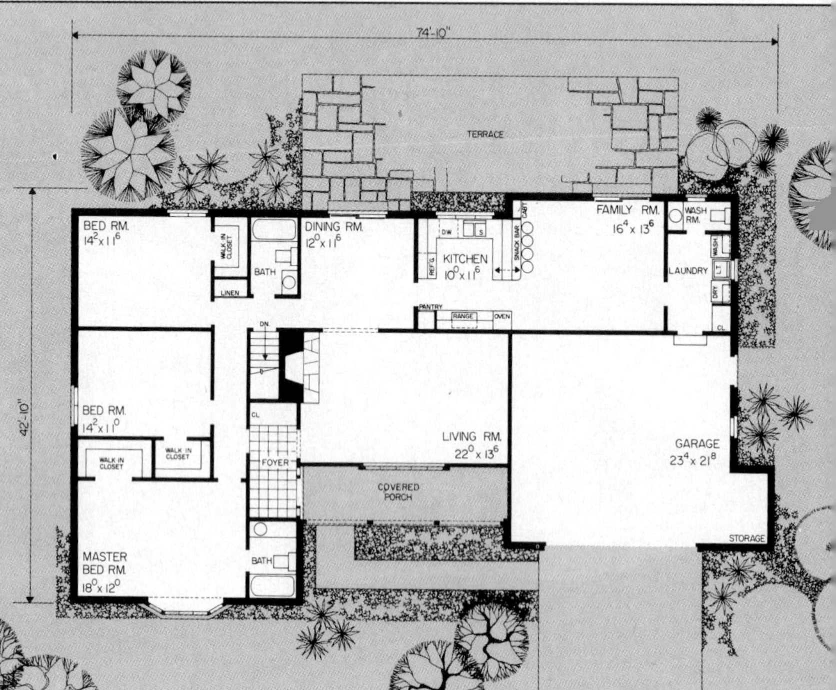

Design T21980

1,901 Sq. Ft.; 36,240 Cu. Ft.

● Planned for easy living, the daily living patterns of the active family will be pleasant ones, indeed. All the elements are present to assure a wonderful family life. The impressive exterior is enhanced by the recessed front entrance area with its covered porch. The center entry results in a convenient and efficient flow of traffic. A secondary entrance leads from the covered side porch, or the garage, into the first floor laundry. Note the powder room nearby.

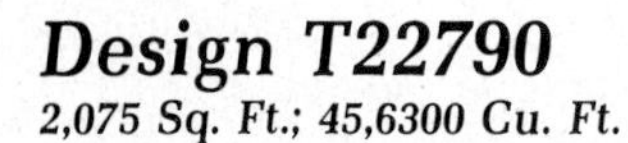

Design T22790

2,075 Sq. Ft.; 45,6300 Cu. Ft.

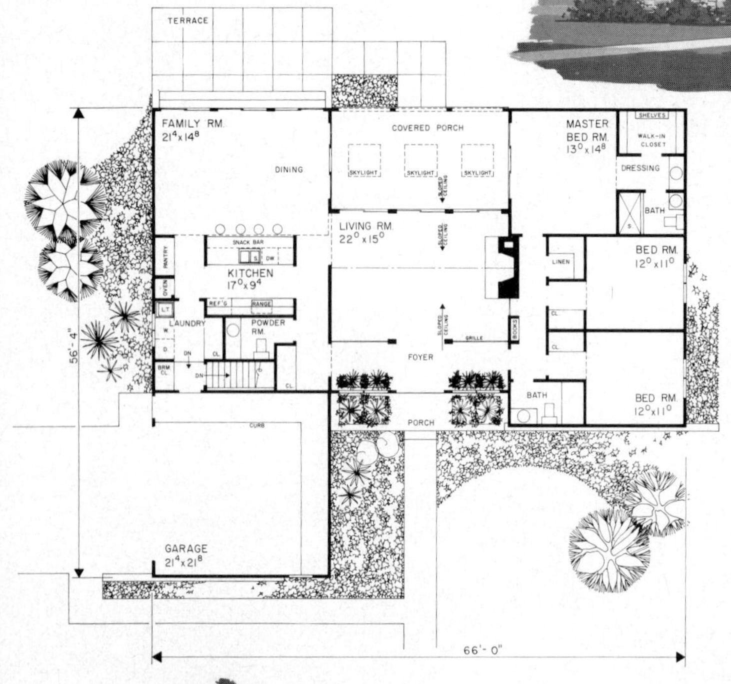

● Enter this contemporary hip-roofed home through the double front doors and immediately view the sloped ceilinged living room with fireplace. This room will be a sheer delight when it comes to formal entertaining. It has easy access to the kitchen and also a powder room nearby. The work area will be convenient. The kitchen has an island work center with snack bar. The laundry is adjacent to the service entrance and stairs leading to the basement. This area is planned to be a real "step saver". The sleeping wing consists of two family bedrooms, bath and master bedroom suite. Maybe the most attractive feature of this design is the rear covered porch with skylights above. It is accessible by way of sliding glass doors in the family/dining area, living room and master bedroom.

Design T22793

2,065 Sq. Ft.; 48,850 Cu. Ft.

● Privacy will be enjoyed in this home both inside and out. The indoor-outdoor living relationships offered in this plan are outstanding: a covered porch at the entrance, a privacy court off the master bedroom divided from the front yard with a privacy wall, a covered porch serving both the living and dining rooms through sliding glass doors (also utilizing a privacy wall) and a covered porch off the kitchen eating area (this one is the largest and has skylights above). Also a large rear terrace. Study the other features of this delightful contemporary design.

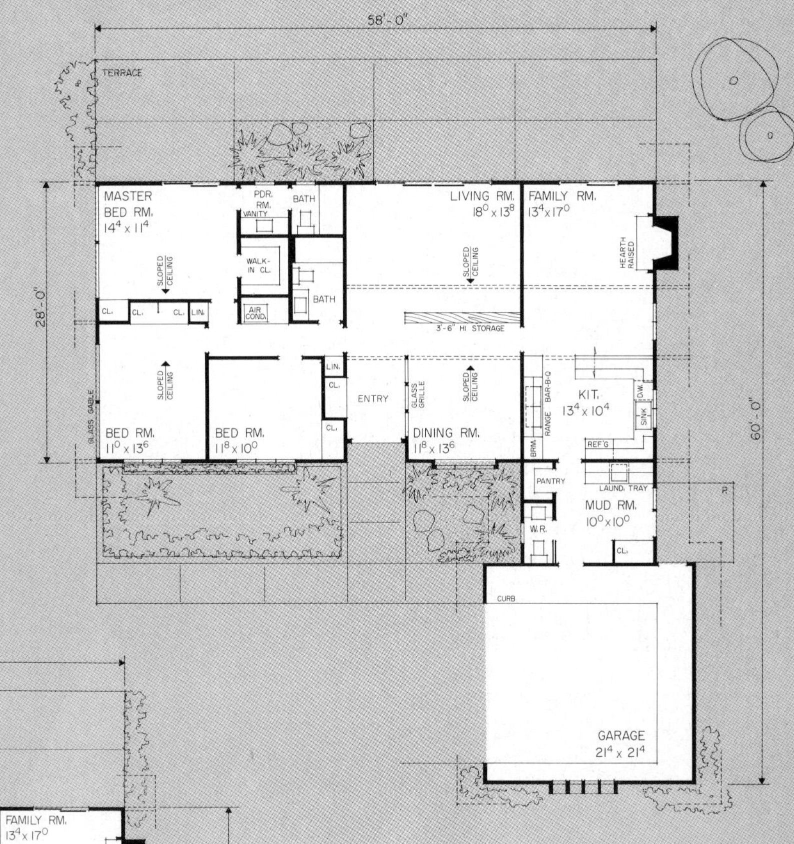

Design T21947 1,764 Sq. Ft.; 18,381 Cu. Ft.

● When it comes to housing your family, if you are among the contemporary-minded, you'll want to give this L-shaped design a second, then even a third, or fourth, look. It is available as either a three or four bedroom home. If you desire the three bedroom, 58 foot wide design order blueprints for T21947; for the four bedroom, 62 foot wide design, order T21948. Inside, you will note a continuation of the contemporary theme with sloping ceilings, exposed beams and a practical 42 inch high storage divider between the living and dining rooms. Don't miss the mud rooms.

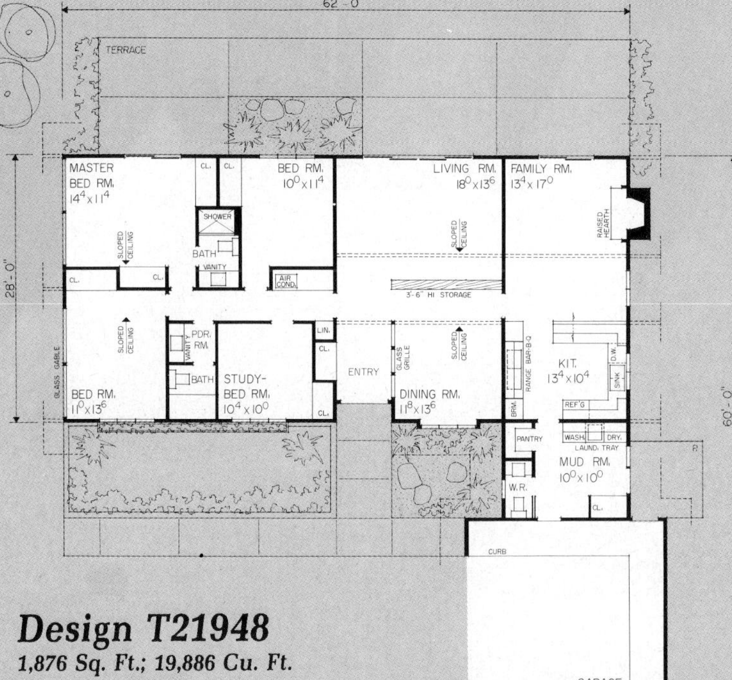

Design T21948
1,876 Sq. Ft.; 19,886 Cu. Ft.

Design T22741

1,842 Sq. Ft.; 37,045 Cu. Ft.

● Here is another example of what 1,800 square feet can deliver in comfort and convenience. The setting reminds one of the sun country of Arizona. However, this design would surely be an attractive and refreshing addition to any region. The covered front porch with its adjacent open trellis area shelters the center entry. From here traffic flows efficiently to the sleeping, living and kitchen zones. There is much to recommend each area. The sleeping with its fine bath and closet facilities; the living with its spaciousness, fireplace and adjacent dining room; the kitchen with its handy nook, excellent storage, nearby laundry and extra wash room.

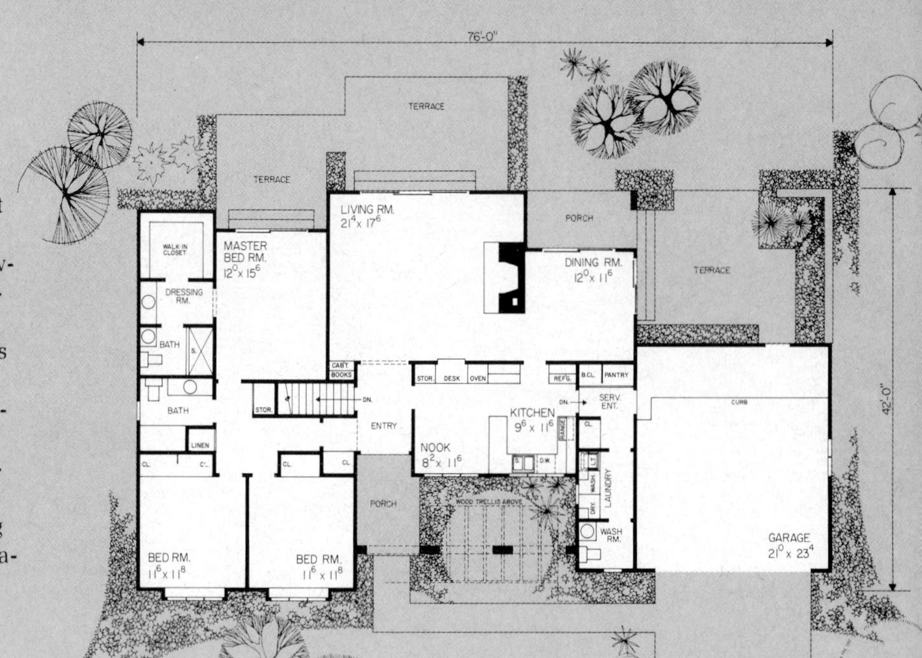

Design T22386

1,994 Sq. Ft.; 22,160 Cu. Ft.

● This distinctive home may look like the Far West, but don't let that inhibit you from enjoying the great livability it has to offer. Wherever built, you will surely experience a satisfying pride of ownership. Imagine, an entrance court in addition to a large side courtyard! A central core is made up of the living, dining and family rooms, plus the kitchen. Each functions with an outdoor living area. The younger generation has its sleeping zone divorced from the master bedroom. The location of the attractive attached garage provides direct access to the front entry. Don't miss the vanity, the utility room with laundry equipment, the snack bar and the raised hearth fireplace. Note three pass-thrus from the kitchen. Observe the beamed and sloping ceilings of the living areas.

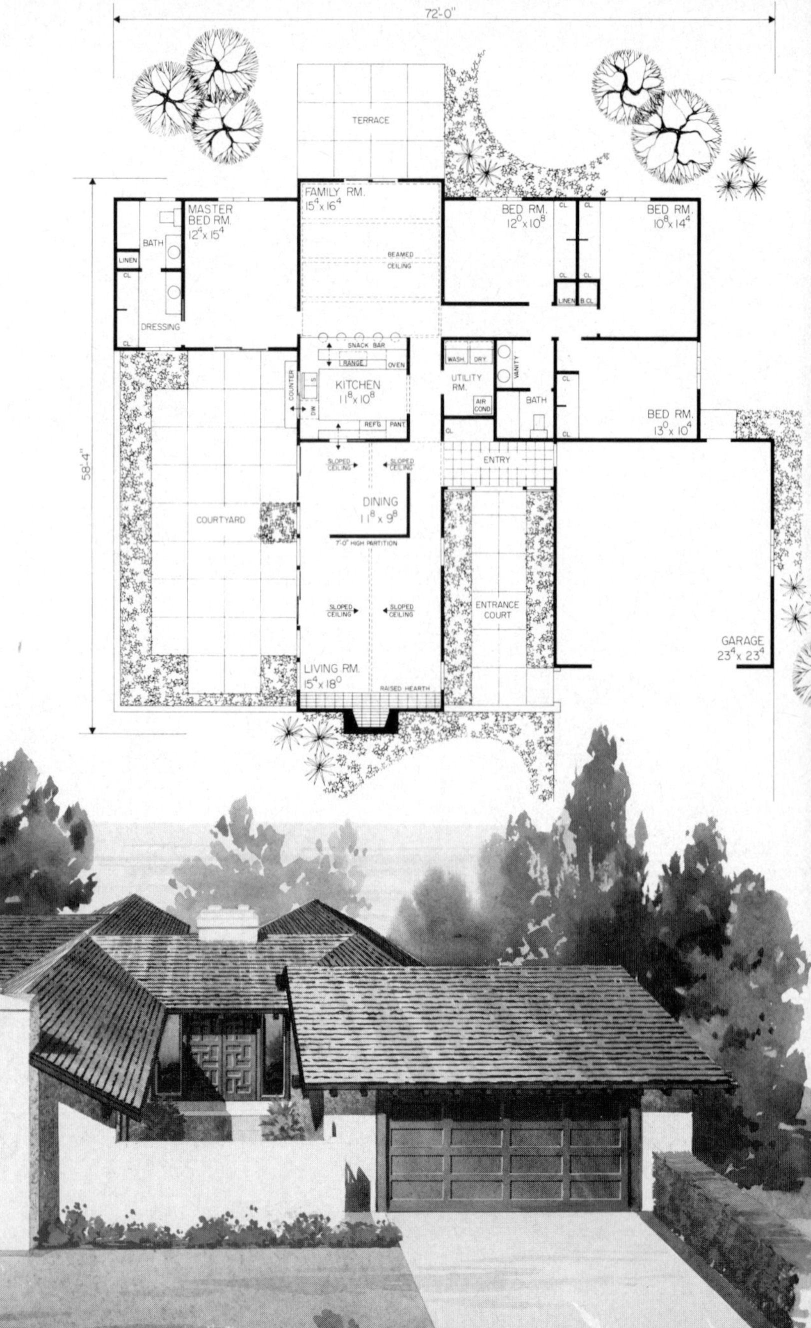

Design T22743

1,892 Sq. Ft.; 23,300 Cu. Ft.

● For those who feel they really don't require both a living and a family room, this refreshing contemporary will serve its occupants well, indeed. Ponder deeply its space and livability; for this design makes a lot of economic sense, too. First of all, placing the attached garage at the front cuts down on the size of a site required. It also represents an appealing design factor. The privacy wall and overhead trellis provide a pleasant front courtyard. Inside, the gathering room satisfies the family's more gregarious instincts, while there is always the study nearby to serve as a more peaceful haven. The separate dining room and the nook offer dining flexibility. The two full baths highlight the economical back-to-back plumbing feature. Note the rear terraces.

Design T22858

2,231 Sq. Ft.; 28,150 Cu. Ft.

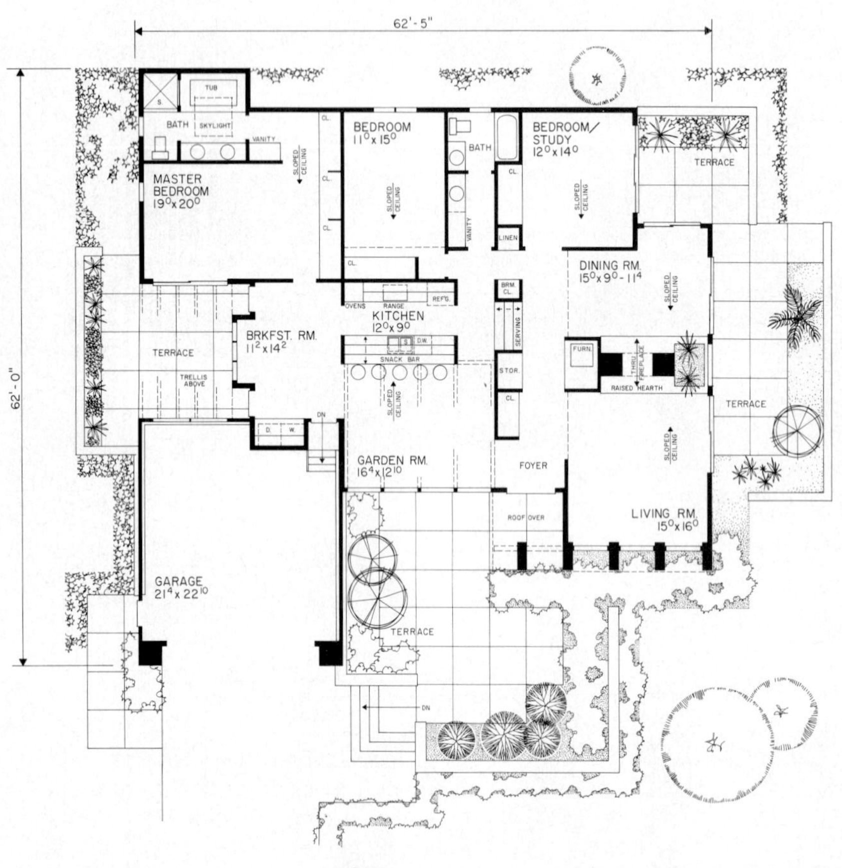

● This sun oriented design was created to face the south. By doing so, it has minimal northern exposure. It has been designed primarily for the more temperate U.S. latitudes using 2 x 6 wall construction. The morning sun will brighten the living and dining rooms along with the adjacent terrace. Sun enters the garden room by way of the glass roof and walls. In the winter, the solar heat gain from the garden room should provide relief from high energy bills. Solar shades allow you to adjust the amount of light that you want to enter in the warmer months. Interior planning deserves mention, too. The work center is efficient. The kitchen has a snack bar on the garden room side and a serving counter to the dining room. The breakfast room with laundry area is also convenient to the kitchen. Three bedrooms are on the northern wall. The master bedroom has a large tub and a separate shower with a four foot square skylight above. When this design is oriented toward the sun, it should prove to be energy efficient and a joy to live in.

Multi-Level Homes

For Functional Split & Bi-Level Living

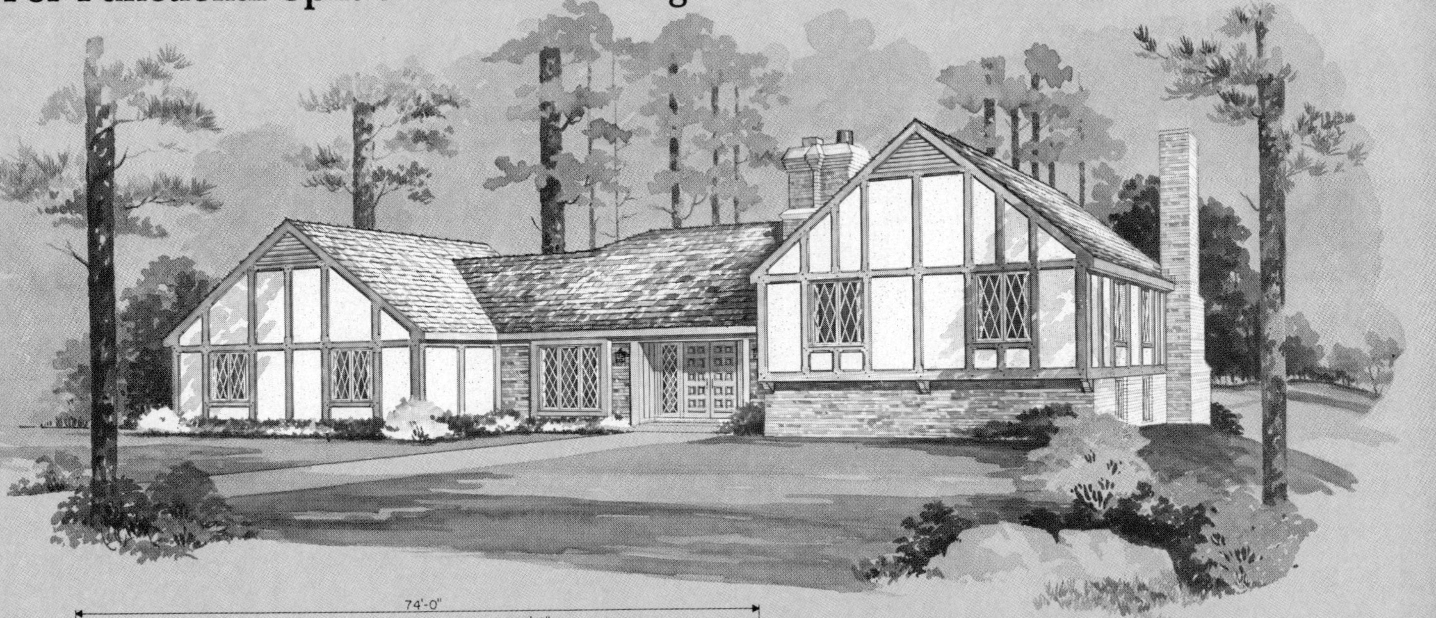

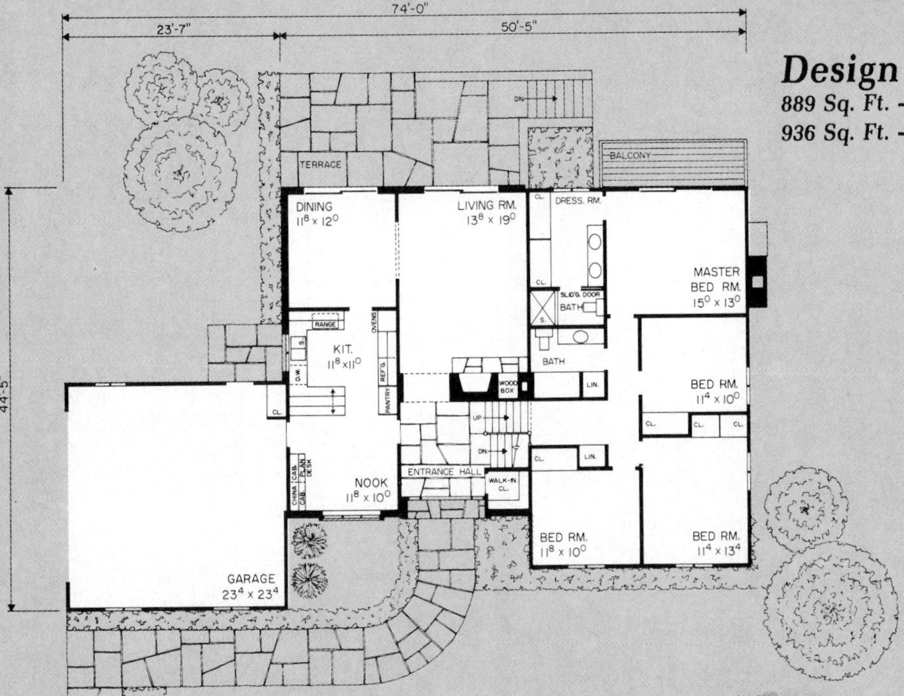

74'-0"
23'-7"
50'-5"
44'-5"
TERRACE
BALCONY
DN
DINING 11⁸ x 12⁰
LIVING RM. 13⁸ x 19⁰
DRESS. RM.
MASTER BED RM. 15⁰ x 13⁰
SLID'G. DOOR
BATH
RANGE
KIT. 11⁸ x 11⁰
OVENS
REF'S.
PANTRY
D.W.
WOOD BOX
BED RM. 11⁴ x 10⁰
CL.
LIN.
UP
DN
ENTRANCE HALL
WALK-IN CL.
NOOK 11⁸ x 10⁰
CHINA CAB.
PLAN DESK
GARAGE 23⁴ x 23⁴
BED RM. 11⁸ x 10⁰
BED RM. 11⁴ x 13⁴

Design T22218

889 Sq. Ft. - Main Level; 960 Sq. Ft. - Upper Level
936 Sq. Ft. - Lower Level; 33,865 Cu. Ft.

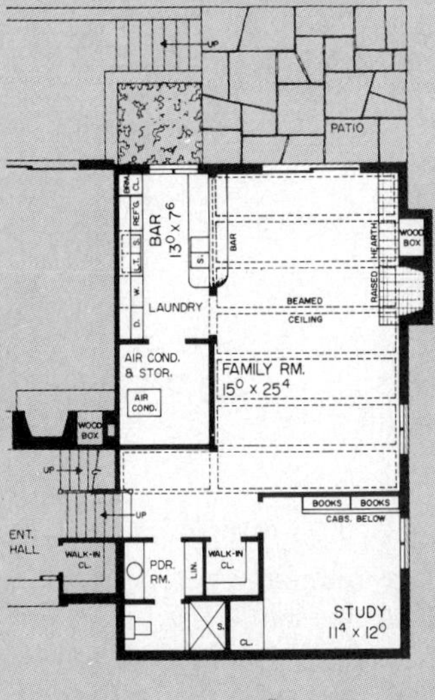

UP
PATIO
BAR 13⁰ x 7⁶
REF'S.
LAUNDRY
BEAMED CEILING
HEARTH
WOOD BOX
AIR COND. & STOR.
AIR COND.
FAMILY RM. 15⁰ x 25⁴
WOOD BOX
UP
BOOKS
BOOKS
CABS. BELOW
ENT. HALL
WALK-IN CL.
PDR. RM.
WALK-IN CL.
STUDY 11⁴ x 12⁰

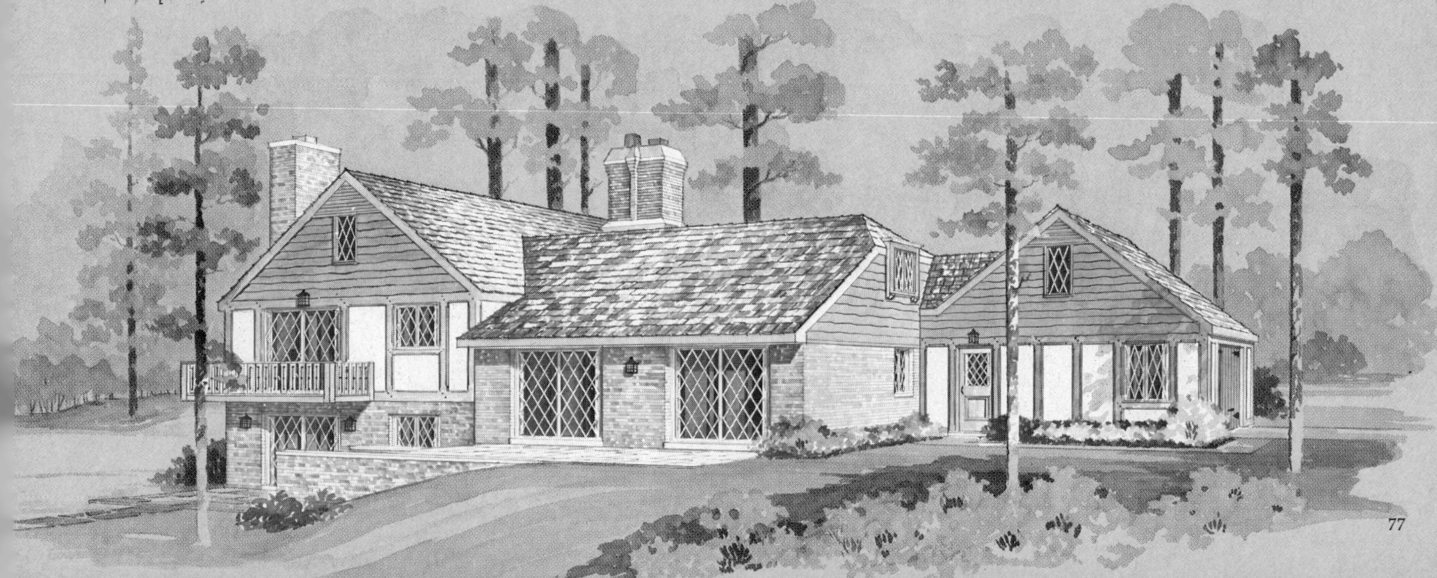

Design T22868

1,203 Sq. Ft. - Upper Level
1,317 Sq. Ft. - Lower Level; 29,595 Cu. Ft.

Common Living Areas – Sleeping Privacy

● Two couples sharing the expense of a house has got to be ideal and, of course, economical. The occupants of this house could do just that. The lower level, housing the kitchen, dining room, family and living rooms and the laundry facilities, is the common area to be shared by both couples. Centrally located, the kitchen and dining room act as a space divider to the living and family rooms so both couples can enjoy privacy.

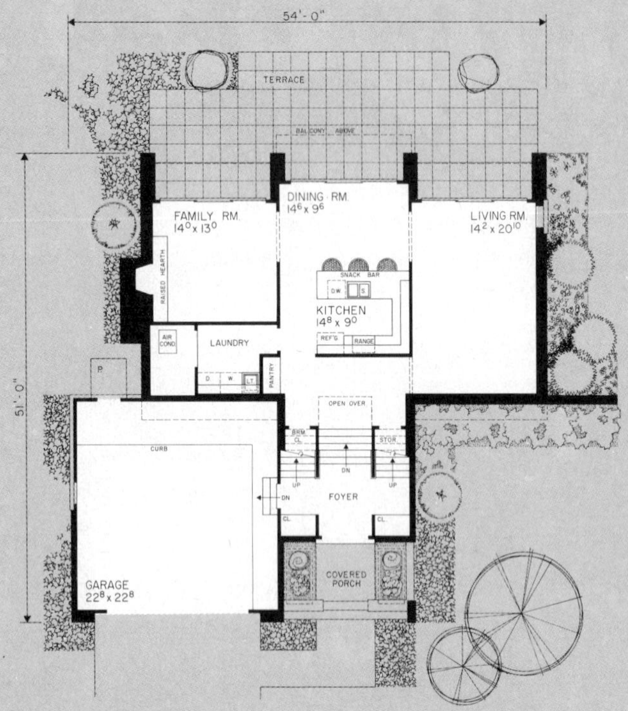

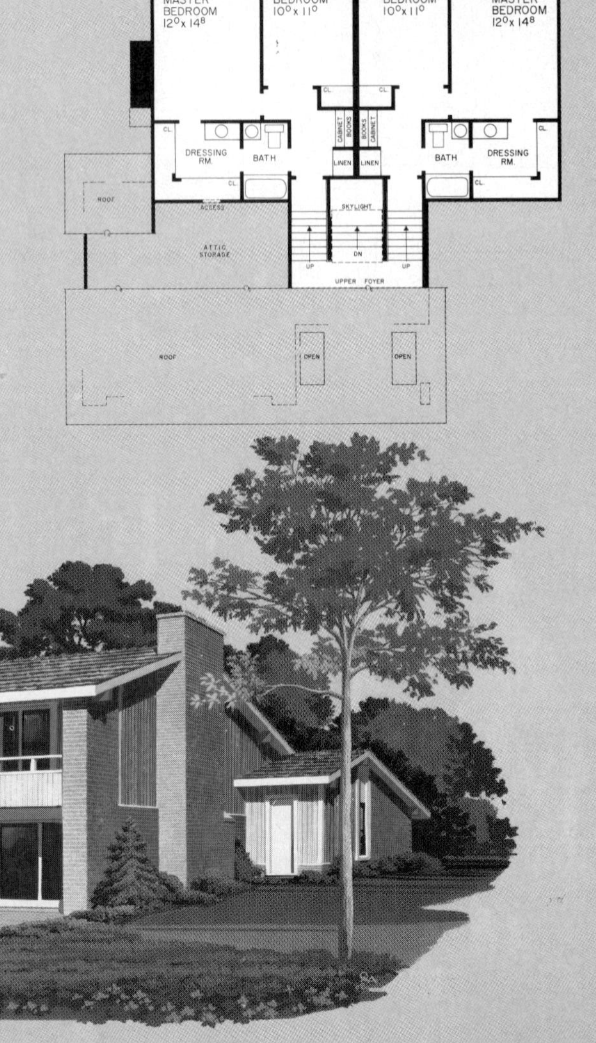

Separate stairways lead to the upper level from the skylit foyer. Each private area has two bedrooms, a dressing room and a full bath. Individual entrances can be locked for additional privacy. Sliding glass doors are in each of the rear rooms on both levels so the outdoors can be enjoyed to its fullest.

Design T22827 *1,618 Sq. Ft. - Upper Level*
1,458 Sq. Ft. - Lower Level; 41,370 Cu. Ft.

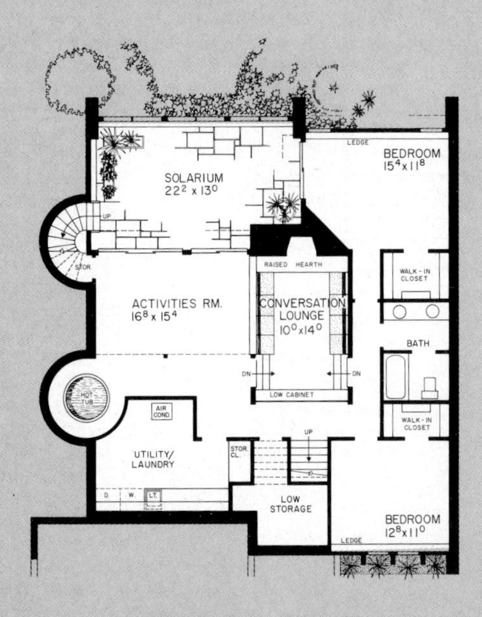

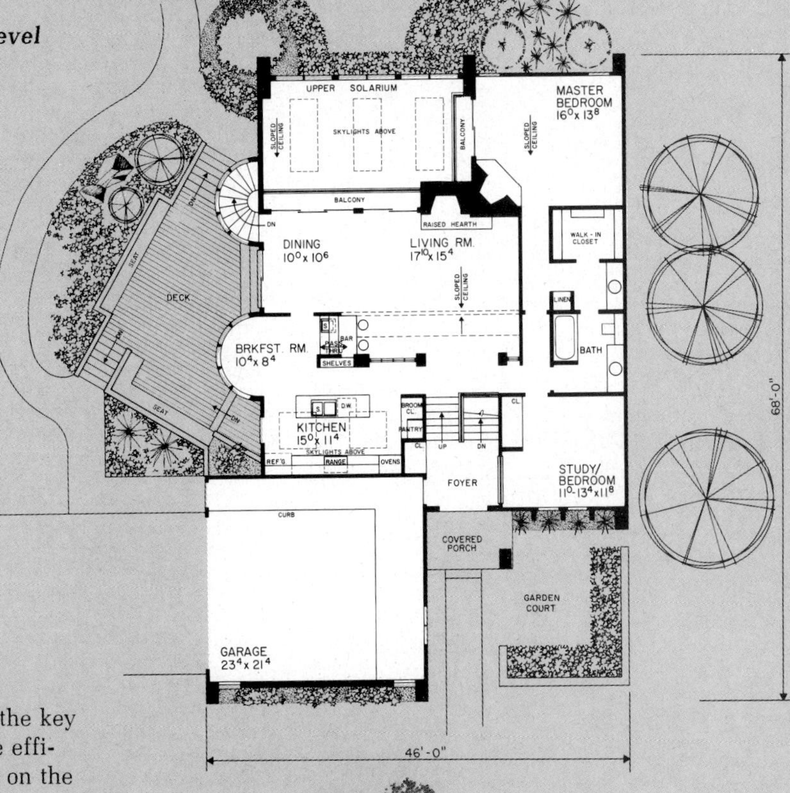

● The two-story solarium with skylights above is the key to energy savings to this bi-level design. Study the efficiency of this floor plan. The conversation lounge on the lower level is a unique focal point.

Design T21977

896 Sq. Ft. - Main Level; 884 Sq. Ft. - Upper Level
896 Sq. Ft. - Lower Level; 36,718 Cu. Ft.

● This split-level with its impressive two-story center portion flanked by a projecting living wing on one side and a two-car garage on the other side, still maintains that very desirable ground-hugging quality. Built entirely of frame with narrow horizontal siding (brick veneer could be substituted), this home will sparkle with a New England flavor. Upon passing through the double front doors, you'll be impressed by an orderly flow of traffic. You'll go up to the sleeping zone; down to the hobby/recreation level; straight ahead to the kitchen and breakfast room; left to the quiet living room. Noteworthy are the extra baths, bedrooms and beamed ceiling family room with fireplace on lower level.

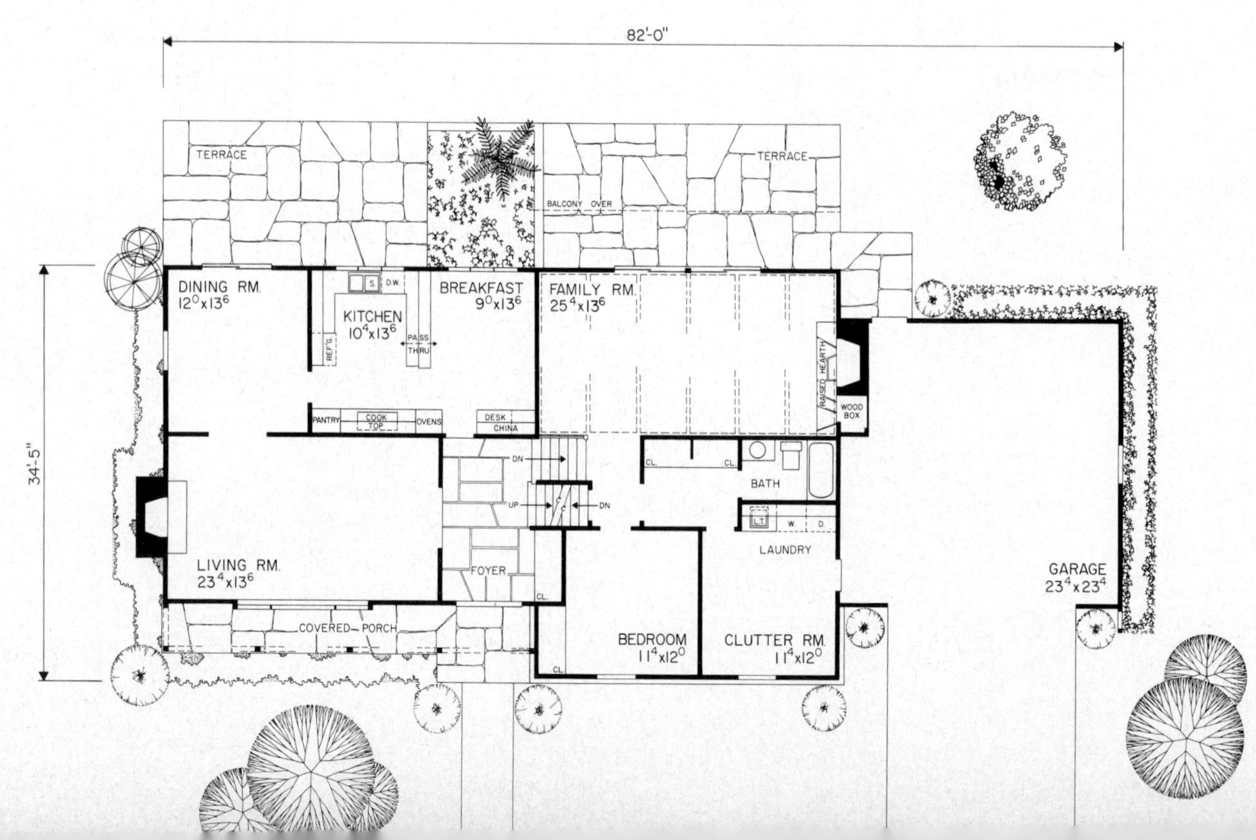

Design T22727 *506 Sq. Ft. - Entry Level; 1,288 Sq. Ft. - Upper Level; 1,241 Sq. Ft. - Lower Level; 38,590 Cu. Ft.*

● Tri-level living at its glorious best. This Colonial facade is picturesque, indeed. The double front doors with their flanking side panels of glass are protected by the overhanging roof. The overhang of the upper level is an appealing detail and adds extra footage. Noteworthy is the size of the four bedrooms, the various storage facilities and the master bedroom balcony. Observe how the entry hall is utilized to receive traffic from both garage and front entrance. The gathering room has a dramatic planter/fireplace wall and functions through two sets of sliding glass doors with the big, L-shaped, upper terrace. The lower, main living level is wonderfully planned. Don't miss the extra bedroom, or study, located on the lower level, with a nearby powder room.

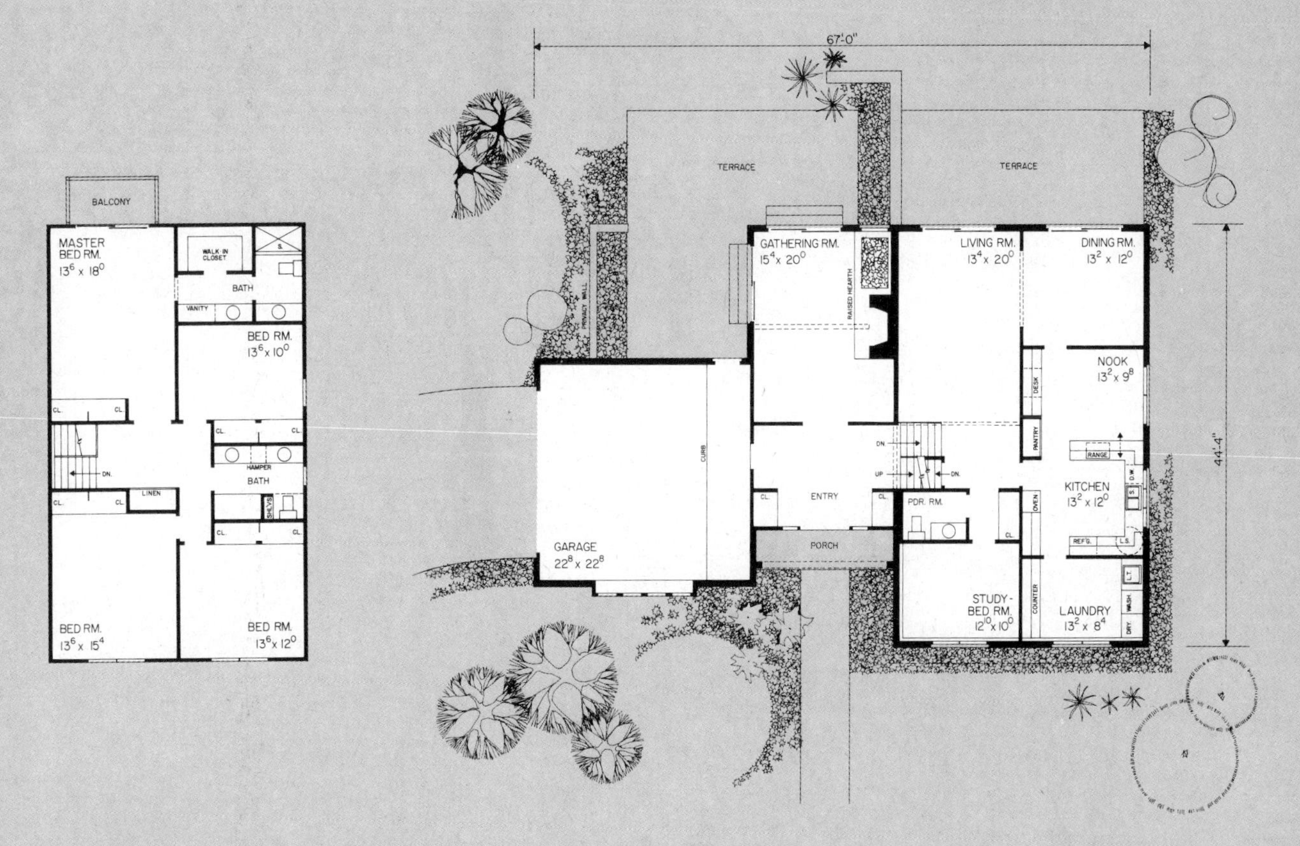

Design T22143 *832 Sq. Ft. - Main Level; 864 Sq. Ft. - Upper Level; 864 Sq. Ft. - Lower Level; 27,473 Cu. Ft.*

● Here the Spanish Southwest comes to life in the form of an enchanting multi-level home. There is much to rave about. The architectural detailing is delightful, indeed. The entrance courtyard, the twin balconies and the roof treatment are particularly noteworthy. Functioning at the rear of the house are the covered patio and the balcony with its lower patio. Well zoned, the upper level has three bedrooms and two baths; the main level has its formal living and dining rooms to the rear and kitchen area looking onto the courtyard; the lower level features the family room, study and laundry. Be sure to notice the extra wash room and the third full bath. There are two fireplaces each with a raised hearth. A dramatic house wherever built!

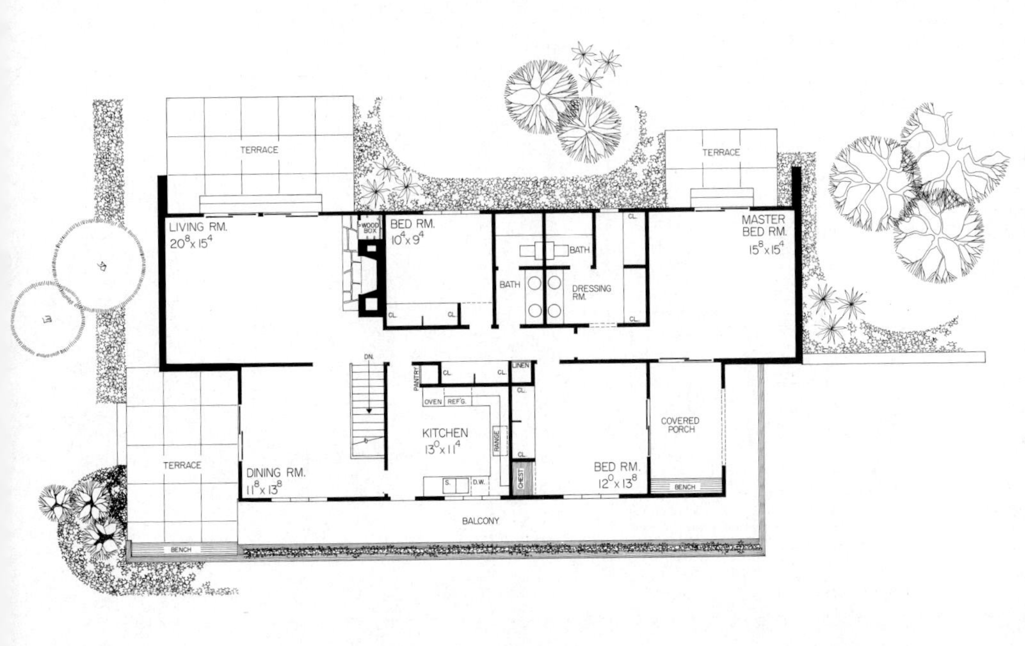

Design T22601

1,724 Sq. Ft. - Upper Level
986 Sq. Ft. - Lower Level
28,240 Cu. Ft.

● Surely it would be difficult to improve upon the refreshing appeal of this contemporary bi-level design. Built into a sloping site, its lower level has direct grade access at the rear. With four bedrooms and three full baths, the large family will be well-served. Each of the living areas has a fireplace. The family dining room is but a step or two from the side terrace for convenient, outdoor dining. The kitchen is handy to the balcony for ease of caring for those potted plants. Worthy of particular note, is the covered porch which functions with two of the upper level bedrooms. Don't miss the oversized garage with all those storage facilities and the work bench. While the blueprints call for an exterior of stone and stucco, you may wish to substitute your own choice of materials.

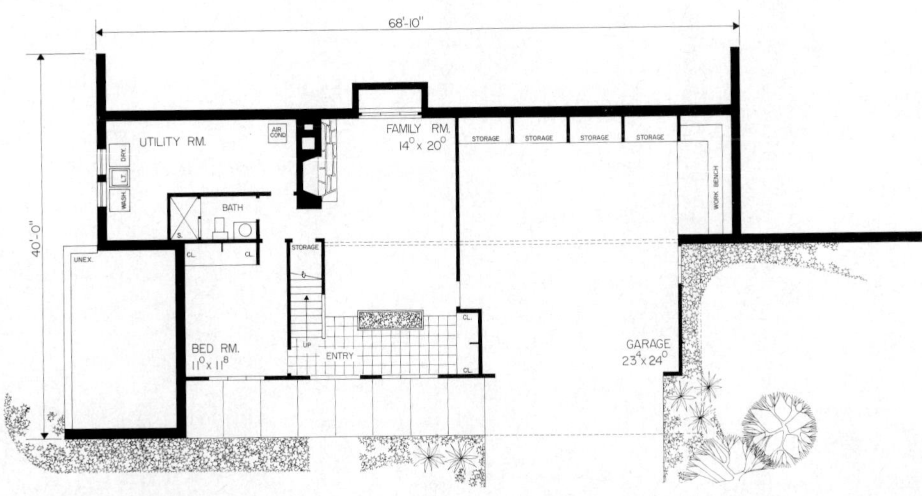

Design T21935 *904 Sq. Ft. - Main Level; 864 Sq. Ft. - Upper Level; 840 Sq. Ft. - Lower Level; 26,745 Cu. Ft.*

● If there was ever a design that looked a part of the ground it was built on, this particular multi-level looks just that. This design will adapt equally well to a flat or sloping site. There would be no question about the family's ability to adapt to what the interior has to offer. Everything is present to satisfy the family's desire to "live a little". Features include: a covered porch, balcony, two fireplaces, extra study, family room with a beamed ceiling, complete laundry and a basement level for added recreational and storage space. Blueprints include non-basement details.

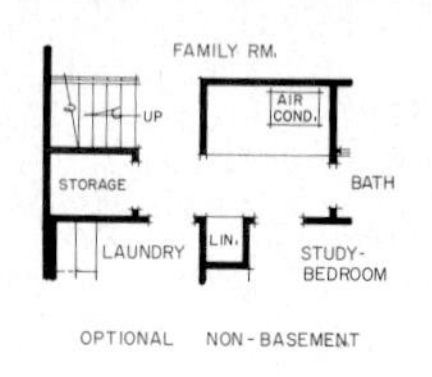

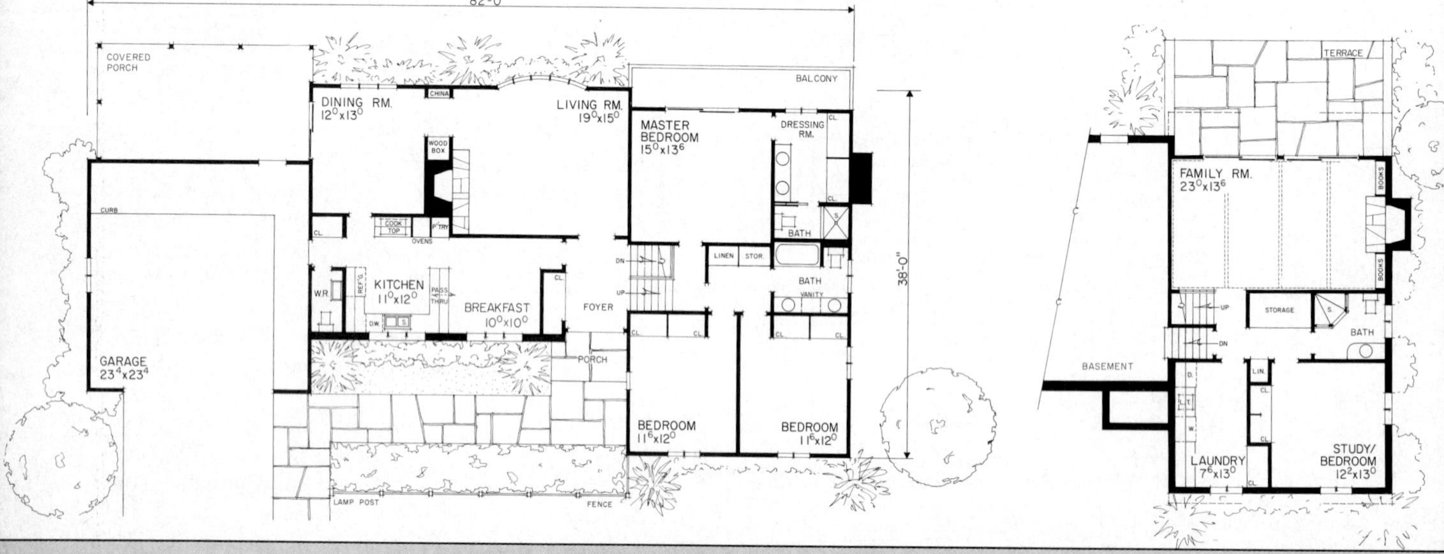

Design T21930 *947 Sq. Ft. - Main Level; 768 Sq. Ft. - Upper Level; 740 Sq. Ft. - Lower Level; 25,906 Cu. Ft.*

● The warmth of this inspiring Colonial adaptation of the split-level idea is not restricted to the exterior. Its homey charm is readily apparent upon stepping through the double front doors. The sunken living room and the beamed ceiling family room with its raised hearth fireplace will be cozy, indeed. The kitchen, powder room and closet, just inside the door from the garage, will be three added conveniences of this design that you should not overlook. There are three bedrooms on the upper level, while there is a fourth to be found on the lower level. Don't miss the big laundry and extra wash room.

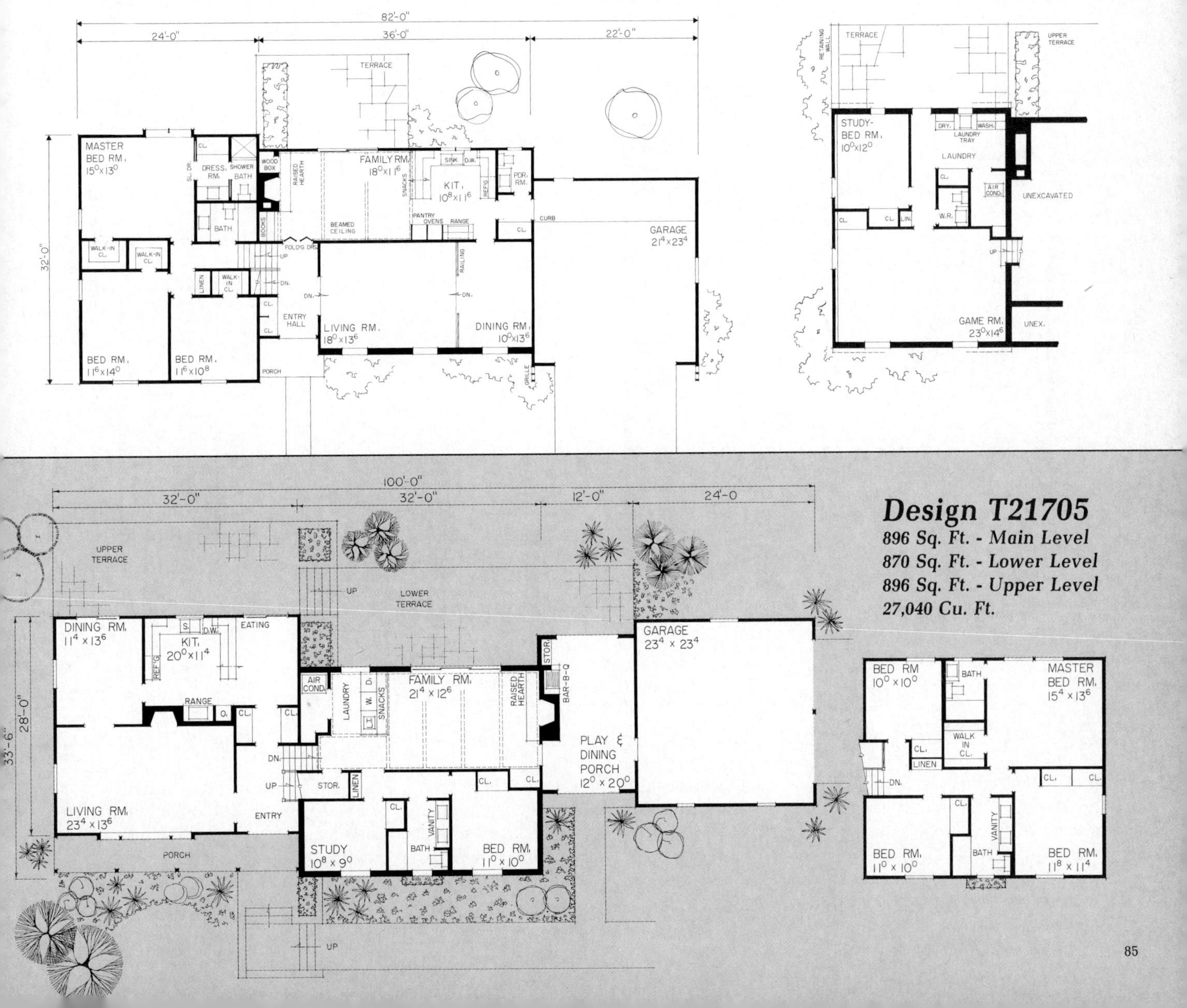

Design T21705

896 Sq. Ft. - Main Level
870 Sq. Ft. - Lower Level
896 Sq. Ft. - Upper Level
27,040 Cu. Ft.

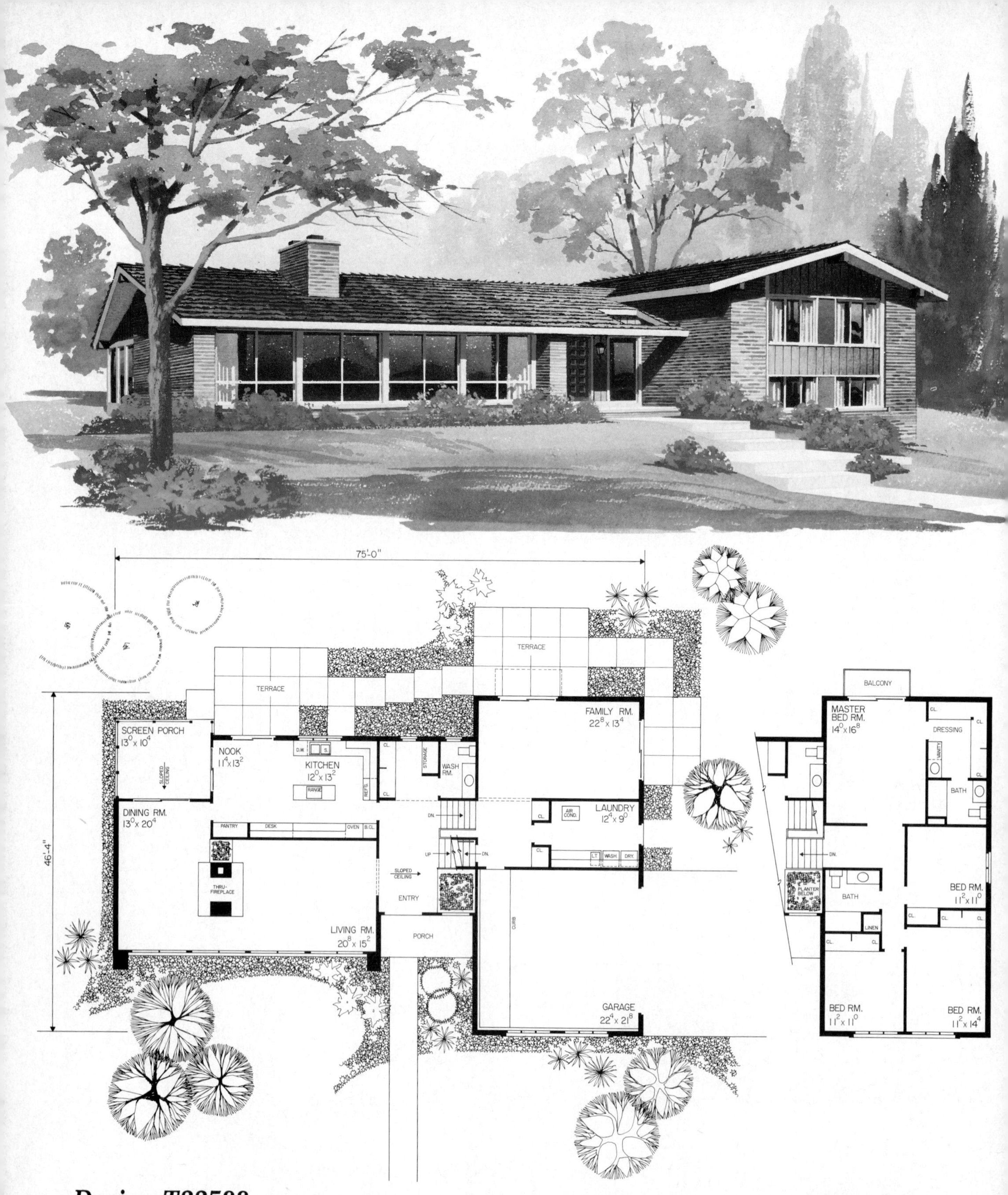

Design T22588 *1,354 Sq. Ft. - Main Level; 1,112 Sq. Ft. - Upper Level; 562 Sq. Ft. - Lower Level; 46,925 Cu. Ft.*

● A thru-fireplace with an accompanying planter for the formal dining room and living room. That's old-fashioned good cheer in a contemporary home. The dining room has an adjacent screened-in porch for outdoor dining in the summertime. There are companions for these two formal areas, an informal breakfast nook and a family room. Each having sliding glass doors to separate rear terraces. Built-in desk, pantry, ample work space and island range are features of the L-shaped kitchen. The large laundry on the lower level houses the heating and cooling equipment. Three family bedrooms, bath and master bedroom suite are on the upper level.

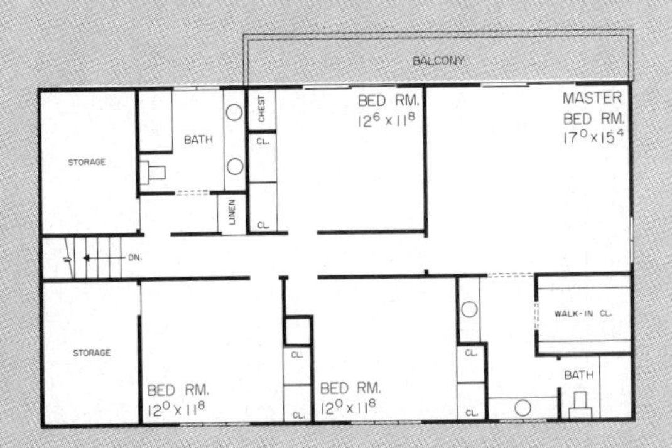

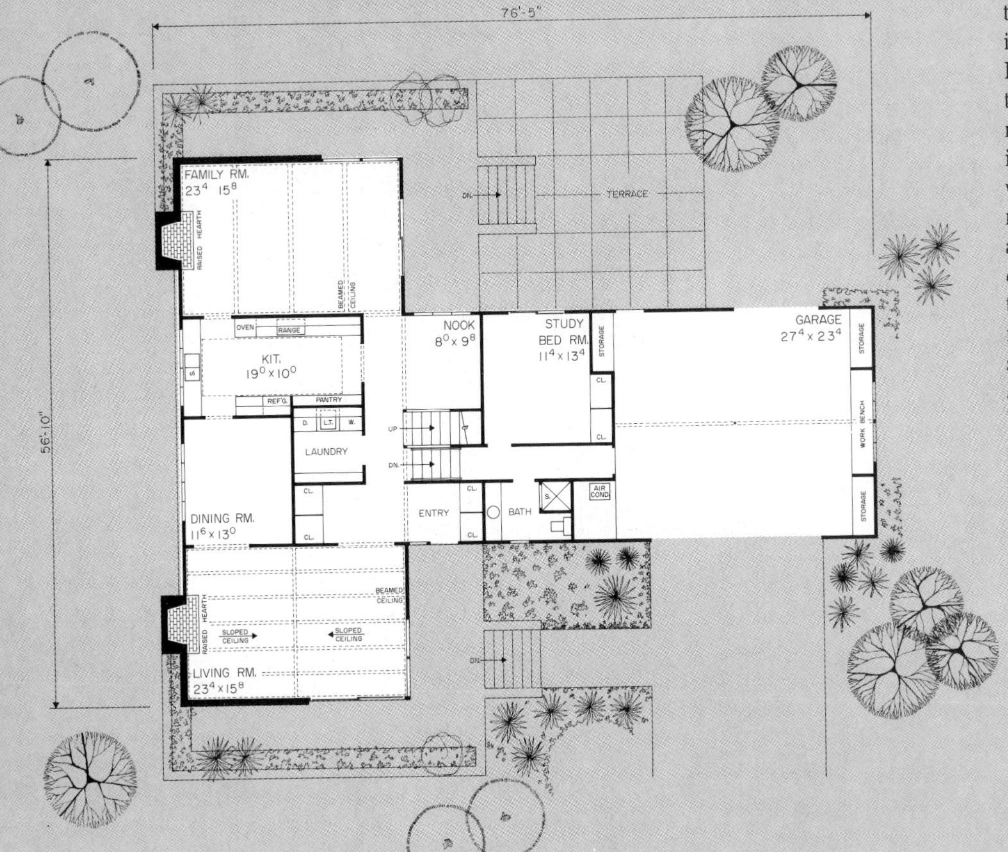

Design T22300

1,579 Sq. Ft. - Main Level
1,176 Sq. Ft. - Upper Level
321 Sq. Ft. - Lower Level
34,820 Cu. Ft.

● A T-shaped contemporary with just loads of livability. You may enter this house on the lower level through the garage, or by ascending the steps to the delightful terrace which leads to the main level front entry. Zoning of the interior is wonderful. Projecting to the front and functioning with the formal dining room is the living room. Projecting to the rear and functioning with the kitchen is the family room. Each of these two living areas features a fireplace, beamed ceiling and sliding glass doors to the outside. Also notice the nook, the laundry and the closet space. On the upper level there are four large bedrooms, two full baths, two storage rooms and an outdoor balcony. The lower level offers that fifth bedroom with a full bath nearby. Don't miss the storage facilities of the garage. Truly fine livability.

Design T22844 *1,882 Sq. Ft. - Upper Level 1,168 Sq. Ft. - Lower Level; 37,860 Cu. Ft.*

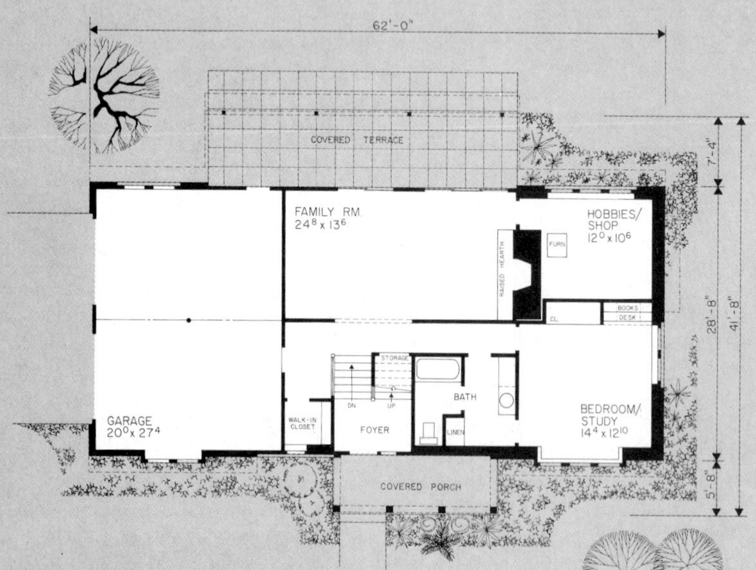

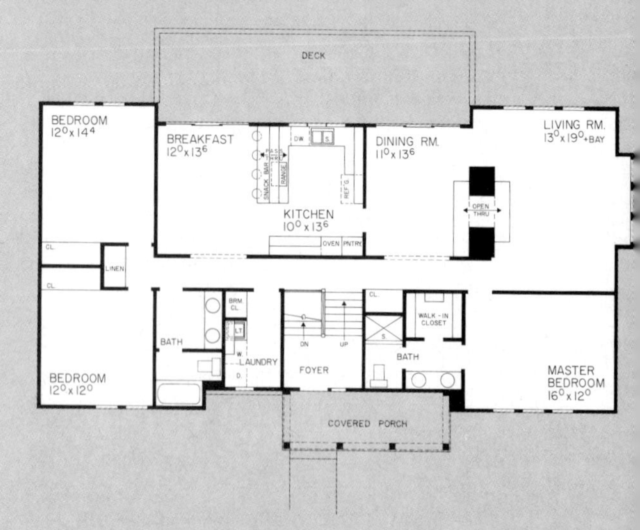

● Bi-level living will be enjoyed to the fullest in this Túdor design. The split-foyer type design will be very efficient for the active family. Three bedrooms are on the upper level, a fourth on the lower level.

Design T22843

1,861 Sq. Ft. - Upper Level
1,181 Sq. Ft. - Lower Level; 32,485 Cu. Ft.

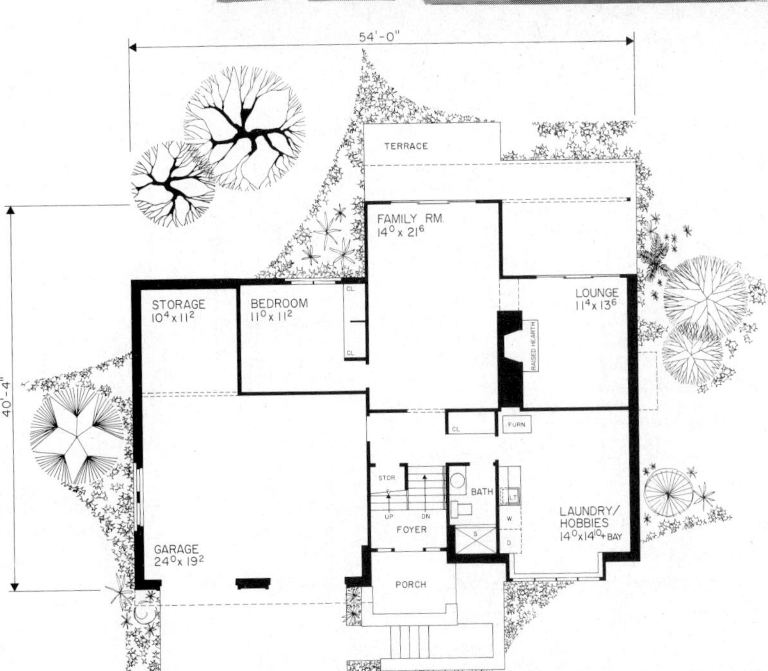

● Bi-level living will be enjoyed to its fullest in this Spanish styled design. There is a lot of room for the various family activities. Informal living will take place on the lower level in the family room and lounge. The formal living and dining rooms, sharing a thru-fireplace, are located on the upper level.

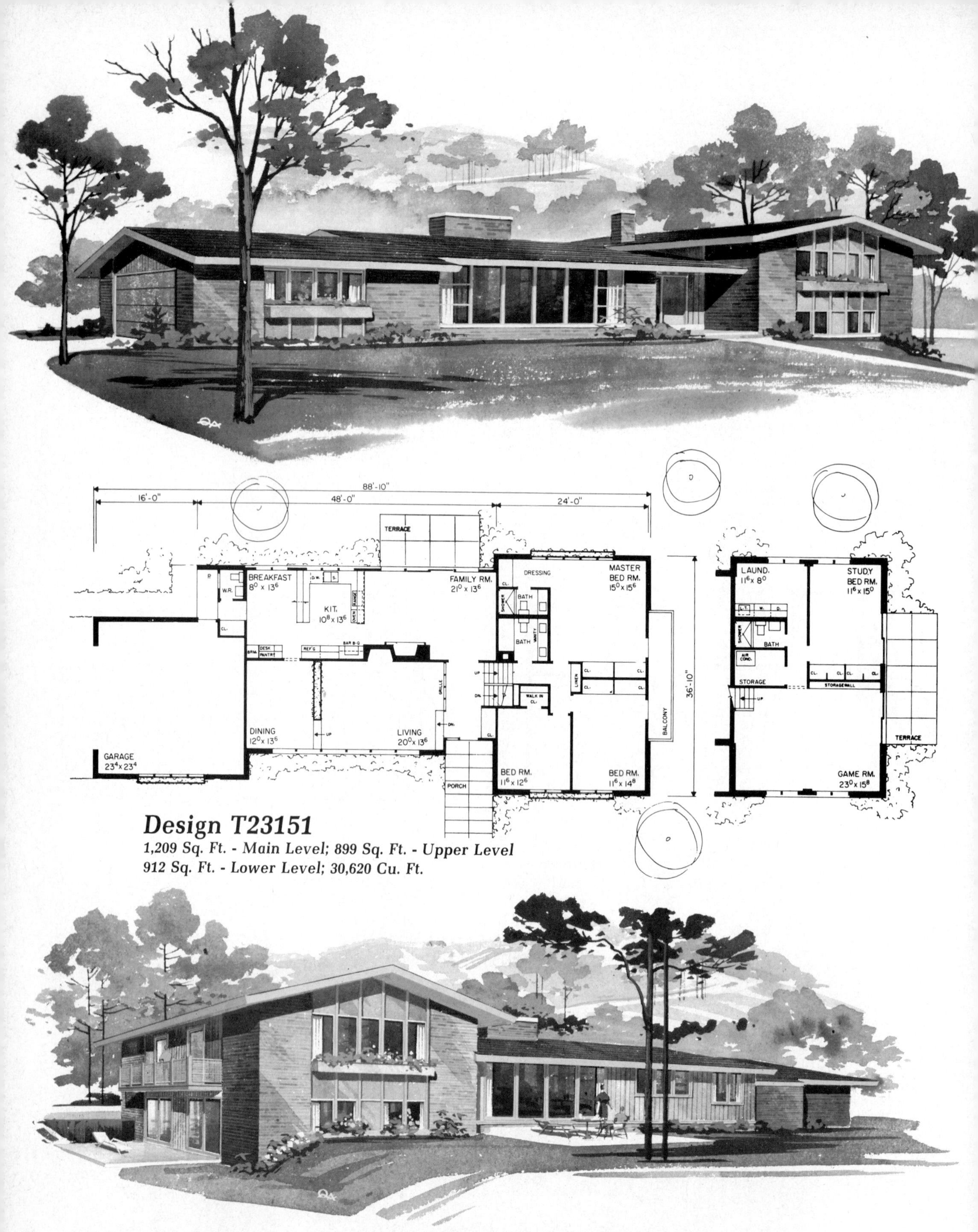

Design T23151

1,209 Sq. Ft. - Main Level; 899 Sq. Ft. - Upper Level
912 Sq. Ft. - Lower Level; 30,620 Cu. Ft.

● Split-level living can be great fun. And it certainly will be for the occupants of this impressive house. First and foremost, you and your family will appreciate the practical zoning. The upper level is the quiet sleeping level. List the features. They are many. The main level is zoned for both formal and informal living. Don't miss the sunken living room or the twin fireplaces. The lower level provides that extra measure of livability for all to enjoy.

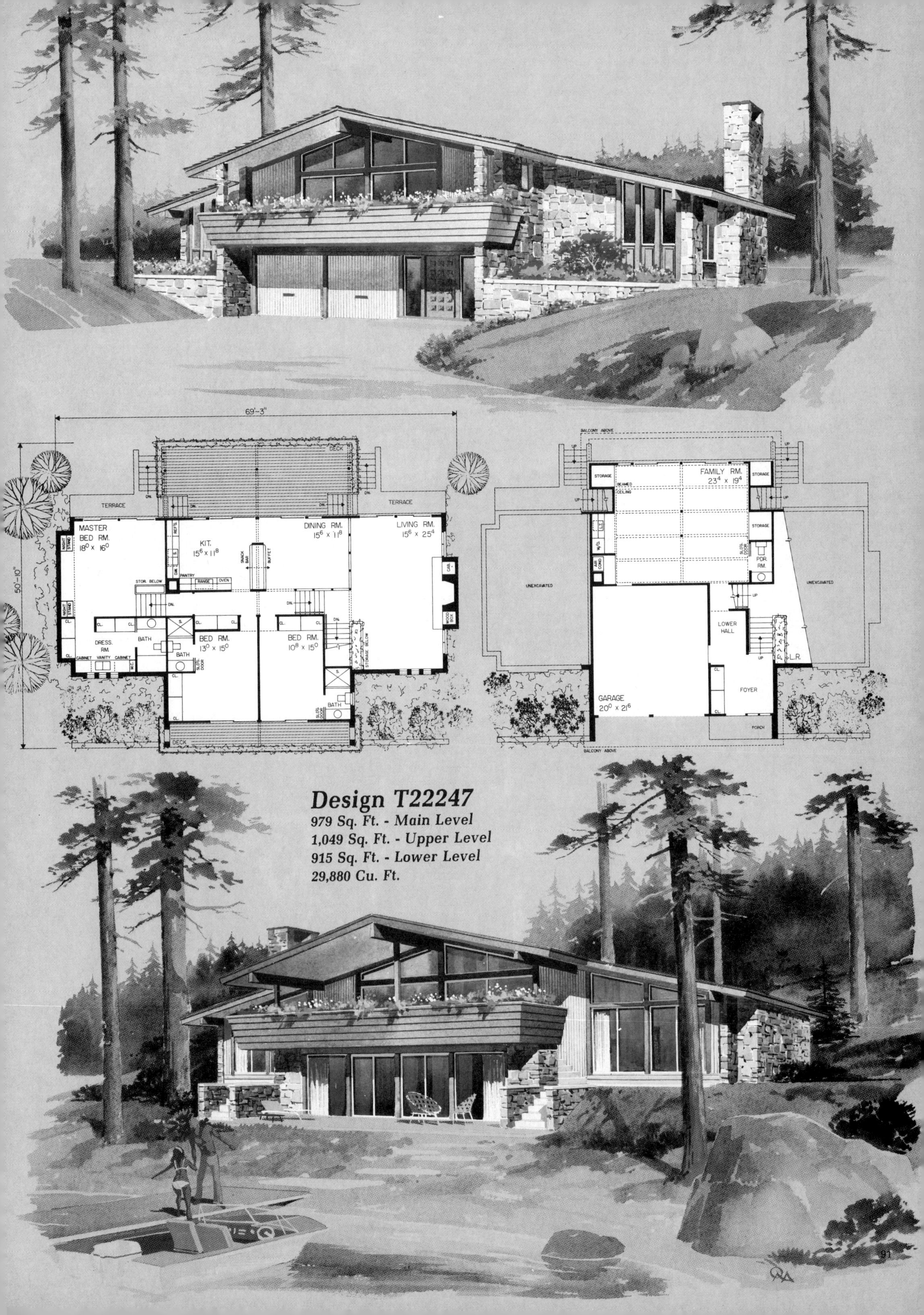

Design T22247

979 Sq. Ft. - Main Level
1,049 Sq. Ft. - Upper Level
915 Sq. Ft. - Lower Level
29,880 Cu. Ft.

Design T22758

1,143 Sq. Ft. - Main Level
792 Sq. Ft. - Upper Level
770 Sq. Ft. - Lower Level
43,085 Cu. Ft.

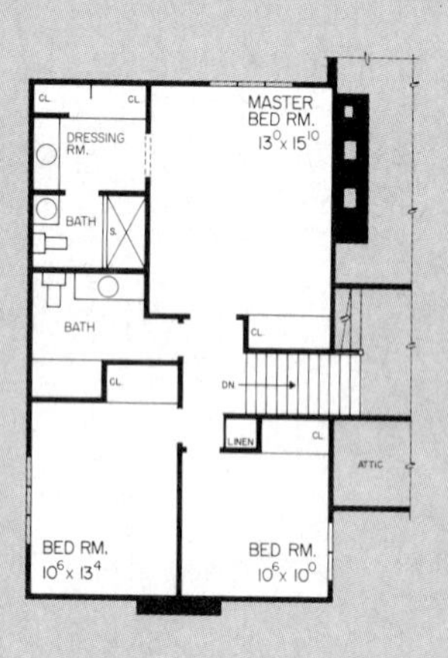

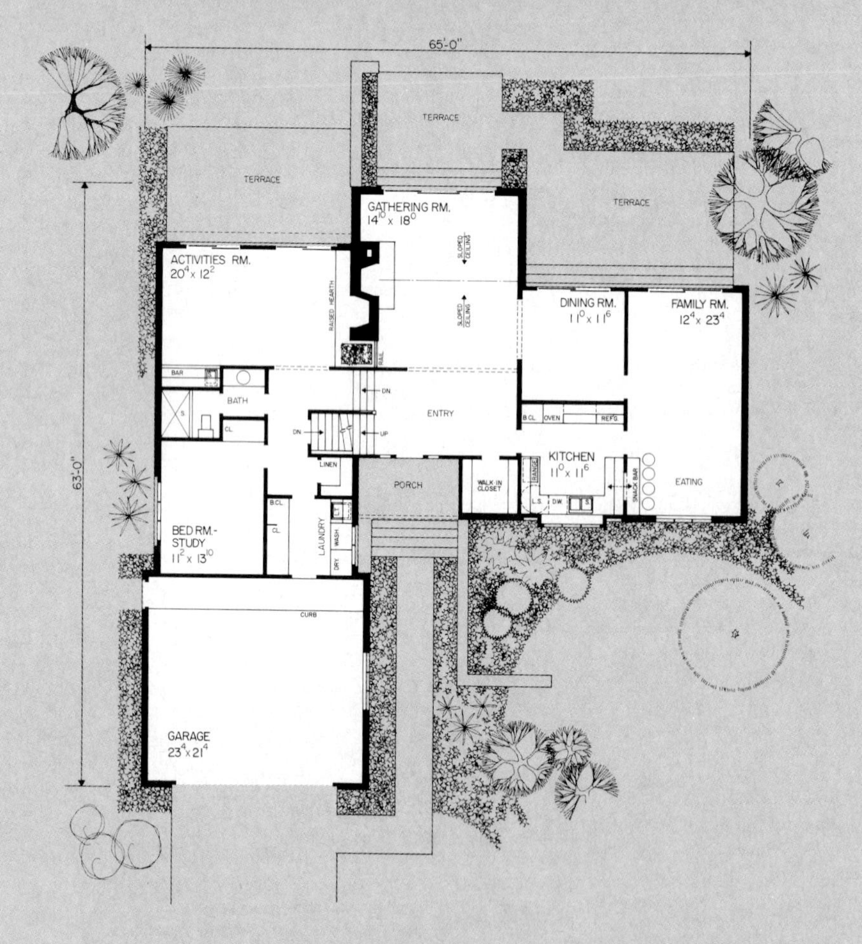

● An outstanding Tudor with three levels of exceptional livability, plus a basement. A careful study of the exterior reveals many delightful architectural details which give this home a character of its own. Notice the appealing recessed front entrance. Observe the overhanging roof with the exposed rafters. Don't miss the window treatment, the use of stucco and simulated beams, the masses of brick and the stylish chimney. Inside, the living potential is unsurpassed. Imagine, there are three living areas - the gathering, family and activities rooms. Having a snack bar, informal eating area and dining room, eating patterns can be flexible. In addition to the three bedrooms, two-bath upper level, there is a fourth bedroom with adjacent bath on the lower level.

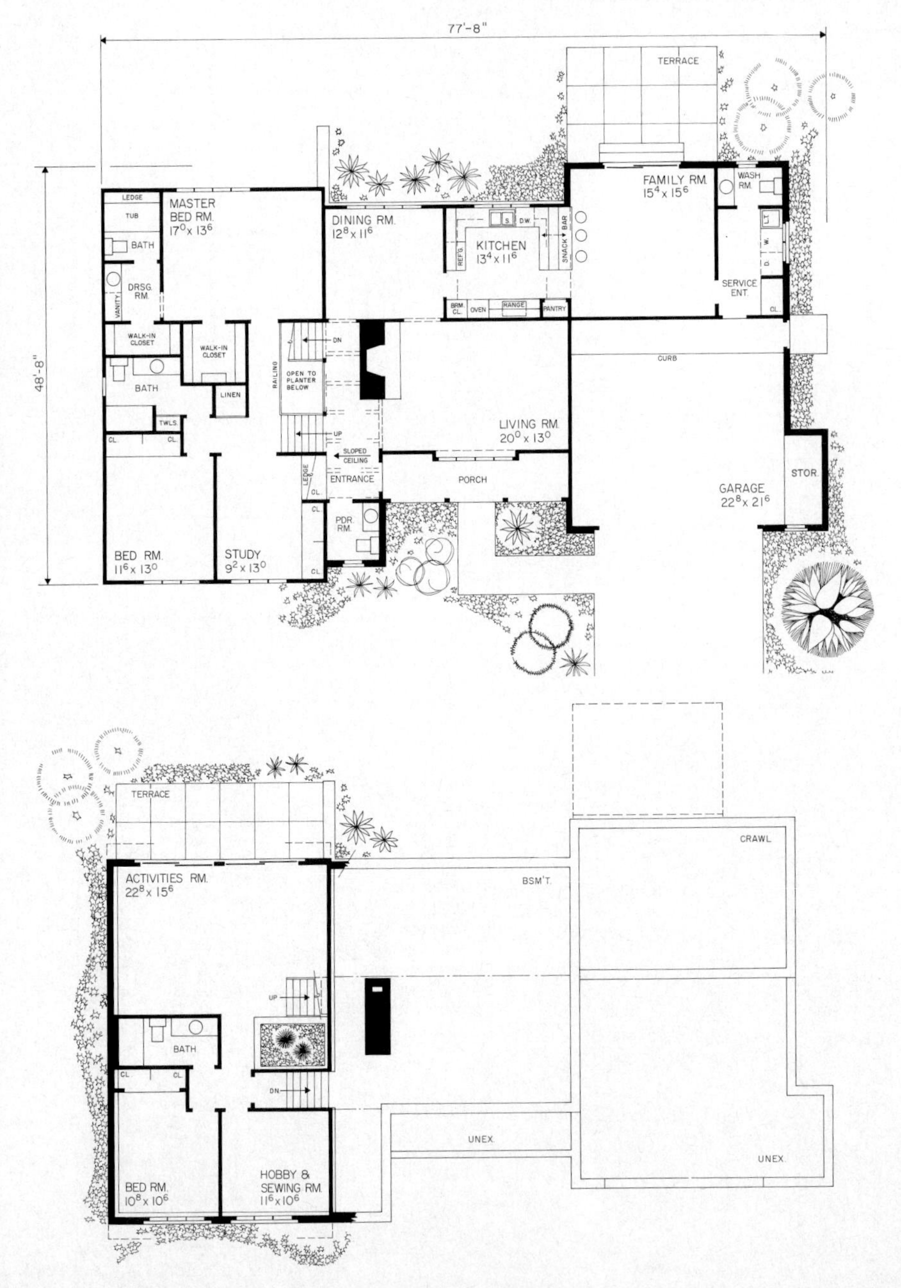

Design T22773

1,157 Sq. Ft. - Main Level
950 Sq. Ft. - Upper Level
912 Sq. Ft. - Lower Level
44,354 Cu. Ft.

● Here is another exquisitely styled Tudor tri-level designed to serve its happy occupants for many years. The contrasting use of material surely makes the exterior eye-catching. Another outstanding feature will be the covered front porch. A delightful way to enter this home. Many fine features also will be found inside this design. Formal living and dining room, U-shaped kitchen with snack bar and family room find themselves located on the main level. Two of the three bedrooms are on the upper level with two baths. Activities room, third bedroom and hobby/sewing room are on the lower level. Notice the built-in planter on the lower level which is visible from the other two levels. A powder room and a wash room both are on the main level. A study is on the upper level which is a great place for a quiet retreat. The basement will be convenient for the storage of any bulk items.

● This multi-level design will be ideal on a sloping site, both in the front and the rear of the house. The contemporary exterior is made up of vertical wood siding. The sloping roofline adds to the exterior appeal and creates a sloped ceiling in the formal living and dining rooms. An attractive bay window highlights the living room as will sliding glass doors in the dining room. The U-shaped kitchen and breakfast room also are located on this main level. The lower level houses the family room, wash room, laundry and access to the two-car garage. All of the sleeping facilities will be found on the upper level: three bedrooms and an exceptional master bedroom suite. Note two fireplaces, island range, two leveled terraces, covered porch, two balconies, etc.

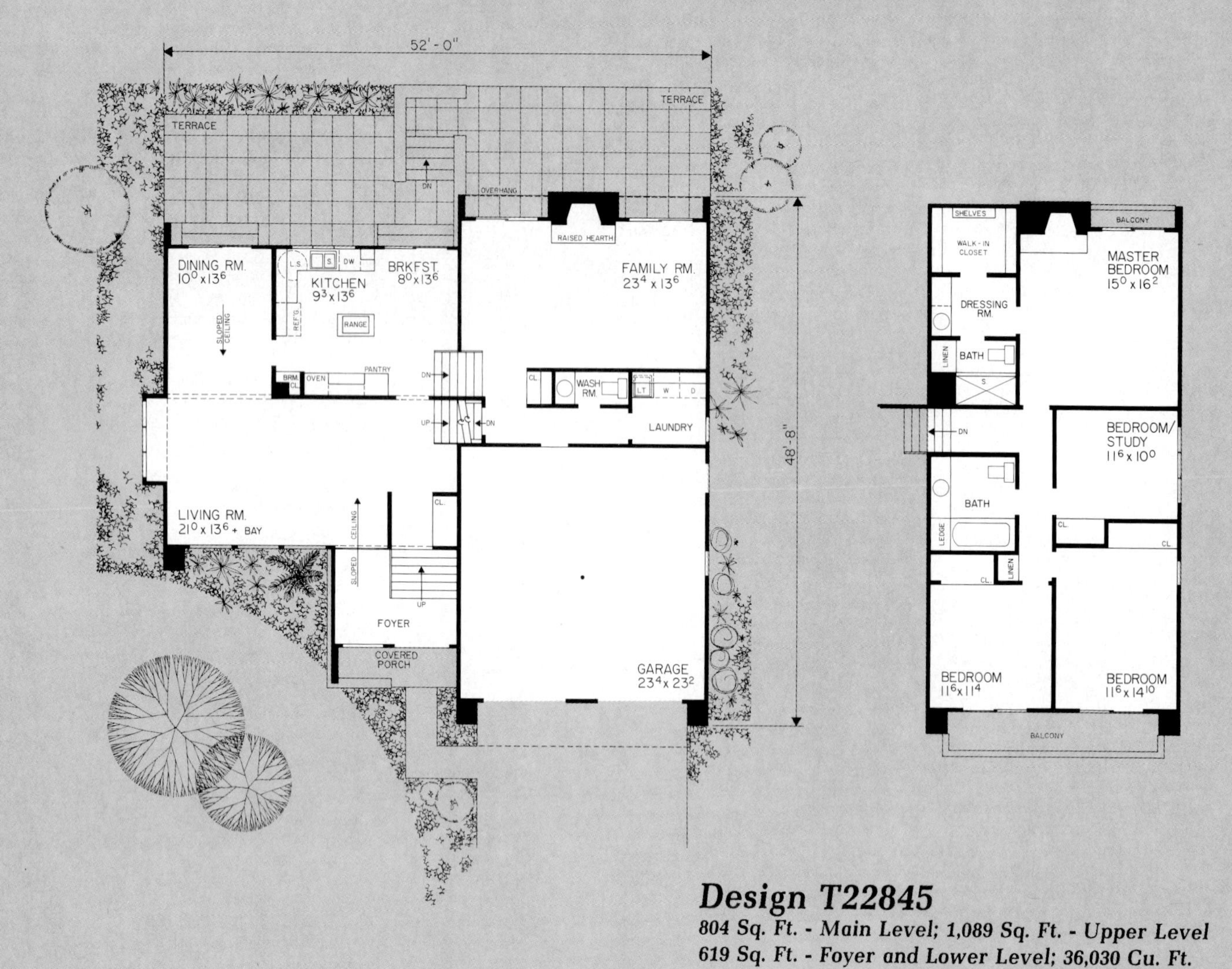

Design T22845

804 Sq. Ft. - Main Level; 1,089 Sq. Ft. - Upper Level
619 Sq. Ft. - Foyer and Lower Level; 36,030 Cu. Ft.

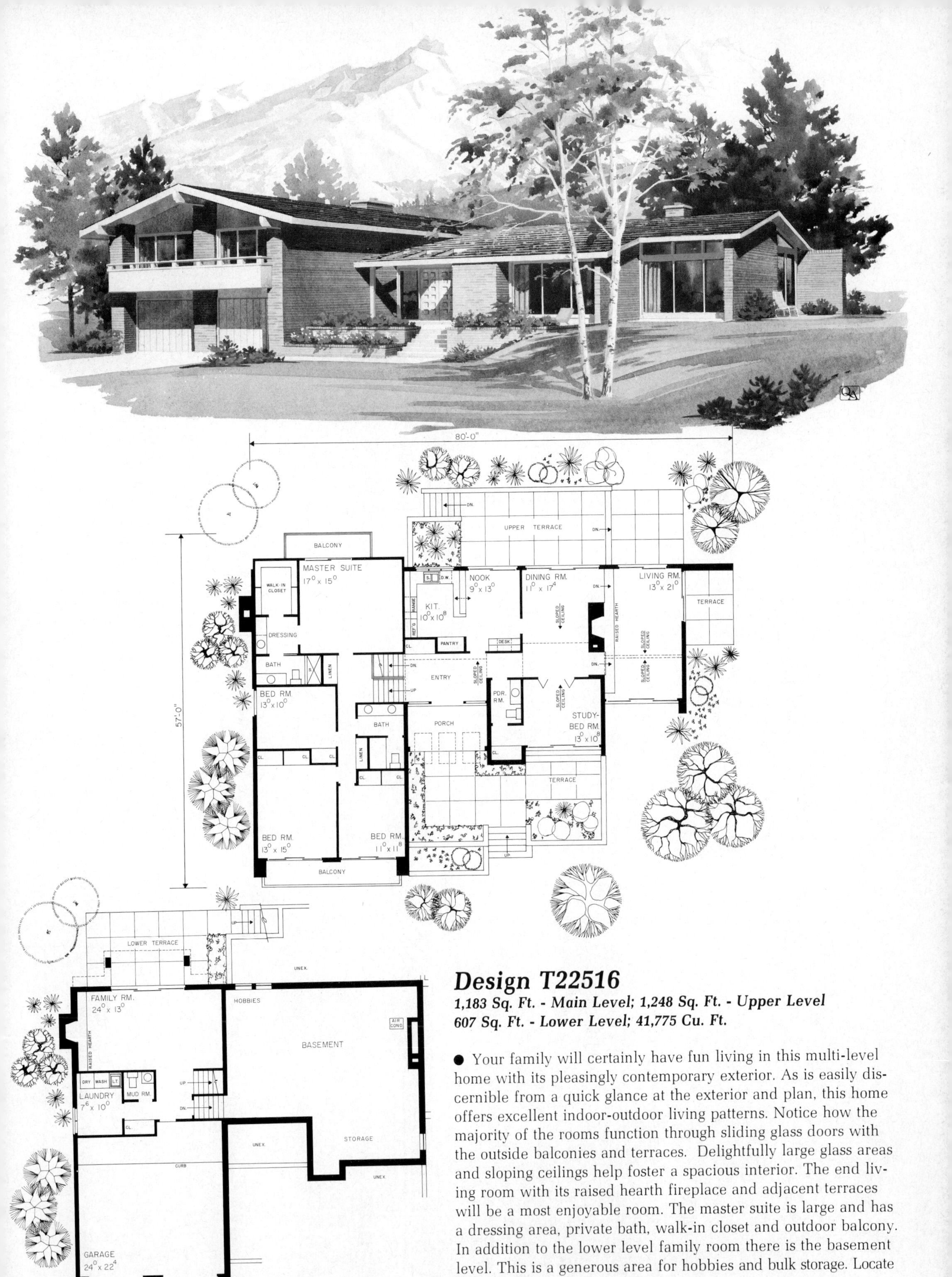

Design T22516

1,183 Sq. Ft. - Main Level; 1,248 Sq. Ft. - Upper Level 607 Sq. Ft. - Lower Level; 41,775 Cu. Ft.

● Your family will certainly have fun living in this multi-level home with its pleasingly contemporary exterior. As is easily discernible from a quick glance at the exterior and plan, this home offers excellent indoor-outdoor living patterns. Notice how the majority of the rooms function through sliding glass doors with the outside balconies and terraces. Delightfully large glass areas and sloping ceilings help foster a spacious interior. The end living room with its raised hearth fireplace and adjacent terraces will be a most enjoyable room. The master suite is large and has a dressing area, private bath, walk-in closet and outdoor balcony. In addition to the lower level family room there is the basement level. This is a generous area for hobbies and bulk storage. Locate pool table here.

● Enter into the front foyer of this traditional design and you will be impressed by the dramatic sloped ceiling. Sunken two steps is the formal living room. This room is highlighted by a fireplace with adjacent wood box, sloped ceiling and multi-paned bay window. Formal and informal dining, kitchen, laundry and wash room also share the main level with the living room and foyer. The lower level houses the family room, bedroom/study, full bath and mechanical room; the upper level three bedrooms and two more full baths. Notice the excellent indoor-outdoor living relationships offered throughout the plan. There is a side terrace accessible from each of the dining areas plus a rear terrace which the lower level opens up to by sliding glass doors. The projection of the garage to the front of the house reduces the size of the lot required for this delightful multi-level home.

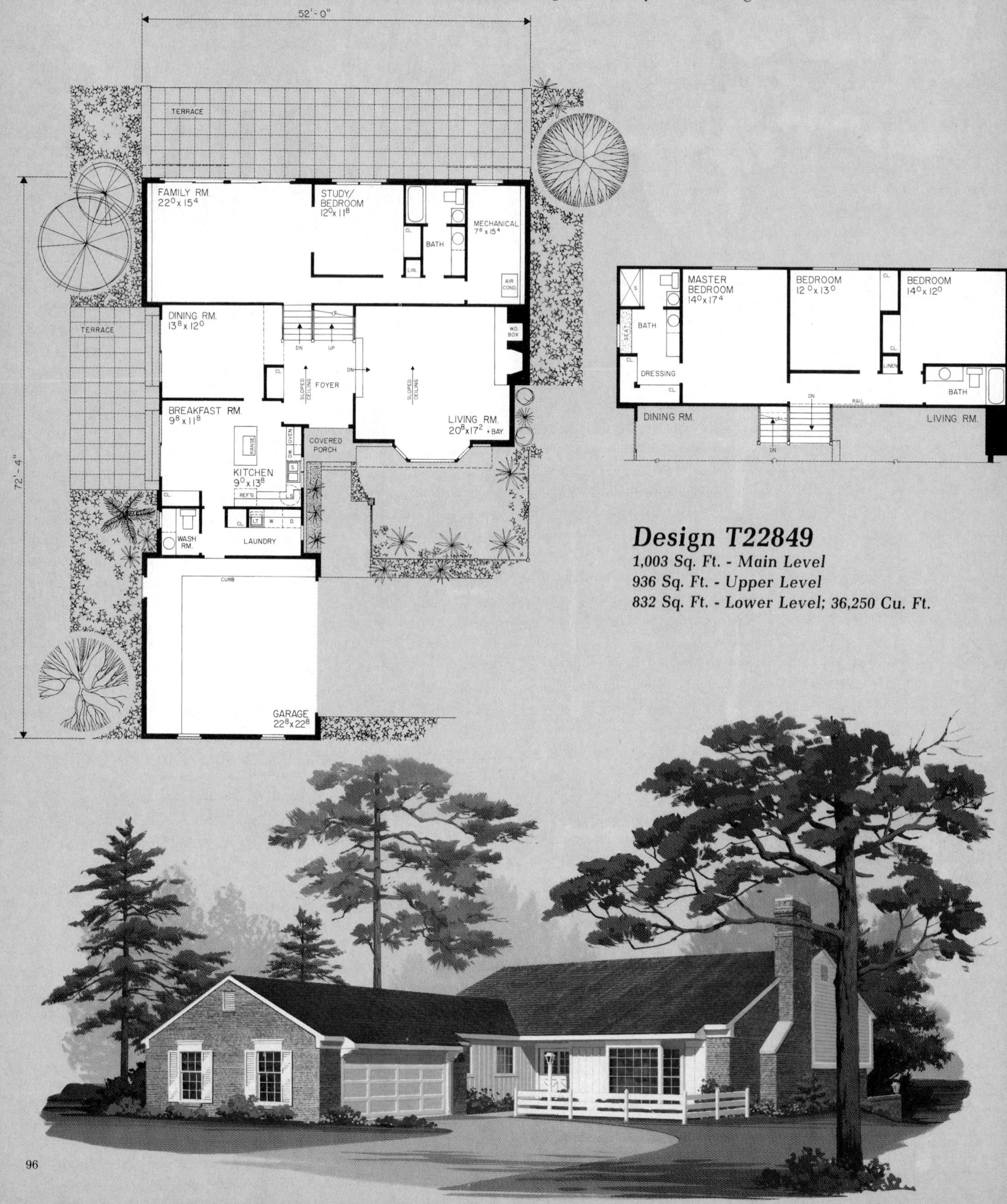

Design T22849

1,003 Sq. Ft. - Main Level
936 Sq. Ft. - Upper Level
832 Sq. Ft. - Lower Level; 36,250 Cu. Ft.

All The "TOOLS" You And Your Builder Need. . .

1. THE PLAN BOOKS

Home Planners' unique Design Category Series makes it easy to look at and study only the types of designs for which you and your family have an interest. Each of six plan books features a specific type of home, namely: Two-Story, 1½ Story, One-Story Over 2000 Sq. Ft., One-Story Under 2000 Sq. Ft., Multi-Levels and Vacation Homes. In addition to the convenient Design Category Series, there is an impressive selection of other current titles. While the home plans featured in these books are also to be found in the Design Category Series, they, too, are edited for those with special tastes and requirements. Your family will spend many enjoyable hours reviewing the delightfully designed exteriors and the practical floor plans. Surely your home or office library should include a selection of these popular plan books. Your complete satisfaction is guaranteed.

2. THE CONSTRUCTION BLUEPRINTS

There are blueprints available for each of the designs published in Home Planners' current plan books. Depending upon the size, the style and the type of home, each set of blueprints consists of from five to ten large sheets. Only by studying the blueprints is it possible to give complete and final consideration to the proper selection of a design for your next home. The blueprints provide the opportunity for all family members to familiarize themselves with the features of all exterior elevations, interior elevations and details, all dimensions, special built-in features and effects. They also provide a full understanding of the materials to be used and/or selected. The low-cost of our blueprints makes it possible and indeed, practical, to study in detail a number of different sets of blueprints before deciding upon which design to build.

3. THE MATERIALS LIST

A list of materials is an integral part of the plan package. It comprises the last sheet of each set of blueprints and serves as a handy reference during the period of construction. Of course, at the pricing and the material ordering stages, it is indispensable.

4. THE SPECIFICATION OUTLINE

Each order for blueprints is accompanied by one Specification Outline. You and your builder will find this a time-saving tool when deciding upon your own individual specifications. An important reference document should you wish to write your own specifications.

5. THE PLUMBING & ELECTRICAL PACKAGE

The construction blueprints you order from Home Planners, Inc. include locations for all plumbing fixtures — sinks, lavatories, tubs, showers, water closets, laundry trays, hot water heaters, etc. The blueprints also show the locations of all electrical switches, plugs, and outlets. These plumbing and electrical details are sufficient to present to your local contractor for discussions about your individual specifications and subsequent installations in conformance with local codes. However, for those who wish to acquaint themselves with many of the intricacies of residential plumbing and electrical details and installations, Home Planners, Inc. has made available this package. We do not recommend that the layman attempt to do his own plumbing and electrical work. It is, nevertheless, advisable that owners be as knowledgeable as possible about each of these disciplines. The entire family will appreciate the educational value of these low-cost, easy-to-understand details.

The Design Category Series

1.

360 TWO STORY HOMES

English Tudors, Early American Salt Boxes, Gambrels, Farmhouses, Southern Colonials, Georgians, French Mansards, Contemporaries. Interesting floor plans for both small and large families. Efficient kitchens, 2 to 6 bedrooms, family rooms, libraries, extra baths, mud rooms. Homes for all budgets.

288 Pages, $6.95

2.

150 1½ STORY HOMES

Cape Cod, Williamsburg, Georgian, Tudor and Contemporary versions. Low budget and country-estate feature sections. Expandable family plans. Formal and informal living and dining areas along with gathering rooms. Spacious, country kitchens. Indoor-outdoor livability with covered porches and functional terraces.

128 Pages, $3.95

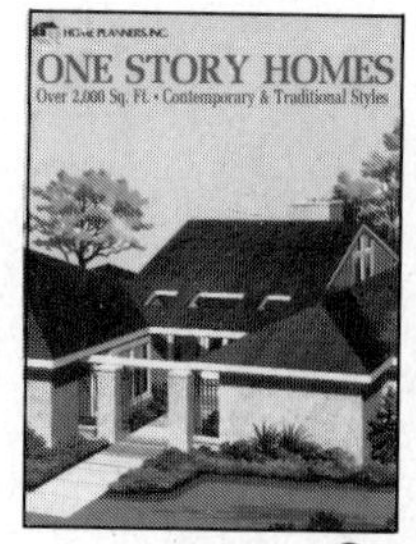

3.

210 ONE STORY HOM OVER 2,000 Sq. Ft.

All popular styles. Includi Spanish, Western, Tud French, and other traditio versions. Contemporari Gracious, family living p terns. Sunken living roor master bedroom suites, at ums, courtyards, pools. Fi indoor-outdoor living re tionships. For modest country-estate budgets.

192 Pages, $4.95

4.

315 ONE STORY HOMES UNDER 2,000 Sq. Ft.

A great selection of traditional and contemporary exteriors for medium and restricted budgets. Efficient, practical floor plans. Gathering rooms, formal and informal living and dining rooms, mud rooms, indoor-outdoor livability. Economically built homes. Designs with bonus space livability for growing families.

192 Pages, $4.95

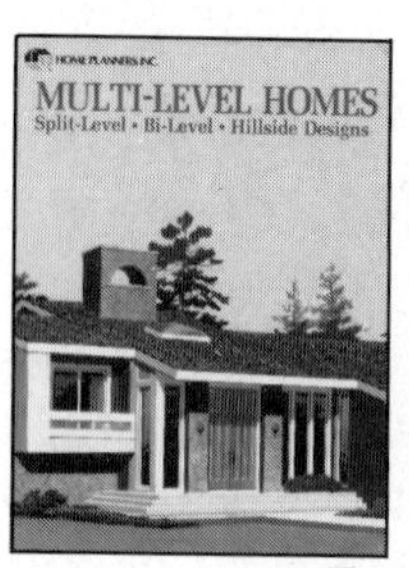

5.

215 MULTI-LEVEL HOMES

For new dimensions in family living. A captivating variety of exterior styles, exciting floor plans for flat and sloping sites. Exposed lower levels. Balconies, decks. Plans for the active family. Upper level lounges, excellent bath facilities. Sloping ceilings. Functional outdoor terraces. For all building budgets.

192 Pages, $4.95

6.

223 VACATION HOME

Features A-Frames, Chale Hexagons, economical recta gles. One and two stories pl multi-levels. Lodges for ye 'round livability. From 480 3238 sq. ft. Cottages sleeping to 22. For flat or sloping site Spacious, open planning. Ov 600 illustrations. 120 Pages full color. Cluster hom selection. For lakeshore woodland leisure living.

176 Pages, $4.95

The Exterior Style Series

7.

330 EARLY AMERICAN PLANS

Our new *Essential Guide to Early American Home Plans* traces Early American architecture from our Colonial Past to Traditional styles popular today with a written history of designs and colorful sections devoted to styles. Many of our designs are patterned after historic homes.

304 Pages, $9.95

8.

335 CONTEMPORARY HOME PLANS

Our new *Essential Guide to Contemporary Home Plans* offers a colorful directory to modern architecture, including a history of American Contemporary styling and more than 335 home plans of all sizes and popular designs. 304 colorful pages! Must reading.

304 Pages, $9.95

9.

135 ENGLISH TUDOR HOMES

and other Popular Fami Plans is a favorite of man The current popularity of th English Tudor home design phenomenal. Here is a boo which is loaded with Tudo for all budgets. There ar one-story, 1½ and two-sto designs, plus multi-levels an hillsides from 1,176–3,849 sq.

104 Pages, $3.95

The Budget Series

11.

175 LOW BUDGET HOMES

A special selection of home designs for the modest or restricted building budget. An excellent variety of Traditional and Contemporary designs. One-story, 1½ and two-story and split-level homes. Three, four and five bedrooms. Family rooms, extra baths, formal and informal dining rooms. Basement and non-basement designs. Attached garages and covered porches.

96 Pages, $2.95

12.

165 AFFORDABLE HOME PLANS

This outstanding book was specially edited with a wide selection of houses and plans for those with a medium building budget. While none of these designs are considered low-cost; neither do they require an unlimited budget to build. Square footages range from 1,428. Exteriors of Tudor, French, Early American, Spanish and Contemporary are included.

112 Pages, $2.95

13.

142 HOME DESIGNS FOR EXPANDED BUILDING BUDGETS

A family's ability to financ and need for a larger hom grows as its size and incom increases. This selection high lights designs which house a average square footage o 2,551. One-story plans averag 2,069; two-stories, 2,735 multi-levels, 2,825. Spaciou homes featuring raised heart fireplaces, open planning an efficient kitchens.

112 Pages, $2.95

General Interest Titles

15.

ENCYCLOPEDIA - 450 PLANS

For those who wish to review and study perhaps the largest selection of designs available in a single volume. Varying exterior styles, plus interesting and practical floor plans for all building budgets. Formal, informal living patterns; indoor-outdoor livability; small, growing and large family facilities.

320 Pages, $9.95

16.

244 HOUSE PLANS FOR BETTER LIVING

Special 40th Anniversary Edition with over 650 illustrations. Sectionalized to highlight special interest groups of designs. A fine introduction to our special interest titles. All styles, sizes, and types of homes are represented. Designs feature gathering rooms, country kitchens, second-floor lounges.

192 Pages $3.50

17.

255 HOME DESIGNS FOR FAMILY LIVING

In addition to the plans that cater to a variety of family living patterns and budgets, there are special sections on vacation homes, earth-sheltered homes, sun-oriented living, and shared livability. One, 1½, two-story, and multi-level designs. The book includes more than 700 exciting illustrations.

192 Pages, $3.50

18.

COLOR PORTFOLIO - 310 DESIGNS

An expanded full-color guide to our most popular Early American, Spanish, French, Tudor, Contemporary, and modern Trend home designs. 310 home plans of all popular styles and sizes. Includes energy-efficient designs. Plans for varying building budgets. One, 1½, two-story, and split-level designs for all terrain. This is our largest full-color book with our newest trend-setting designs and other favorites. It's must reading for the serious home planner.

288 Pages in Full Color, $12.95

10.

136 SPANISH & WESTERN HOME DESIGNS

Stucco exteriors, arches, tile roofs, wide-overhangs, courtyards and rambling ranches are characteristics which make this design selection distinctive. These sun-country designs highlight indoor-outdoor relationships. Solar oriented livability is featured.

120 Pages, $3.95

PLAN BOOKS are a valuable tool for anyone who plans to build a new home. After you have selected a home design that satisifies your list of requirements, you can order blueprints for further study.

14.

115 HOME DESIGNS FOR UNLIMITED BUILDING BUDGETS

This book will appeal to those with large families and the desire and wherewithal to satisfy all the family needs, plus most of their wants. The upscale designs in this portfolio average 3,132 square feet. One-story designs average 2,796 sq. ft.; 1½-story, 3,188 sq. ft.; two-story, 3,477 sq. ft.; multi-level, 3,532 sq. ft. Truly designs for elegant living.

112 Pages, $2.95

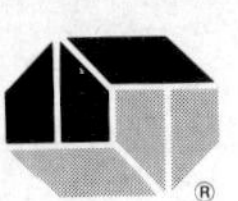

HOME PLANNERS, INC.

Dept. BK, 23761 Research Drive
Farmington Hills, Michigan 48024

Please mail me the following:

THE DESIGN CATEGORY SERIES - A great series of books specially edited by design type and size. Each book features interesting sections to further enhance the study of design styles, sizes and house types. A fine addition to the home or office library. Complete collection - over 1250 designs.

1. ______ 360 Two Story Homes @ $6.95 ea. .... $______
2. ______ 150 1½ Story Homes @ $3.95 ea. .... $______
3. ______ 210 One Story Homes - Over 2,000 Sq. Ft. @ $4.95 ea. . $______
4. ______ 315 One Story Homes - Under 2,000 Sq. Ft. @ $4.95 ea. $______
5. ______ 215 Multi-Level Homes @ $4.95 ea. .... $______
6. ______ 223 Vacation Homes @ $4.95 ea. .... $______

OTHER CURRENT TITLES - The interesting series of plan books listed below have been edited to appeal to various style preferences and budget considerations. The majority of the designs highlighted in these books also may be found in the Design Category Series.

The Exterior Style Series-

7. ______ 330 Early American Home Plans @ $9.95 ea. .... $______
8. ______ 335 Contemporary Home Plans @ $9.95 ea. .... $______
9. ______ 135 English Tudor Homes @ $3.95 ea. .... $______
10. ______ 136 Spanish & Western Home Designs @ $3.95 ea. .... $______

The Budget Series-

11. ______ 175 Low Budget Homes @ $2.95 ea. .... $______
12. ______ 165 Affordable Home Plans @ $2.95 ea. .... $______
13. ______ 142 Home Designs for Expanded Budgets @ $2.95 ea. . $______
14. ______ 115 Home Designs for Unlimited Budgets @ $2.95 ea. . $______

General Interest Titles-

15. ______ Encyclopedia of Home Designs - 450 Designs @ $9.95 ea. $______
16. ______ 244 House Plans for Better Living @ $3.50 ea. .... $______
17. ______ 255 Home Designs for Family Living @ $3.50 ea. ..... $______

Full Color Book-

18. ______ Color Portfolio of Houses & Plans - 310 Designs @ $12.95 ea. $______

Sub Total $______

Michigan Residents kindly add 4% sales tax $______

TOTAL-Check enclosed $______

Your order will be processed and shipped within 48 hours

MAIL TODAY

SATISFACTION GUARANTEED!

Please Print

Name ______________________

Address ______________________

City ______________ State ______________ Zip ______

In Canada Mail To: Home Planners, Inc., 20 Cedar St. North, Kitchener, Ontario N2H 2W8

TB2BK

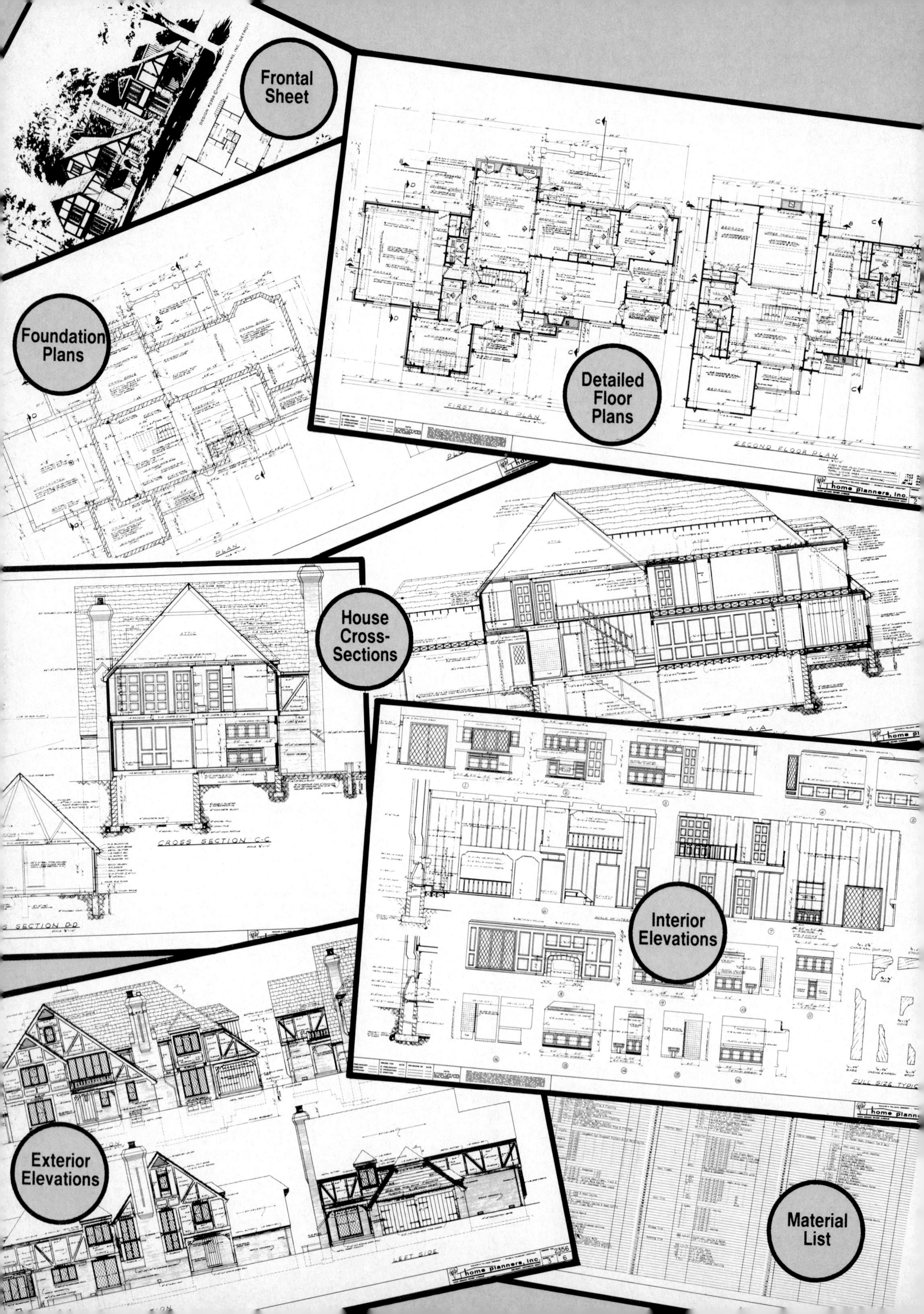
Frontal Sheet
Foundation Plans
Detailed Floor Plans
House Cross-Sections
Interior Elevations
Exterior Elevations
Material List
FIRST FLOOR PLAN
SECOND FLOOR PLAN
CROSS SECTION C-C
home planners, inc.

The Blueprints

1. FRONTAL SHEET.
Artist's landscaped sketch of the exterior and ink-line floor plans are on the frontal sheet of each set of blueprints.

2. FOUNDATION PLAN.
¼" Scale basement and foundation plan. All necessary notations and dimensions. Plot plan diagram for locating house on building site.

3. DETAILED FLOOR PLAN.
¼" Scale first and second floor plans with complete dimensions. Cross-section detail keys. Diagrammatic layout of electrical outlets and switches.

4. HOUSE CROSS-SECTIONS.
Large scale sections of foundation, interior and exterior walls, floors and roof details for design and construction control.

5. INTERIOR ELEVATIONS.
Large scale interior details of the complete kitchen cabinet design, bathrooms, powder room, laundry, fireplaces, paneling, beam ceilings, built-in cabinets, etc.

6. EXTERIOR ELEVATIONS.
¼" Scale exterior elevation drawings of front, rear, and both sides of the house. All exterior materials and details are shown to indicate the complete design and proportions of the house.

7. MATERIAL LIST.
Complete lists of all materials required for the construction of the house as designed are included in each set of blueprints.

THIS BLUEPRINT PACKAGE
will help you and your family take a major step forward in the final appraisal and planning of your new home. Only by spending many enjoyable and informative hours studying the numerous details included in the complete package, will you feel sure of, and comfortable with, your commitment to build your new home. To assure successful and productive consultation with your builder and/or architect, reference to the various elements of the blueprint package is a must. The blueprints, material list and specification outline will save much consultation time and expense. Don't be without them.

The Material List

With each set of blueprints you order you will receive a material list. Each list shows you the quantity, type and size of the non-mechanical materials required to build your home. It also tells you where these materials are used. This makes the blueprints easy to understand.

Influencing the mechanical requirements are geographical differences in availability of materials, local codes, methods of installation and individual preferences. Because of these factors, your local heating, plumbing and electrical contractors can supply you with necessary material take-offs for their particular trades.

Material lists simplify your material ordering and enable you to get quicker price quotations from your builder and material dealer. Because the material list is an integral part of each set of blueprints, it is not available separately.

Among the materials listed:

• Masonry, Veneer & Fireplace • Framing Lumber • Roofing & Sheet Metal • Windows & Door Frames • Exterior Trim & Insulation • Tile Work, Finish Floors • Interior Trim, Kitchen Cabinets • Rough & Finish Hardware

The Specification Outline

This fill-in type specification lists over 150 phases of home construction from excavating to painting and includes wiring, plumbing, heating and air-conditioning. It consists of 16 pages and will prove invaluable for specifying to your builder the exact materials, equipment and methods of construction you want in your new home. One Specification Outline is included free with each order for blueprints. Additional Specification Outlines are available at $3.00 each.

CONTENTS
• General Instructions, Suggestions and Information • Excavating and Grading • Masonry and Concrete Work • Sheet Metal Work • Carpentry, Millwork, Roofing, and Miscellaneous Items • Lath and Plaster or Drywall Wallboard • Schedule for Room Finishes • Painting and Finishing • Tile Work • Electrical Work • Plumbing • Heating and Air-Conditioning

The Plumbing & Electrical Package

Consists of Large 24" x 36" Sheets for Easy Reference.
Color-Coded for Quick Recognition
of Details.

For those who wish to acquaint themselves with many of the intricacies of residential plumbing and electrical details and installations. An invaluable tool and great supplement to the blueprint package.

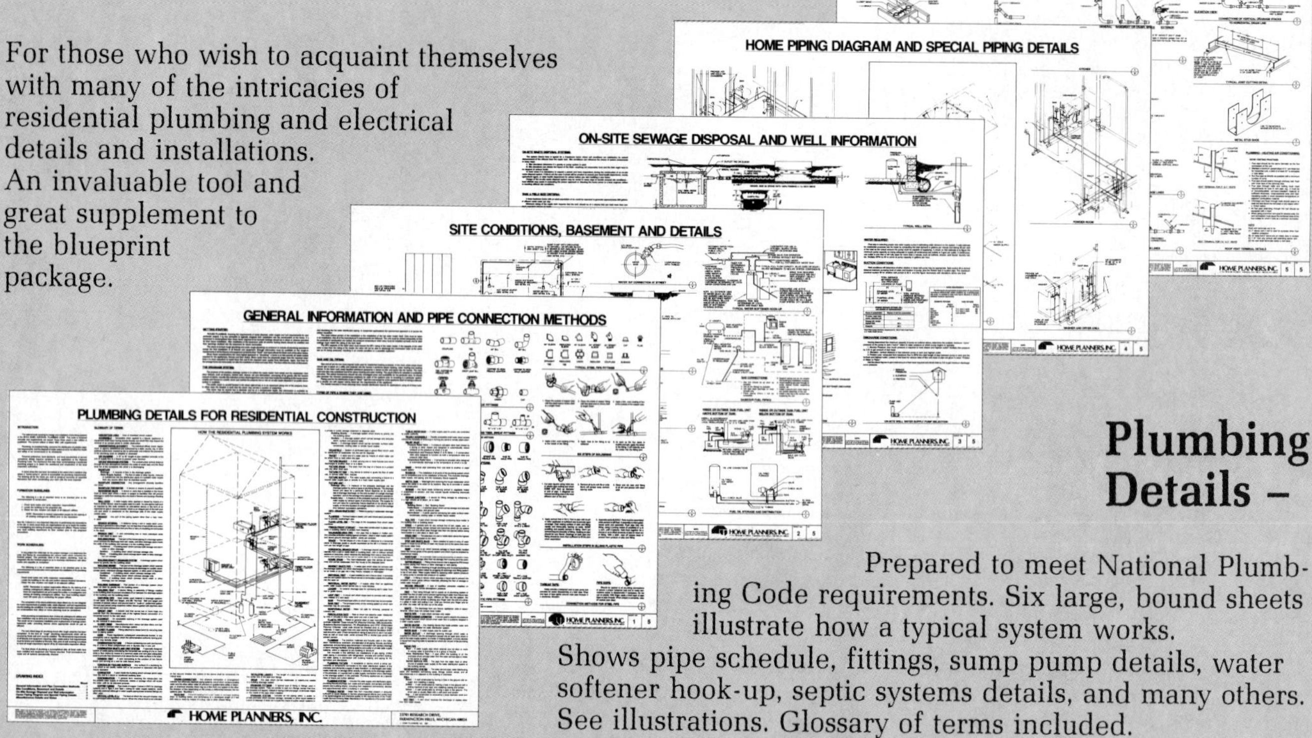

Plumbing Details –

Prepared to meet National Plumbing Code requirements. Six large, bound sheets illustrate how a typical system works. Shows pipe schedule, fittings, sump pump details, water softener hook-up, septic systems details, and many others. See illustrations. Glossary of terms included.

Only $12.95

Of Great Educational Value to the Entire Family. Order Both Sets

only

$19.95

(Save $5.95)

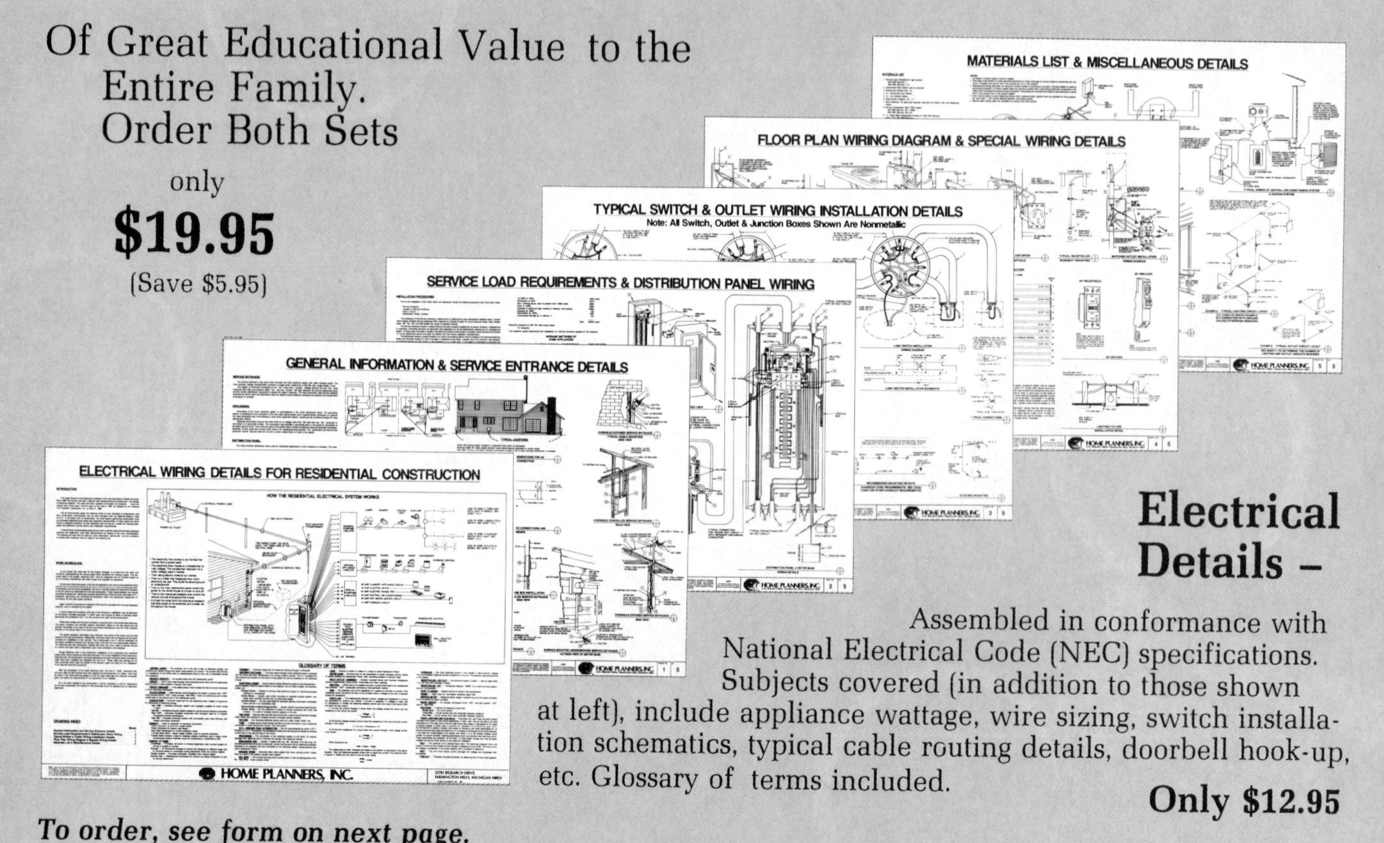

Electrical Details –

Assembled in conformance with National Electrical Code (NEC) specifications. Subjects covered (in addition to those shown at left), include appliance wattage, wire sizing, switch installation schematics, typical cable routing details, doorbell hook-up, etc. Glossary of terms included.

Only $12.95

To order, see form on next page.

Before You Order

1. STUDY THE DESIGNS . . . found in Home Planners books. As you review these delightful custom homes, you should keep in mind the total living requirements of your family — both indoors and outdoors. Although we do not make changes in plans, many minor changes can be made prior to the period of construction. If major changes are involved to satisfy your personal requirements, you should consider ordering one set of blueprints and having them redrawn locally. Consultation with your architect is strongly advised when contemplating major changes.

2. HOW TO ORDER BLUEPRINTS . . . After you have chosen the design that satisfies your requirements, or if you have selected one that you wish to study in more detail, simply clip the accompanying order blank and mail with your remittance. However, if it is not convenient for you to send a check or money order, you can use your credit card, or merely indicate C.O.D. shipment. Postman will collect all charges, including postage and C.O.D. fee. C.O.D. shipments are not permitted to Canada or foreign countries. Should time be of essence, as it sometimes is with many of our customers, your telephone order usually can be processed and shipped in the next day's mail. Simply call toll free 1-800-521-6797, (Michigan residents call collect 0-313-477-1850).

3. OUR SERVICE . . . Home Planners makes every effort to process and ship each order for blueprints and books within 48 hours. Because of this, we have deemed it unnecessary to acknowledge receipt of our customers orders. See order coupon for the postage and handling charges for surface mail, air mail or foreign mail.

4. A NOTE REGARDING REVERSE BLUEPRINTS . . . As a special service to those wishing to build in reverse of the plan as shown, we do include an extra set of reversed blueprints for only $30.00 additional with each order. Even though the lettering and dimensions appear backward on reversed blueprints, they make a handy reference because they show the house just as it's being built in reverse from the standard blueprints — thereby helping you visualize the home better.

5. OUR EXCHANGE POLICY . . . Since blueprints are printed up in specific response to your individual order, we cannot honor requests for refunds. However, the first set of blueprints in any order (or the one set in a single set order) for a given design may be exchanged for a set of another design at a fee of $20.00 plus $3.00 for postage and handling via surface mail; $4.00 via air mail.

How many sets of blueprints should be ordered?

This question is often asked. The answer can range anywhere from 1 to 8 sets, depending upon circumstances. For instance, a single set of blueprints of your favorite design is sufficient to study the house in greater detail. On the other hand, if you are planning to get cost estimates, or if you are planning to build, you may need as many as eight sets of blueprints. Because the first set of blueprints in each order is $125.00, and because additional sets of the same design in each order are only $30.00 each (and with package sets even more economical), you save considerably by ordering your total requirements now. To help you determine the exact number of sets, please refer to the handy check list.

How Many Blueprints Do You Need?

___**OWNER'S SET(S)**

___**BUILDER** (Usually requires at least 3 sets: 1 as legal document; 1 for inspection; and at least 1 for tradesmen — usually more.)

___**BUILDING PERMIT** (Sometimes 2 sets are required.)

___**MORTGAGE SOURCE** (Usually 1 set for a conventional mortgage; 3 sets for F.H.A. or V.A. type mortgages.)

___**SUBDIVISION COMMITTEE** (If any.)

___**TOTAL NO. SETS REQUIRED**

Blueprint Ordering Hotline–

Phone toll free: 1-800-521-6797.
Orders received by 11 a.m. (Detroit time) will be processed the same day and shipped to you the following day. Use of this line restricted to blueprint ordering only. Michigan residents simply call collect 0-313-477-1850.

Kindly Note: When ordering by phone, please state Order Form Key No. located in box at lower left corner of blueprint order form.

In Canada Mail To:
Home Planners, Inc., 20 Cedar St. North
Kitchener, Ontario N2H 2W8
Phone: (519) 743-4169

TO: **HOME PLANNERS, INC., 23761 RESEARCH DRIVE**
FARMINGTON HILLS, MICHIGAN 48024

Please rush me the following:

____ SET(S) BLUEPRINTS FOR DESIGN NO(S). ______________ $________
Single Set, $125.00; Additional Identical Sets in Same Order $30.00 ea.
4 Set Package of Same Design, $175.00 (Save $40.00) 8 Set Package of Same Design, $225.00 (Save ($110.00) Material Lists & Specification Outline included.

____ SPECIFICATION OUTLINES @ $3.00 EACH .... $________

____ DETAIL SETS @ $12.95 ea. or both @ $19.95: ☐ PLUMBING ☐ELECTRICAL $________

Michigan Residents add 4% sales tax $________

FOR POSTAGE AND HANDLING PLEASE CHECK ✓ & REMIT
☐ $3.00 Added to Order for Surface Mail (UPS) - Any Mdse.
☐ $4.00 Added for Priority Mail of One-Three Sets of Blueprints.
☐ $6.00 Added for Priority Mail of Four or more Sets of Blueprints.
☐ For Canadian orders add $2.00 to above applicable rates.
$________

☐ C.O.D. PAY POSTMAN (C.O.D. Within U.S.A. Only) TOTAL in U.S.A. funds $________

PLEASE PRINT
Name ________________
Street ________________
City ________________ State ________ Zip ________

CREDIT CARD ORDERS ONLY: Fill in the boxes below **Prices subject to change without notice**

Credit Card No. ☐☐☐☐☐☐☐☐☐☐☐☐☐☐☐☐ Expiration Date Month/Year ☐☐☐☐

CHECK ONE: ☐ VISA ☐ MasterCard

Your Signature ________________

Order Form Key TB2BP

BLUEPRINT ORDERS SHIPPED WITHIN 48 HOURS OF RECEIPT!

TO: **HOME PLANNERS, INC., 23761 RESEARCH DRIVE**
FARMINGTON HILLS, MICHIGAN 48024

Please rush me the following:

____ SET(S) BLUEPRINTS FOR DESIGN NO(S). ______________ $________
Single Set, $125.00; Additional Identical Sets in Same Order $30.00 ea.
4 Set Package of Same Design, $175.00 (Save $40.00) 8 Set Package of Same Design, $225.00 (Save $110.00) Material Lists & Specification Outline included.

____ SPECIFICATION OUTLINES @ $3.00 EACH .... $________

____ DETAIL SETS @ $12.95 ea. or both @ $19.95: ☐ PLUMBING ☐ELECTRICAL $________

Michigan Residents add 4% sales tax $________

FOR POSTAGE AND HANDLING PLEASE CHECK ✓ & REMIT
☐ $3.00 Added to Order for Surface Mail (UPS) - Any Mdse.
☐ $4.00 Added for Priority Mail of One-Three Sets of Blueprints.
☐ $6.00 Added for Priority Mail of Four or more Sets of Blueprints.
☐ For Canadian orders add $2.00 to above applicable rates.
$________

☐ C.O.D. PAY POSTMAN (C.O.D. Within U.S.A. Only) TOTAL in U.S.A. funds $________

PLEASE PRINT
Name ________________
Street ________________
City ________________ State ________ Zip ________

CREDIT CARD ORDERS ONLY: Fill in the boxes below **Prices subject to change without notice**

Credit Card No. ☐☐☐☐☐☐☐☐☐☐☐☐☐☐☐☐ Expiration Date Month/Year ☐☐☐☐

CHECK ONE: ☐ VISA ☐ MasterCard

Your Signature ________________

Order Form Key TB2BP

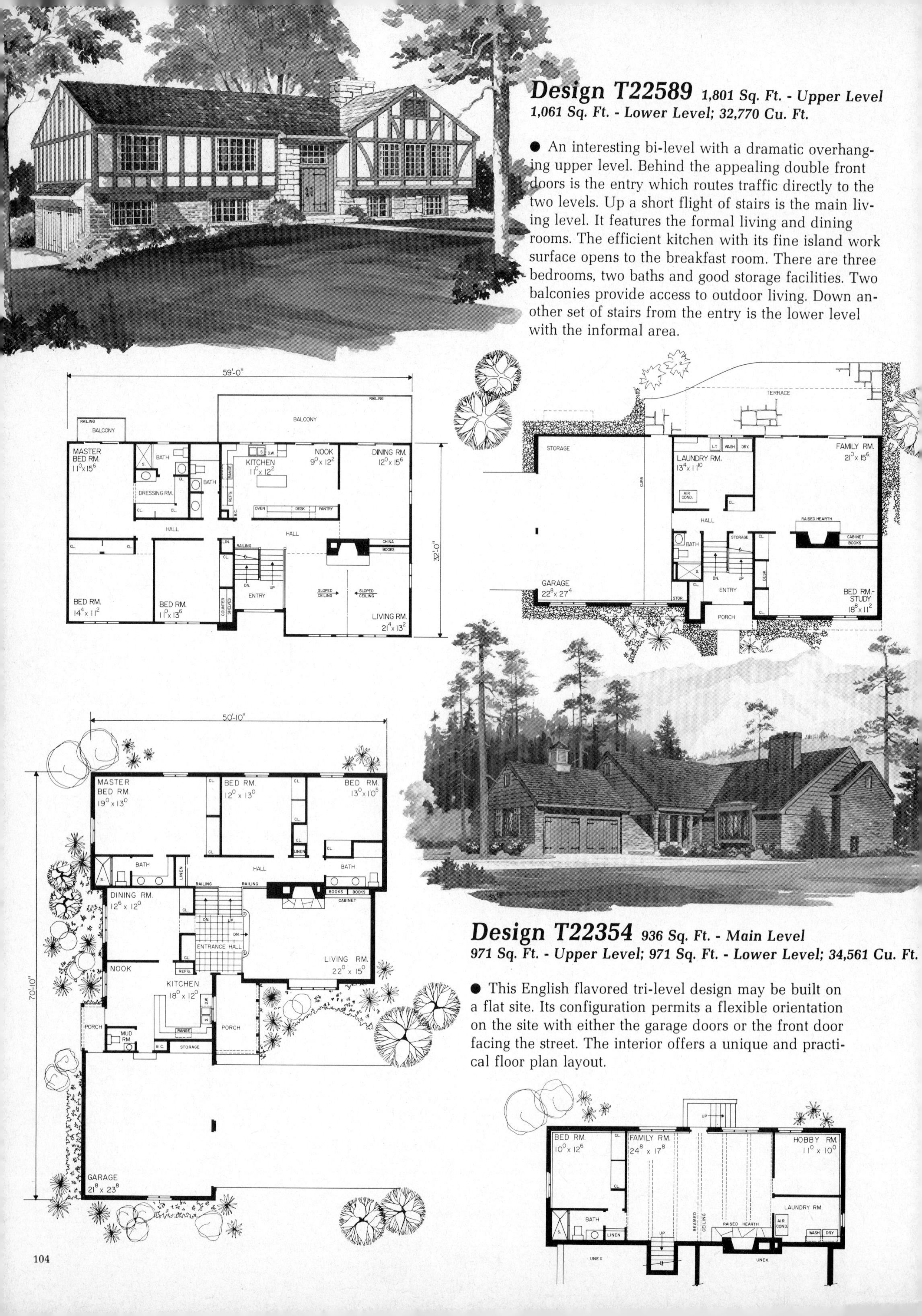

Design T22589 *1,801 Sq. Ft. - Upper Level 1,061 Sq. Ft. - Lower Level; 32,770 Cu. Ft.*

● An interesting bi-level with a dramatic overhanging upper level. Behind the appealing double front doors is the entry which routes traffic directly to the two levels. Up a short flight of stairs is the main living level. It features the formal living and dining rooms. The efficient kitchen with its fine island work surface opens to the breakfast room. There are three bedrooms, two baths and good storage facilities. Two balconies provide access to outdoor living. Down another set of stairs from the entry is the lower level with the informal area.

Design T22354 *936 Sq. Ft. - Main Level 971 Sq. Ft. - Upper Level; 971 Sq. Ft. - Lower Level; 34,561 Cu. Ft.*

● This English flavored tri-level design may be built on a flat site. Its configuration permits a flexible orientation on the site with either the garage doors or the front door facing the street. The interior offers a unique and practical floor plan layout.

Hillside Homes
With Exposed Lower Levels

Design T21812

1,726 Sq. Ft. - Main Level
1,320 Sq. Ft. - Lower Level
30,142 Cu. Ft.

● A home with two faces! The street view of this contemporary design presents a most pleasingly formal facade. The wide overhanging roof, the projecting masonry piers, the attractive glass treatment and the recessed front entrance all go together to form a perfectly delightful image. The rear terrace view is a picture of informality. The upper level outdoor balcony, overhanging the sweeping lower level terrace, will make summer entertaining an occasion to look forward to. The balcony gives way to the spacious deck which will be an ideal spot on which to sunbathe or dine. The plan is interesting, indeed. A two-way fireplace separates the big living/dining area. Observe the work center; study the lower level layout. Be sure to note the extra bedroom.

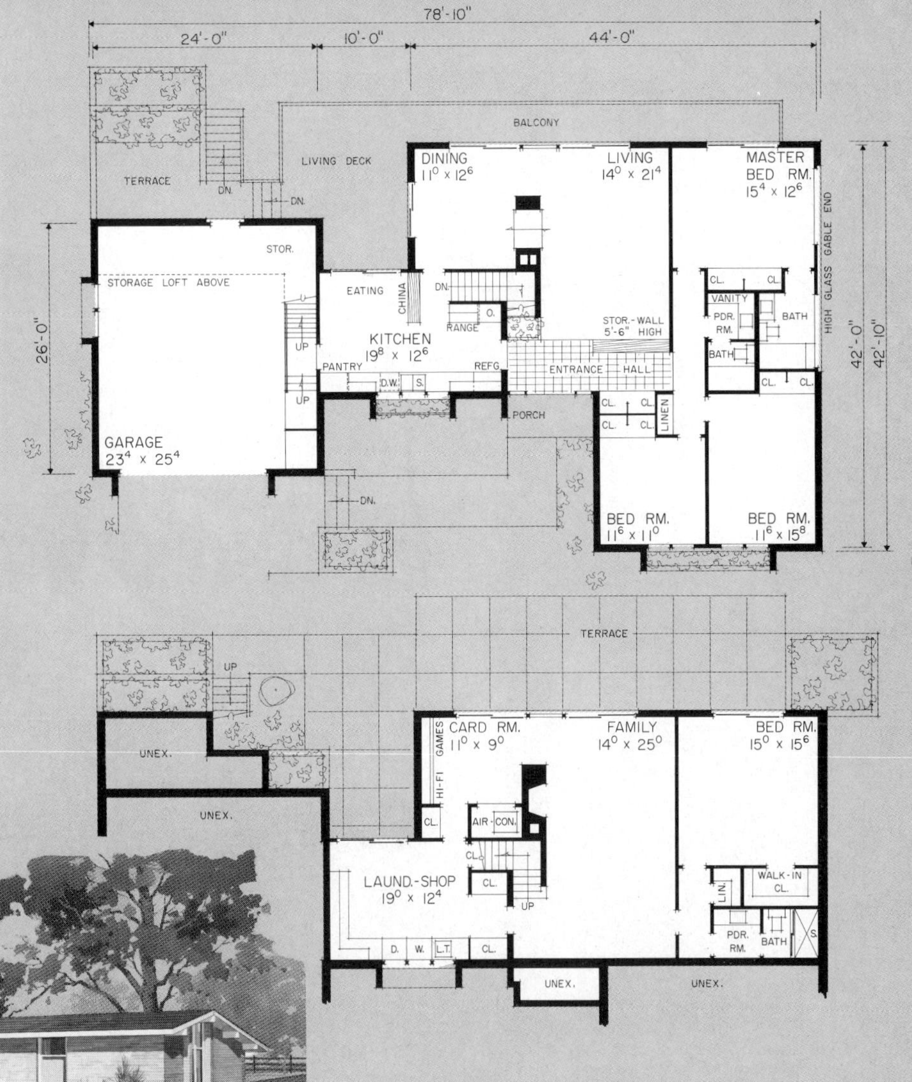

Design T22847 ***1,874 Sq. Ft. - Main Level***
1,131 Sq. Ft. - Lower Level; 44,305 Cu. Ft.

● This is an exquisitely styled Tudor, hillside design, ready to serve its happy occupants for many years. The contrasting use of material surely makes the exterior eye-catching.

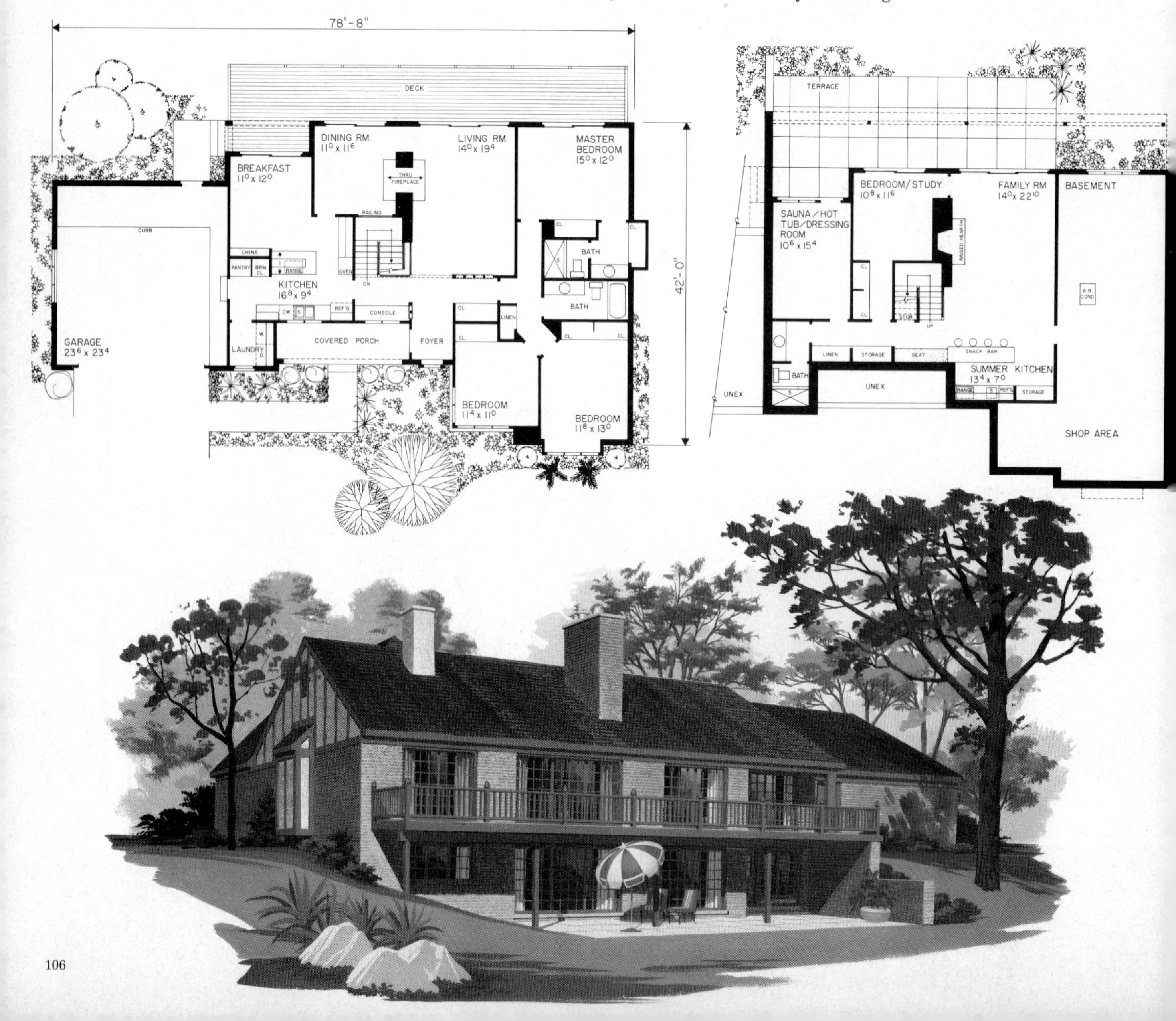

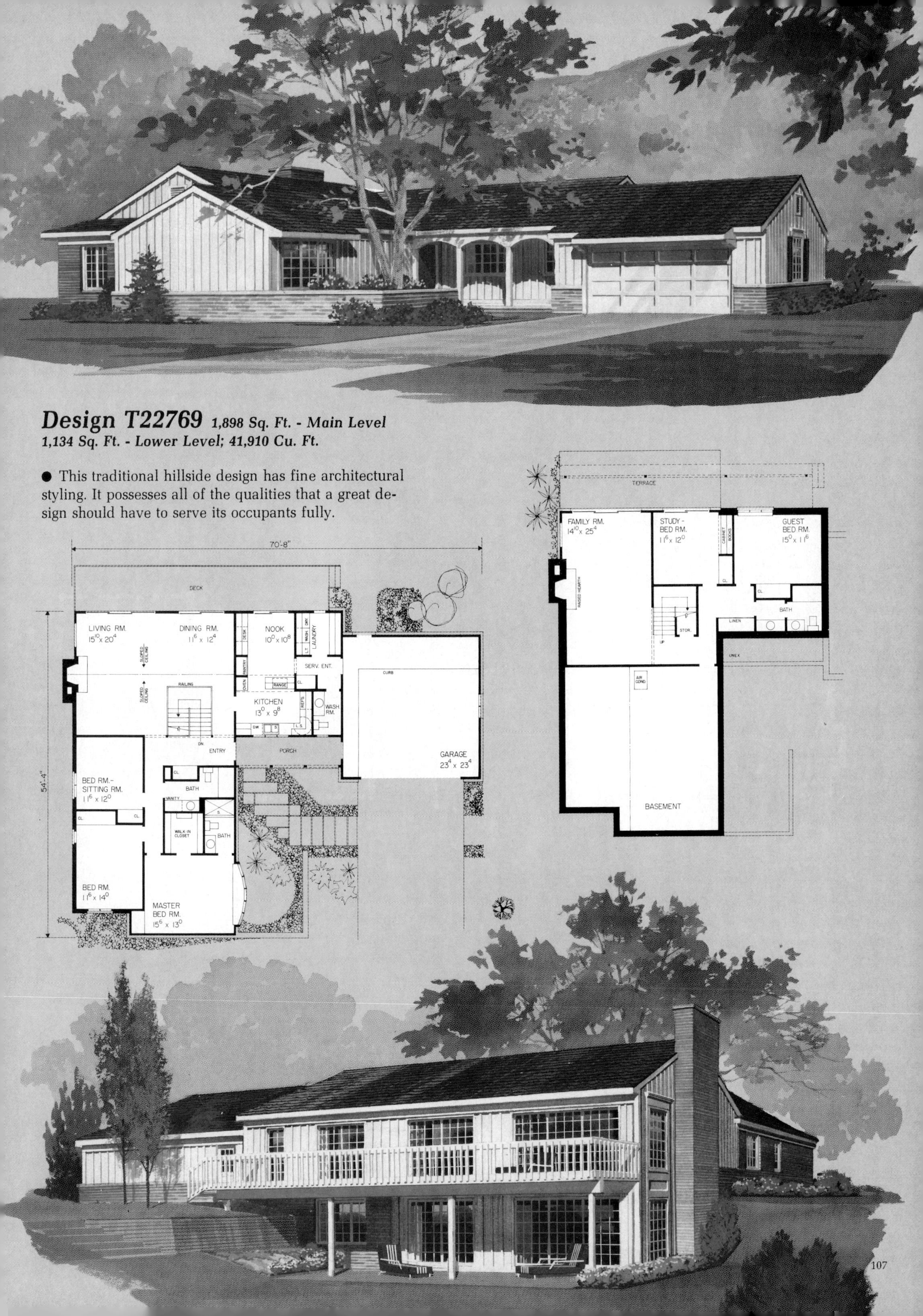

Design T22769 *1,898 Sq. Ft. - Main Level*

1,134 Sq. Ft. - Lower Level; 41,910 Cu. Ft.

● This traditional hillside design has fine architectural styling. It possesses all of the qualities that a great design should have to serve its occupants fully.

Design T21853 *1,274 Sq. Ft. - Main Level; 784 Sq. Ft. - Upper Level; 792 Sq. Ft. - Lower Level; 34,982 Cu. Ft.*

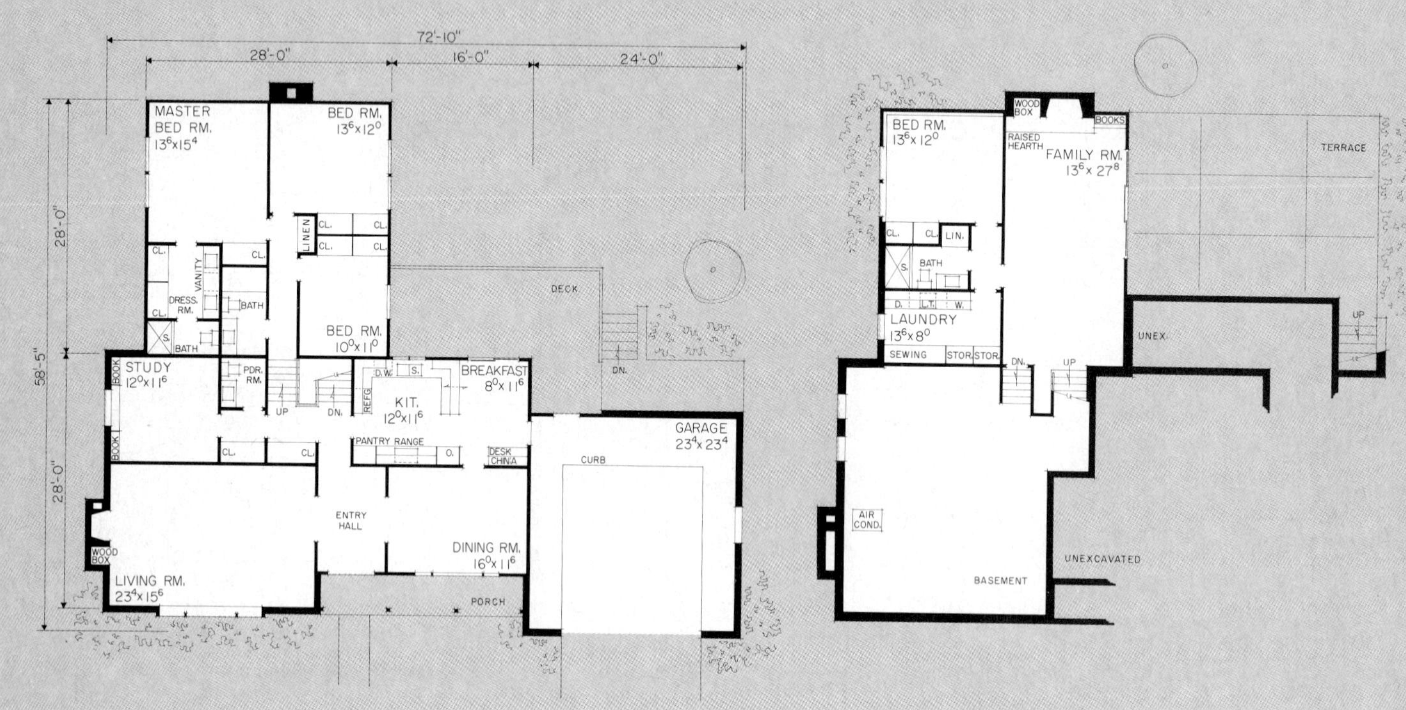

● Here, on these two pages, are two traditional homes designed specifically with the hillside site in mind. From the street they appear to be cozy one-story homes. From the rear, however, their appearance is pleasingly different. The lower level is exposed and opens onto the outdoor terrace area. The decks provide the main levels with outdoor living facilities which will be everyone's favorite area for relaxation. Study the floor plans with care. The convenient living potential of each design is outstanding. Which house satisfies your family living requirements?

Design T21739 *1,281 Sq. Ft. - Main Level; 857 Sq. Ft. - Sleeping Level; 687 Sq. Ft. - Lower Level; 37,624 Cu. Ft.*

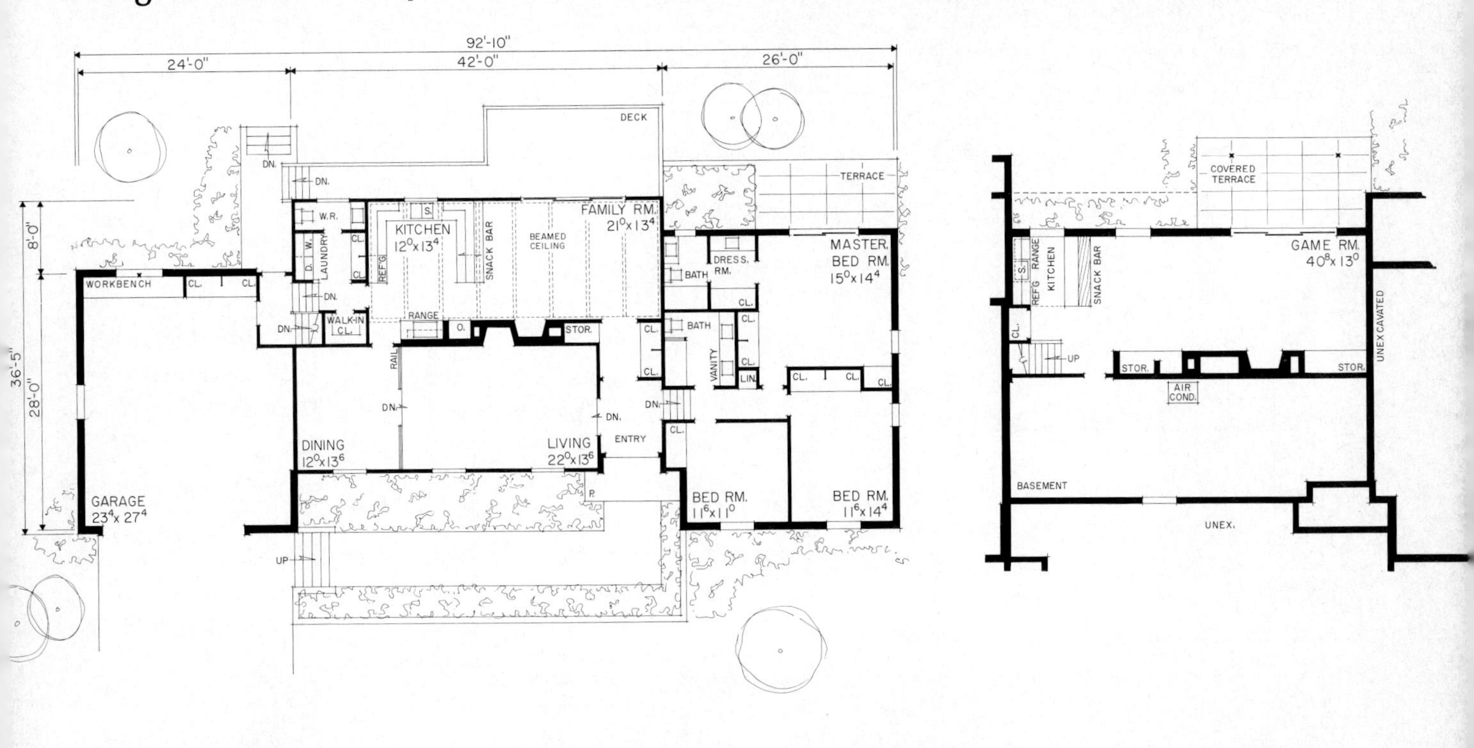

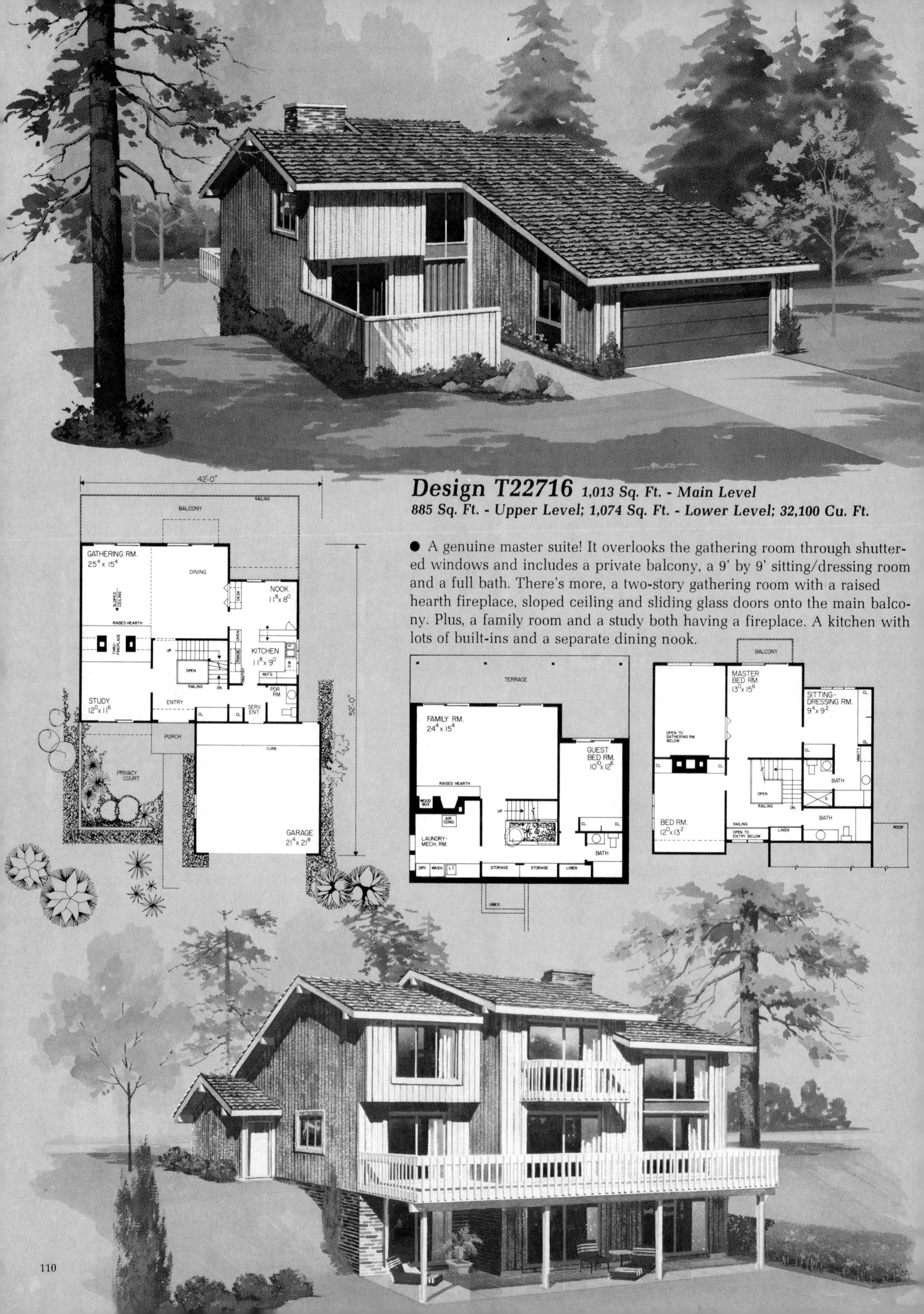

Design T22716 *1,013 Sq. Ft. - Main Level*
885 Sq. Ft. - Upper Level; 1,074 Sq. Ft. - Lower Level; 32,100 Cu. Ft.

● A genuine master suite! It overlooks the gathering room through shuttered windows and includes a private balcony, a 9' by 9' sitting/dressing room and a full bath. There's more, a two-story gathering room with a raised hearth fireplace, sloped ceiling and sliding glass doors onto the main balcony. Plus, a family room and a study both having a fireplace. A kitchen with lots of built-ins and a separate dining nook.

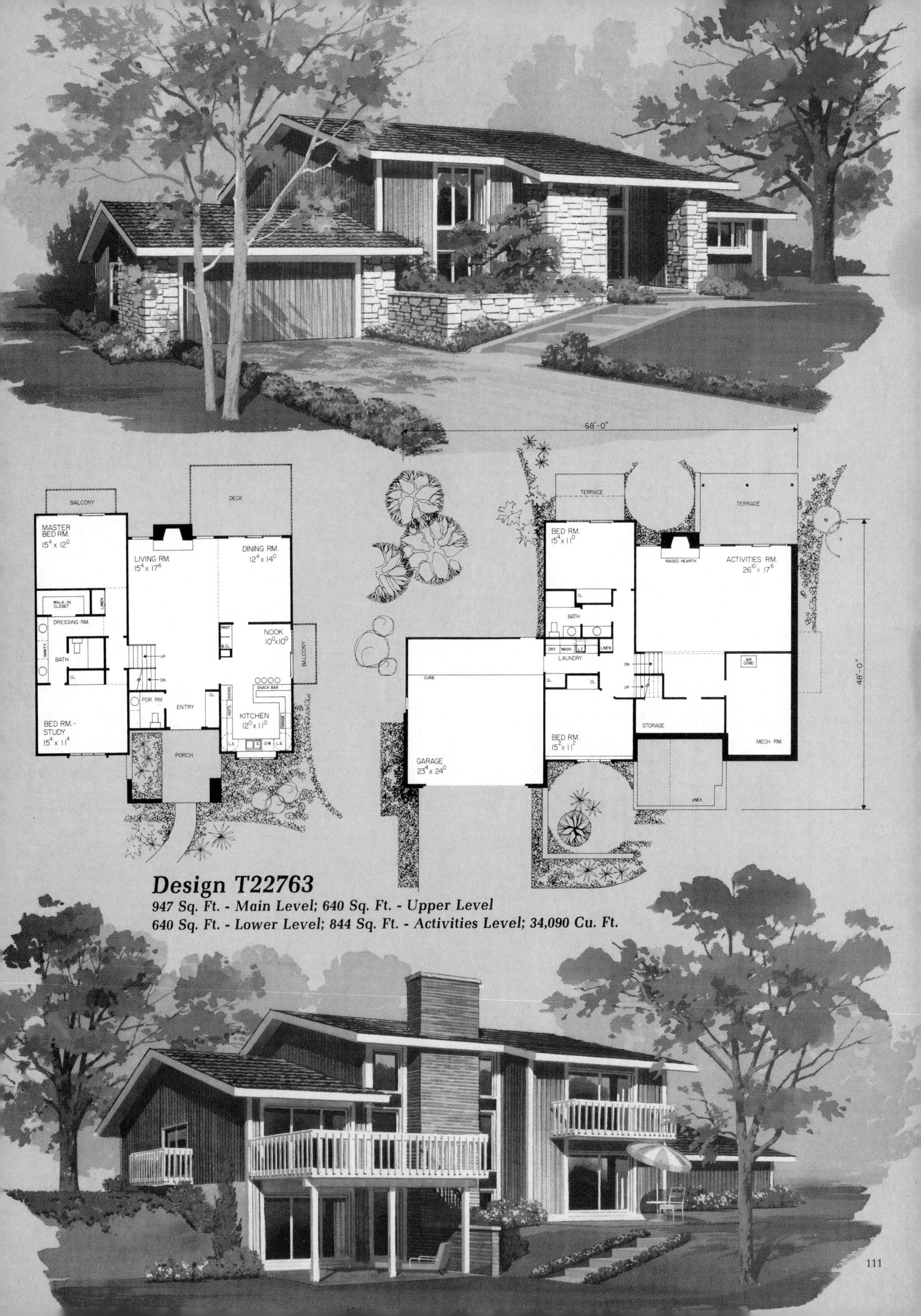

Design T22763

947 Sq. Ft. - Main Level; 640 Sq. Ft. - Upper Level
640 Sq. Ft. - Lower Level; 844 Sq. Ft. - Activities Level; 34,090 Cu. Ft.

Design T22760

1,483 Sq. Ft. - Main Level
1,483 Sq. Ft. - Lower Level; 33,080 Cu. Ft.

● Here is contemporary design at its simple, yet dramatic, best. The modern adaptation of the mansard roof produces results that are interesting, indeed. The top of the roof itself is virtually flat and built-up with a gravel surface. The overhanging portion is made up of metal. While this is predominantly a frame house with vertical siding, there are brick masses which offer an attractive contrast. The rear view is unique with glass areas effectively shaded by overhanging roofs and balconies. Two of the terraces are covered, thus permitting inclement weather use. No rained-out cookouts here! A thru-fireplace separates the dining room from the sunken living room.